New Dynamics of
Urban Sociology

New Dynamics of Urban Sociology

Dr. Suresh Chandra

JNANADA PRAKASHAN (P&D)
NEW DELHI

Published by :
JNANADA PRAKASHAN (P&D)
4837/2, 24, Ansari Road, Daryaganj
New Delhi-110002
Phone : 011-23272047
Mobile : 9212137080
Email: jnanadabooksdelhi@yahoo.com
Website: www.jnanadabooks.com; text.ind.in

Assisted by :
TEXT BOOK PROMOTION SOCIETY OF INDIA
4837/2, 24, Ansari Road, Daryaganj
New Delhi-110002
Phone : 011-23272047
Mobile : 9212137080

Edition : 2017

New Dynamics of Urban Sociology

ISBN : 978-81-7139-440-1

Typesetting by :
Vardhman Computers
New Delhi-110 017, India

Published by Mrs. S. Chowdhary for M/s. Jnanada Prakashan (P&D) Daryaganj, Ansari Road, New Delhi-110002, India and printed at Balaji Offset, Navin Shahdara, Delhi-110032, India.

PREFACE

City has always played a significant role in both the rise as well as fall of the great human civilizations. As a result, the study of city or for that matter urban sociology has always attracted the attention of social scientists, especially geographers and sociologists.

The book "New Dynamics of Urban Sociology" is a serious attempt to understand the forces and factors determining the parameters of urban sociology. The very first chapter introduces urban sociology. The next chapter deals with contemporary urban sociology.

Globalisation definitely is a major force of social change. The study of the relationship between urbanisation and social change has been made in the third chapter. Issues and challenges for the urban family and challenges for sustainable urbanisation have been discussed and analysed in the fourth and fifth chapter respectively. There exits a relationship among culture, politics and sexuality. The study of this crucial linkages has been made in the sixth chapter.

The study of urban poverty in India, gender perspective of urbanisation and poverty and women workforce in urban India has been made in the seventh, eighth and ninth chapter respectively. The linkages among poverty, migration and urbanisation have been examined in the tenth chapter. Globalisation as a process involves multiple economies and work cultures, which has significant implication for urban landscape. The various challenges experienced by urban sociology has been covered in the final chapter.

The author has made an attempt to explore the approaches, methods and strategies for making the urban sociology more dynamic in the coming years. Despite all the challenges, the crucial fact remains that urbanisation is a continuing process and more importantly, the growth of urbanisation especially in the developing world is on the rise. The author is fully convinced that this work would be a significant contribution to the literature on urban sociology.

CONTENTS

1

INTRODUCING URBAN SOCIOLOGY

You can only express things properly by details.... Yet, a detail ceases to mean anything when it becomes nothing but a colour and a shape, when we feel it's a detail and nothing more.[1] In recent years, scholarly accounts of urban modernity in Europe have focused increasingly on historical processes that transcended the boundaries of the local. The emergence of modern forms of state power and urban governance, the growth of civil society and the rise of the public sphere have emerged as key themes in the historiography. In turn, this has led to a growing recognition of the comparative possibilities afforded by the analytical study of these transnational developments. Historians have been especially keen to explore the similarities and differences that characterised the modernisation of urban society in diverse European contexts.

However, there has been relatively muted recognition of the extent to which imperial expansion and overseas colonisation lent a global dimension to many of these historical processes. Yet, even a cursory survey would show that many of the contemporary megacities in the former colonial societies of Asia and Africa acquired their recognisably modern characteristics during the 'imperial globalisation' of the nineteenth and early twentieth centuries. The fabric of urban life in many colonial cities was transformed by the rise of a global economic system based on industrial capitalism and its attendant technologies of power. At the same time, the dense concentration of modern factories, commercial firms, western-educated local intelligentsia and culturally diverse migrant communities rendered colonial cities decisive sites of the encounter between European and non-European societies.[2] A vigorous public culture emerged in these cities, buoyed by a thriving print industry and a variety of associational activities. The experience of urban modernity in the colonial context thus offers fertile terrain for the comparative analysis of processes and ideas that may have originated in Europe but became truly global in reach and scope during the age of empire.

These themes and their scholarly appraisal constitute the point of departure for this book, which explores the dynamics of urban change in a premier colonial city at a pivotal juncture in its emergence as a modern metropolis, drawing together strands that have hitherto been treated in an isolated and piecemeal manner, this micro-study investigates the social history of Bombay in the late Victorian and Edwardian eras. In examining the colonial experience of historical processes that have attracted considerable attention in recent European scholarship, the inquiry seeks to highlight the global dimension to a comparative discussion of these themes. At the same time, the book does not construe modernisation in the colonial context as the inexorable unfolding of industrial capitalism, 'westernisation' or 'governmentality'. Rather, it is interpreted here as a contested and contingent set of outcomes that flowed from the contradictory currents generated by the market, state and politics against a background of rapid technological change, demographic growth, urbanisation and mass migration.[3] In particular, the book highlights the manner in which the turbulent changes unleashed by European modernity were negotiated, appropriated or resisted by the colonised.

This book also seeks to contribute to the current revitalisation of urban studies in India. For long, as scholars have noted, the perception that the defining feature of Indian society was its predominantly agrarian character had tended to obscure the significance of its cities.[4] It was the village rather than the modern city that dominated the Indian intellectual landscape. As with many other representations of the subcontinent, the notion that India had been since time immemorial a land of self-contained village communities was a construct of nineteenth-century colonial discourse.[5] However, it was embraced by educated Indians of differing ideological persuasions and exerted a profound influence on their cultural and political imagination in the twentieth century.[6] The village was regarded as the authentic repository of the timeless values and virtues of Indian civilisation, whereas the modern city was viewed with profound ambivalence as a spurious Western implant.[7] These attitudes also suffused the scholarship within the social sciences: anthropologists, sociologists and political scientists largely focused on the countryside since the 'real' India was believed to reside, literally as well as figuratively, in her villages.[8]

There were, of course, intermittent flashes of interest in the modern Indian city. One of the earliest attempts at studying processes of contemporary urbanism in the subcontinent was undertaken not very long after the embryonic field of 'urban planning' had begun to crystallise in Britain at the dawn of the twentieth century. This was initiated by Patrick Geddes (1854-1932), the renowned Scottish polymath, 'social evolutionist' and civic visionary who spent prolonged periods of time in India between 1914 and 1924. Having initially arrived in the country on the eve of the First World War with his peripatetic City and Town Planning Exhibition, Geddes stayed on to investigate the effects of economic and social change on its cities. In the years that followed, he prepared over fifty 'town-planning' reports on Indian urban centres.

In 1919, Geddes also took up a professorship in the newly-created department of Sociology and Civics at the University of Bombay. In his writings and lectures, Geddes questioned many of the prevailing shibboleths of urban 'improvement' that he encountered in colonial India, regarding them as historically ill-informed and destructive. Instead, he advocated ecologically sensitive forms of town planning that were attuned to the rich architectural, civic and cultural traditions of the Indian urban environment.[9] Geddes's work triggered a short-lived burst of enthusiasm for studying Indian urbanism. In particular, it produced an interest in indigenous traditions of urbanism and spawned attempts to search for solutions to contemporary civic problems in the prescriptions of the past. But, on the whole, his influence was restricted to a few individuals and did not have a lasting impact.[10] Indeed, one of the intriguing features of the late colonial period is that even though the leading lights of the Indian intelligentsia were products of the city, they 'devoted most of their energies to the task of producing an idea not of the future Indian city but of a rural India fit for the modern age'.[11] This seeming paradox has yet to be satisfactorily accounted for, but any plausible explanation would surely have to consider the impact of Gandhi on Indian intellectual life in these years.

The contemporary Indian city resurfaced as an object of intellectual scrutiny in the 1950s. The nationalist endeavour to construct fitting capital cities for newly-created regional states,[12] the need to accommodate within towns and cities the massive influx of Partition-affected refugees and the burgeoning international interest in processes of 'modernisation' in post-colonial societies, all combined to create new political situations in which urban issues attracted scholarly attention. Several developments attest to this newfound interest in the city. A number of theoretically-driven anthropological and sociological accounts of Indian cities were published in this decade.[13] The topic of 'urbanisation' also came to form a separate segment within the Indian Sociological Association and the Indian Economic Association,[14] while 'Town-Planning' became a recognised subject in the undergraduate curriculum.[15] Equally significant was the decision of the Indian Planning Commission's Research Programmes Committee to initiate and sponsor socio-economic surveys of a number of major cities.[16]

The urban surveys of the 1950s inaugurated an enduring tradition of descriptive studies detailing the economic, demographic and morphological features of contemporary Indian cities.[17] But, their wealth of detail was rarely matched by a depth of historical perspective. Historians, for their part, did not begin to engage with the modern Indian city until the 1960s. Two developments in that decade served to awaken their interest. First, scholars embarking on the serious study of the Indian nationalist movement were drawn to the urban centres in which 'modern' politics emerged. Thus, a number of studies sought to locate the rise of Indian nationalism within specific urban contexts.[18] Second, a growing interest in the 'industrialisation' of developing societies led some scholars to undertake the historical investigation of these themes in relation to particular cities.[19] Common to all these works was a tendency to view the city merely as the backdrop for the larger economic and political processes that were the principal focus of analysis.

In the following two decades, however, scholars began to pursue fresh lines of enquiry that construed the social history of the modern Indian city as an important object of study in its own right. Three noteworthy strands can be discerned within this historiography. First, historians began to explore the ways in which the built environment and public architecture of Indian cities under colonial rule was shaped by the ideology and cultural values of the European ruling elite.[20] Some works within this genre emphasised the centrality of the events of 1857 in reshaping colonial attitudes to urban governance in the cities of North India.[21] Second, scholars began to explore the social history of a variety of urban groups. Some focused on particular intermediate classes or ethnic communities;[22] others examined the social formation and political culture of the urban working classes.[23] Finally, there emerged a new interest in the public culture of Indian cities during the colonial period. There was an attempt to reconsider the political culture of Indian elites in the light of the analytical perspectives drawn from cultural anthropology and 'ethnohistory'.[24] At the same time, the growing incidence of 'communal' violence in contemporary Indian cities, as well as wider intellectual trends, prompted a new interest in urban 'popular culture' and collective mentalities.[25]

Notwithstanding the interest exhibited in the modern Indian city by individual scholars and the formation of the Urban History Association of India,[26] the countryside continued to dominate the scholarly agenda in the 1970s and 1980s. Village studies revolving around caste, kinship and ritual held sway over the disciplines of anthropology and sociology.[27] Historians investigating the rural order under colonial rule focused especially on the mechanisms and effects of colonial tenurial systems, the social formation of various agrarian strata and the different modes of peasant protest.[28] As one distinguished historian pointed out in 1981, the peasant continued to remain 'the favourite subject for research in India'.[29] The appearance shortly thereafter of *Subaltern Studies* as a powerful new intellectual current served further to overshadow urban social history for the rest of the 1980s.[30]

However, over the past decade or so, the modern Indian city has elbowed its way back to the forefront of the academic agenda. A growing number of scholars have begun to explore the unfolding dynamics of contemporary Indian urbanism. Several public initiatives have also been launched in recent years to bring together academics, artists and activists in order to reflect collectively on the economic, political and cultural processes that are rapidly transforming Indian cities. Indeed, the new intellectual ferment surrounding the city has prompted some writers to herald an 'urban turn' in South Asian studies.[31]

Three developments, acting in conjunction, have provided the broader material and intellectual context for the ongoing resuscitation of urban studies in India. First, the rapid increase in the total number of towns and cities as well as the sheer size of the country's urban population has begun to dent the entrenched perception of India as a land of villages. While a majority of Indians continue to live in the countryside, the proportion of town-dwellers has been expanding steadily and currently constitutes about a third of the country's total population. Reckoned in absolute terms, this yields a figure of around three hundred million, a tenth of the world's urban population. Viewed from another perspective, the total number of people living in Indian towns and cities not only outstrips the entire population of some European nations like France and Germany, but also that of more populous countries such as Brazil and the United States of America. Significantly, the larger metropolitan centres have grown the fastest and according to the 2001 census there are 35 Indian cities with a population in excess of a million.[32] Indeed, as one writer recently remarked, 'There will soon be more people living in the city of Bombay than on the continent of Australia'.[33]

Second, the far-reaching changes wrought by economic liberalisation and globalisation since the early 1990s have profoundly altered the face of Indian cities. At one level, these processes have hastened the demise of many of the traditional manufacturing industries that dominated the urban landscape. Cities like Ahmedabad, Bombay and Kanpur have seen their core industries decimated, leading to the retrenchment of millions of workers.[34] Industrial restructuring has led to the contraction of production in the so-called 'formal sector', even as the 'informal economy' has continued steadily to expand in size. Indian towns and cities today are thus teeming with millions of casually employed, low-paid workers who toil in small-scale manufacturing enterprises and seasonal industries that lie outside the purview of any protective labour legislation. These developments have triggered scholarly interest in the workings of India's burgeoning urban 'informal economy'.[35] It has also prompted them to query the classic narratives of industrialisation, which saw the process as inevitably culminating in the modern, large-scale factory system, based on capital-intensive technologies and a commitment to steady levels of production and labour deployment.[36]

At another level, the withering away of many of the staple industries that lay at the heart of India's urban modernity in the twentieth century has been offset by the rise of economically dynamic service-sector activities that have thrived on the revolution in information technology. Indian cities have become part of a new 'inter-metropolitan and global network carrying out information processing and control functions'.[37] They have also emerged as key sites in the refashioning of middle-class identities. Equipped with technical, professional or processing skills, middle-class men and women are the principal beneficiaries of the surge in demand for Indian services in the new global economy. Their visibility and volubility has been enhanced even further by the arrival in India over the past decade of multi-national corporations willing to offer undreamt of salaries to their white-collar employees.[38] In turn, the increased spending power of the middle classes has spawned a new urban consumer culture, amply reflected in the ever-proliferating malls and multiplexes appearing in Indian cities.[39]

Finally, the so-called 'urban turn' has also been impelled by the recognition that the Indian city is now in a 'new, post-nationalist stage' marked by the deepening contradiction between 'economic inequalities' and 'political opportunities', giving rise to new claims and conflicts over its identity.[40] On the one hand, as Chatterjee has suggested, there has been an 'apparent shift in the ruling attitudes towards the big city in India'. A new vision of a global, post-industrial city has come to dominate the fantasies of India's rapidly expanding urban middle classes. The combined effects of the 'intensified circulation of images of global cities through cinema, television, and the internet' and the 'urgent pressure to connect with the global economy and attract foreign investment', Chatterjee argues, has had important consequences for the ways in which the urban poor are now perceived by social elites and the state. Thus, recent years have witnessed a 'growing assertion by organisations of middle-class citizens of their right to unhindered access to public spaces and thoroughfares and to a clean and healthy urban environment'.

Simultaneously, 'manufacturing industries are being moved out of city limits; squatters and encroachers are being evicted; property and tenancy laws are being rewritten to enable market forces to rapidly convert the congested and dilapidated sections of the old city into high-value commercial and residential districts'.[41] On the other hand, Chatterjee contends, the poor have sought to advance their own claims on the city by forging a new domain of 'political society' whose values are antithetical to the norms of middle-class 'civil society'. Many of their 'political' practices are 'founded on violations of the law' and hence very different from the constitutionally sanctioned relations between the state and citizens within civil society.[42] Equally, it has been argued, collective rituals of 'public protest, violence, and local mobilisations' have been integral to their sense of politics. Such 'political spectacles' in public arenas are thus regarded as having played a key role in fashioning new forms of chauvinistic and particularistic identities among the plebeian classes in contemporary Indian cities.[43]

The urgency of the 'urban question' has thus reignited interest in the modern Indian city. Recent perspectives on the postcolonial city have opened up fresh lines of enquiry and brought novel theoretical concerns to bear on the study of contemporary urban trends. At the same time, there has been a tendency in these accounts to posit a rather stark contrast between the turbulent postcolonial city and its seemingly staid colonial predecessor. Yet, there has never been a 'golden age' in the career of the modern city, when it was free of the conflicts generated by the deepening hold of market relations, state power and politics.

This book explores a watershed era in Bombay's evolution as a modern metropolis. Like many other urban centres in the sprawling

Indian Ocean region,[44] the late nineteenth and early twentieth centuries were a tumultuous and fractious period in the city's history: Bombay was transformed from a prosperous port city into a major industrial metropolis. At the heart of this process lay the rapid expansion of the cotton-textile industry, whose profound influence on the city's economy, social structure and political culture has been extensively documented by scholars over the past four decades.[45] But, as this book seeks to demonstrate, there were other ways in which the late Victorian and Edwardian eras were decisive in shaping Bombay's identity as a modern city. Most notably, it was in these decades that the city was restructured in accordance with the dictates of modern urban planning and intrusive modes of governance deployed in response to the challenges posed by rapid industrialisation and massive labour migration. Equally, the city became the site of a vigorous associational culture and 'modernising' social activism that infused its civil society with a new dynamism. The legacy of these developments continues to endure in the built environment and public culture of postcolonial Bombay.

From San Francisco to Singapore, urban modernity in the nineteenth century inaugurated a profound transformation in the techniques of rule. The city was rendered into an object of knowledge in the form of maps, surveys and censuses. New imperatives of rationality, legibility and visibility underpinned the conceptualisation and governance of urban space. The city also came to embody new ideals of order that valorised 'public health' and the unimpeded flow of commodities and people.[46] At the same time, governments and urban elites viewed with anxiety the massed ranks of the poor or racially defined 'others', whose norms and practices were regarded as impediments to the realisation of an ordered society.[47] In turn, this induced strategies of governance aimed at taming and disciplining their supposedly 'lawless' and 'licentious' disposition.

This book addresses some of these themes in the context of a fundamental shift in the political rationalities of colonial governance in *fin de siecle* Bombay. Until the last decade of the nineteenth century the city's rulers had remained largely apathetic to the social and political consequences of industrial urbanisation.[48] In particular, they had cultivated a studied indifference to the emergence in the late nineteenth century of the 'unintended city'.[49] Thus, as the city rapidly industrialised and population expanded, the provision of civic amenities failed to keep pace, leading to excessive overcrowding and insanitary living conditions in its swiftly proliferating 'slums'. Similarly, the authorities had generally refrained from interfering in the affairs of the urban neighbourhoods. Prior to the 1890s, the neighbourhoods had been left to their own self-regulation, with the rulers largely relying on putatively 'traditional' community leaders to maintain order within this domain.

This study show how during the 1890s the city was convulsed by a set of crises that triggered a reappraisal of colonial strategies of governance. Specifically, they focus on the attempts of colonial authorities to order and discipline urban space. The outbreak of a severe and prolonged plague epidemic in the late 1890s jolted Bombay's rulers out of their ostrich-like posture *vis-à-vis* the problems of the city's civic infrastructure. This study considers the ways in which the widely entrenched belief that epidemic diseases were a product of locality-specific conditions of filth and squalor in the city's 'slums' exerted a significant influence over the colonial state's war against plague. In the wake of the epidemic, tackling the problems created by the abysmal living conditions of the urban poor became a critical necessity for the city's ruling elites. The consequence was the establishment in 1898 of a City Improvement Trust. Modelled on the English and Scottish improvement schemes of the nineteenth century, the Trust set about demolishing dilapidated neighbourhoods, opening up overcrowded areas and constructing 'sanitary dwellings' for the city's poor.This intervention of the state in the sphere of urban development, through the creation of a special agency devoted solely to the purpose of civic restructuring, was the first attempt of its kind in colonial India. This study investigates the functioning of the Bombay Improvement Trust, assesses its impact on the city's built environment and underscores the diverse ways in which the city's residents sought to contest, subvert or deflect its operations.

If colonial civic renewal sought to reorder urban space, colonial policing focused on its regulation. Chapter argues that the outbreak of major episodes of collective violence in the 1890s, as well as the simultaneous emergence of a plebeian casual economy and public culture centred on the street, produced a significant shift in the strategies of urban policing. Attempts were initiated to modernise the police in line with metropolitan models and practices. Furthermore, the traditional colonial mode of exercising 'indirect' influence yielded to more authoritarian methods of 'top-down' control. The shift in emphasis was facilitated by a new City Police Act that was introduced in 1902. This piece of legislation vastly enhanced the powers of the police by bringing a range of activities in public spaces under their surveillance. In particular, the Act vested the police with an exhaustive array of 'special powers' for regulating and controlling collective activities in public spaces. It also consolidated and extended the formal powers of regulation vested in the police by criminalising a range of activities in 'public' sites. In turn, their newly consolidated powers embroiled the police more directly than before in the conflicts of the street and the neighbourhood and amplified the repercussions of such intervention.

The city's rulers adopted a more interventionist approach to urban governance. Integral to this shift were the crises of the 1890s, which prompted colonial authorities to set about reordering and regulating urban space. In highlighting the connection between these two developments, the book proposes an analytical framework within which the disparate events of these years, hitherto studied in an episodic fashion, can be located. As in the metropolitan context, centralising governmental agencies intervened in unprecedented ways. However, while this book focuses on the augmentation and application of colonial power, it queries the view that the state was a monolithic and omnipotent entity with an unlimited or unchallenged capacity to mould the spaces of the city to its will.[50] It suggests that far from constituting a unitary institution, the state was the dispersed locus of contending logics and internal contradictions. The chapters that follow also demonstrate how their strategies and mechanisms of governance ensnared colonial authorities in conflicts that they were unable easily to resolve. Furthermore, by documenting the numerous ways in which indigenous agents countered the policies and actions of their rulers—ranging from outright defiance to the subtlest forms of subversion—one may highlight how the city was a 'contested terrain', shaped as much by acts of resistance as by the operations of power.[51]

At the same time, the book seeks to qualify recent accounts which have suggested that the boundaries between state and society were contingent, fuzzy and porous.[52] While the state cannot be regarded as a discrete organisation that was external to society, the practices of its various agencies nonetheless produced a 'structural effect', simultaneously material and ideological, that set it apart as a transcendental entity.[53] In other words, the 'idea' of the state became more firmly entrenched within local society. And no matter how indistinct the dividing lines between state and society might have been, they were nonetheless regarded as boundaries.[54]

Another key feature of global modernity in the 'long' nineteenth century was the rise and consolidation of new forms of urban public culture. This was symbolised by the proliferation of clubs, societies and other kinds of voluntary associations, which became a characteristic feature of towns and cities across the globe. It was through such associational activities, central to 'civil society', that men and women from diverse social backgrounds negotiated the pressures and possibilities of modern life. At the same time, urban associational culture transformed cities into veritable theatres of popular politics.[55] The emergent public sphere of civil society enabled the liberal critique of modern state power as well as the articulation of collective identities.

The period from the 1890s to the end of the First World War, it is now widely accepted, marked an important watershed in the public culture of the Indian subcontinent. These years witnessed a spectacular surge in associational activities ranging from caste societies to nationalist organisations, as well as the rise of a dynamic print industry that churned out books, newspapers, journals, tracts, pamphlets and posters. There also arose new forms of collective action in public arenas: reasoned debates in the press, as well as memorials, meetings and public demonstrations.[56] Importantly, these developments were a product of the urban context. It was in the city that Indians encountered and came to terms with new definitions of the 'public' and the 'private' and it was here too that they began to recognise the potential of novel modes of association and sociability.[57]

Chapters trace the crystallisation of 'civil society' in colonial Bombay during the late Victorian and Edwardian eras. The growing density and diversity of the modern associational culture that was fostered in the city. In particular, it highlights the countervailing trends that were a distinctive feature of Indian civil society. On the one hand, a vast proportion of the clubs, societies and trusts established in these years were organisational 'hybrids' that combined voluntary and a scriptive criteria of membership. On the other hand, there also developed paradigmatic forms of voluntary association that adhered to the principle of open access based on secular criteria of membership. In focusing on the simultaneous rise and co-existence of different kinds of associations, this chapter treats within the same analytical framework forms of collective sociability that hitherto have been considered discretely. It also demonstrates how the city's varied associational life helped to create a richly textured public culture marked by multiplicity and multivalence.

At the same time, the chapter seeks to highlight the ambiguous and contradictory effects of this associational culture. The clubs and societies that proliferated in this period served to promote in their members feelings of mutual fellowship and goodwill as well as a concern for the 'common good'. They also helped to entrench within Indian public life a remarkably enduring commitment to debate and discussion. Yet, the voluntary associations did not always adhere to the values of autonomy, equality and deliberative decision-making. Nor were they free of tensions and conflicts.[58] At times, internal rivalries ripped apart associations as their members competed against each other for power and prestige. In other instances, associational activity produced deep fissures within urban society that even resulted in riots. Furthermore, 'modern' forms of collective sociability served to refashion a variety of putatively primordial attachments and 'traditional' identities.

This study also draws attention to two features of associational life in Bombay that were central to contemporary Indian civil society. First, it focuses not only on the associations founded by the liberal-nationalist elite, but also those formed to espouse communities defined by caste or religion. It, thus, questions the view that the term civil society is 'best used to describe those institutions of modern associational life set up by nationalist elites in the era of colonial modernity'. This restrictive understanding of the concept is premised on a 'normative model presented by Western modernity'. The defining features of associational culture in this ideal-typical version of civil society are 'equality, autonomy, freedom of entry and exit, contract, deliberative procedures of decision-making, recognised rights and duties of members, and other such principles'.[59] However, many of these characteristics can also be discerned in associations that were based on putatively ascribed identities of caste or religion, but which nevertheless adopted the same forms, principles and practices as the ideal-typical voluntary organisation.[60] Indeed, such 'hybrid' societies were as much a product of colonial modernity as the purely voluntary associations that are the *sine qua non* of liberal models of civil society.

Second, the study also challenges the widely entrenched perception that the norms and practices of civil society were solely internalised by the Anglophone intelligentsia and were more or less alien to the cultural world-view and dispositions of the lower orders.[61] It shows how the associational ventures in colonial Bombay were borne aloft by the initiatives of individuals and groups drawn from diverse social strata. In particular, it suggests that in spite of their lack of basic entitlements and the severe political constraints that they faced, the city's working classes displayed a willingness to commit themselves 'partially and transiently to others with the same sectional interests' and were not unaware of the niceties of 'associational civility'. Conversely, their awareness of the 'advantages of social individuation' notwithstanding, English-educated Indians were not always able to transcend their attachment to 'a world of more complete commitments'.[62]

The final considers a novel departure in the history of Bombay's nascent civil society. Conscious of their self-proclaimed status as the new leaders of Indian society and the arbiters of new norms of 'respectable' public conduct, the city's educated elites initiated and participated in forms of social activism that sought to 'uplift' and 'improve' the masses. In particular, there developed among sections of the Indian intelligentsia a newfound enthusiasm for 'social service'. For long, it was assumed that this concern for the poor first emerged in the Gandhian era of Indian nationalism. In recent years, however, the importance of pre-Gandhian 'constructive nationalism' has attracted scholarly attention. In particular, historians have begun to examine the voluntary organisations animated by the ideals of 'active citizenship' and 'selfless service' that emerged prior to the Great War.[63]

While sharing their interest in the specific local and global conjunctures within which these developments occurred, the analytical perspective adopted in this study is distinctive in at least two ways. First, it locates the new concern about the poor within broader processes of urban middle-class formation in colonial India. Second, the study seeks to disentangle the specific connotations of 'social service' from the generic category of 'social reform' to which it has usually been consigned. In particular, it argues that while 'social reform' during the late nineteenth century had largely denoted the *internal* attempts at 'self-improvement' within particular castes and communities, the emergent discourse and practice of 'social service' articulated by members of the high-status Anglophone intelligentsia was directed at the destitute, the downtrodden and the disadvantaged.

NOTES AND REFERENCES

1. Czeslaw Milosz, *The Seizure of Power* (London, 1985), pp. 42-3.
2. Susan Bayly, 'The Evolution of Colonial Cultures: Nineteenth-Century Asia', in Andrew Porter (ed.), *The Oxford History of the British Empire* (5 vols, Oxford, 1999), III, pp. 447-69.
3. Marshall Berman, *All That is Solid Melts into Air: The Experience of Modernity* (London, 1983), p. 16.
4. Rajnarayan Chandavarkar, *The Origins of Industrial Capitalism in India: Business Strategies and the Working Classes in Bombay, 1900-1940* (Cambridge, 1994), p. 2.
5. Thomas R. Metcalf, *The New Cambridge History of India,* vol. III, part 4: *Ideologies of the Raj* (Delhi, 1998), pp. 68-71; Louis dumont, 'The "Village Community" from Maine to Munro', *Contributions to Indian Sociology,* 9 (1966): 67-89; Clive dewey, 'Images of the Village Community: A Study in Anglo-Indian Ideology', *Modern Asian Studies* (hereafter MAS), 6/2 (1972): 291-328.
6. Gyan Prakash, 'The Urban Turn', in Ravi Vasudevan et al. (eds), *Sarai Reader 02: Cities of Everyday Life* (Delhi, 2002), p. 3.

7. Partha Chatterjee, *The Politics of the Governed: Reflections on Popular Politics in Most of the World* (Delhi, 2004), pp. 140-41.
8. Janaki Nair, *The Promise of the Metropolis: Bangalore's Twentieth Century* (Delhi, 2005), pp. 1-10.
9. Helen Meller, *Patrick Geddes: Social Evolutionist and City Planner* (London, 1990). See also Jacqueline Tyrwhitt (ed.), *Patrick Geddes in India* (London, 1947).
10. Narayani Gupta, 'British Town-Planners and India', in Narayani Gupta and Mushirul Hasan (eds), *India's Colonial Encounter: Essays in Honour of Eric Stokes* (Delhi, 1993), pp. 243-4. The most prominent Indian followers of Geddes in the inter-war years were N.A. Toothi, his student at Bombay whom he sent to England for further training, and Radhakamal Mukherjee, who was based in the department of Sociology at Lucknow. However, another student, G.S. Ghurye, became 'violently' disaffected by the 'indoctrination in civic reconstruction' that he received from Geddes. Meller, *Patrick Geddes,* pp. 225-7.
11. Chatterjee, *Politics of the Governed,* p. 140.
12. For an overview, see Sunil Khilnani, *The Idea of India* (Delhi, 1999), pp. 107-149.
13. Khilnani, *Idea of India,* p. 235; Anthony d. King, *Urbanism, Colonialism, and the World- Economy: Cultural and Spatial Foundations of the World Urban System* (London and New York, 1991), pp. 13-14. The most noteworthy of these are Robert Redfield and Milton Singer, 'The Cultural Role of Cities', *Man in India,* 36/3 (1956): 161-94; Milton Singer, 'The Great Tradition in a Metropolitan Centre: Madras', in Milton Singer (ed.), *Traditional India: Structure and Change* (Philadelphia, 1959); and G.S. Ghurye, 'Cities of India', *Sociological Bulletin,* 11/2 (1953): 47-71.
14. Nair, *Promise of the Metropolis,* p. 6.
15. Gupta, 'British Town-Planners and India', p. 244.
16. M.S.A. Rao (ed.), *Urban Sociology in India: Reader and Sourcebook* (Hyderabad, 1974), p. 11.
17. Ibid., pp. 11-12; Nair, *Promise of the Metropolis,* pp. 6-7.
18. J.C. Masselos, *Towards Nationalism: Group Affiliations and the Politics of Public Associations in Nineteenth Century Western India* (Bombay, 1974); Anil Seal, *The Emergence of Indian Nationalism: Competition and Collaboration in the Later Nineteenth Century* (Cambridge, 1968); E.R. Leach and S.N. Mukherjee (eds) *Elites in South Asia* (Cambridge,

1970), pp. 33-78; Christine dobbin, *Urban Leadership in Western India: Politics and Communities in Bombay City, 1840-85* (Oxford, 1972); C.A. Bayly, *The Local Roots of Indian Politics:* Allahabad, 1870-1920 (Oxford, 1975). Even though many of these works were published in the early 1970s, the research on which they were based had in most instances been initiated in the previous decade.

19. Morris d. Morris, *The Emergence of an Industrial Labour Force: A Study of the Bombay Cotton Mills, 1854-1947* (Berkeley, 1965).

20. Anthony d. King, *Colonial Urban Development: Culture, Social Power, and Environment* (London, 1976); Kenneth Ballhatchet and J. Harrison (eds), *The City in South Asia: Premodern and Modern* (London, 1980); Susan Nield, 'Colonial Urbanism: The development of Madras City in the Eighteenth and Nineteenth Centuries', MAS, 13 (1979): 217-46; Thomas Metcalf, *An Imperial Vision: Indian Architecture and Britain's Raj* (Berkeley and Los Angeles, 1989); Mariam dossal, *Imperial Designs and Indian Realities: The Planning of Bombay City, 1845-1875* (Bombay, 1996).

21. Veena Talwar Oldenburg, *The Making of Colonial Lucknow, 1856-1877* (Princeton, 1984); Narayani Gupta, *Delhi Between Two Empires, 1803-1931: Society, Government and Urban Growth* (Delhi, 1981).

22. C.A. Bayly, *Rulers, Townsmen and Bazaars: North Indian Society in the Age of British Expansion, 1770-1870* (Cambridge, 1983); Thomas A. Timberg, *The Marwaris: From Traders to Industrialists* (Delhi, 1978); J.C. Masselos, 'Power in the Bombay "Moholla", 1904-15: An Initial Exploration into the World of the Indian Urban Muslim', *South Asia,* 6 (1976): 75-95.

23. Rajnarayan Chandavarkar, 'Workers' Politics and the Mill districts in Bombay between the Wars', MAS, 15/3 (1981): 603-647; Chitra Joshi, 'Bonds of Community, Ties of Religion: Kanpur Textile Workers in the Early Twentieth Century', *Indian Economic and Social History Review* (hereafter *IESHR),* 22/3 (1985): 251-80; dipesh Chakrabarty, 'Communal Riots and Labour: Bengal's Jute Mill-hands in the 1890s', *Past and Present,* 91/1 (1981): 140-69.

24. Douglas Haynes, *Rhetoric and Ritual in Colonial India: The Shaping of a Public Culture in Surat City, 1852-1928* (Delhi, 1992).

25. Sumanta Banerjee, *The Parlour and the Street: Elite and Popular Culture in Nineteenth Century Calcutta* (Calcutta, 1989); J.C. Masselos, 'Change and Custom in the Format of the Bombay Mohurram during the Nineteenth and Twentieth Centuries', *South Asia,* New Series, 5/2 (1982): 47-67; Sandria Freitag, *Collective Action and Community: Public*

Arenas and the Emergence of Communalism in North India (Delhi, 1990); Sandria Freitag (ed.), *Culture and Power in Banaras* (Berkeley, 1989); Nita Kumar, *The Artisans of Benares, 1880-1980* (Princeton, 1988); Gyanendra Pandey, 'Encounters and Calamities: The history of a north India *qasba* in the nineteenth century', in Ranajit Guha (ed.), *Subaltern Studies III: Writings on South Asian History and Society* (Delhi, 1984), pp. 231-70.

26. For details, see Indu Banga (ed.), *The City in Indian History* (Delhi, 1991).
27. Jonathan P. Parry, 'Introduction', in Jonathan P. Parry, Jan Breman and Karin Kapadia (eds), *The Worlds of Indian Industrial Labour* (Delhi, 1999), pp. ix-xxxvi.
28. See, for instance, Eric Stokes, *The Peasant and the Raj: Studies in Agrarian society and Peasant Rebellion in colonial India* (Cambridge, 1978); Utsa Patnaik (ed.), *Agrarian Relations and Accumulation: The Mode of Production Debate in India* (Bombay, 1990).
29. Narayani Gupta, 'Twelve Years On: Urban History in India', *Urban History Yearbook* (1981), p. 76.
30. C.A. Bayly, 'Introduction: The Connected World of Empires', in Leila Tarazi Fawaz and C.A. Bayly (eds), *Modernity and Culture: From the Mediterranean to the Indian Ocean* (New York, 2002), p. 10. For a representative sample of the early writings of this collective, see Ranajit Guha and Gayatri Chakravorty Spivak (eds), *Selected Subaltern Studies* (Delhi, 1988). Interestingly, dipesh Chakrabarty's monograph on jute mill workers of Calcutta, one of the few works by a member of the group that was set in an urban context, argued that the primordial cultural values of the rural migrants who came to work in the city prevented them from attaining a modern 'class consciousness'. Thus, even in his account the shadow of the countryside continued to loom large over the modern Indian city. See dipesh Chakrabarty, *Rethinking Working-Class History: Bengal, 1890-1940* (Delhi, 1989).
31. Prakash, 'Urban Turn', pp. 2-7.
32. K.C. Sivaramakrishnan, Amitabh Kundu and B.N. Singh, *Handbook of Urbanisation in India: An Analysis of Trends and Processes* (Delhi, 2005), pp. 5-7.
33. Suketu Mehta, *Maximum City: Bombay Lost and Found* (London, 2005), p. 3.
34. Darryl d'Monte, *Ripping the Fabric: The Decline of Mumbai and its Mills* (Delhi, 2002); Chitra Joshi, *Lost Worlds: Indian Labour and its*

Forgotten Histories (Delhi, 2000). Of course, the signs of impending crisis were evident even before the era of economic liberalisation commenced. Through the 1970s and 1980s there were attempts, both in the private and public sectors, to 'downsise' firms and rationalise production strategies. Employers increasingly took recourse to casual labour, which could be hired and fired in keeping with their requirements. The new era of privatisation that was inaugurated by economic liberalisation in the early 1990s only served further to accentuate these trends. See Jan Breman, 'The study of industrial labour in post-colonial India—the informal sector: A concluding review', in Parry et al. (eds), *Worlds of Indian Industrial Labour,* pp. 407-429.

35. Jan Breman, *Footloose Labour: Working in India's Informal Economy* (Cambridge, 1996). For a historical exploration of these themes in the context of late colonial north India, see Nandini Gooptu, *The Politics of the Urban Poor in Early Twentieth-Century India* (Cambridge, 2001), pp. 27-65.
36. Rajnarayan Chandavarkar, *Imperial Power and Popular Politics: Class, Resistance and the State in India, c. 1850-1950* (Cambridge, 1998), pp. 30-73; Prabhu P. Mahapatra, 'Situating the Renewal: Reflections on Labour Studies in India', Integrated Labour History Research Programme, Working Paper No. 2 (Noida, 1998).
37. Chatterjee, *Politics of the Governed,* pp. 142-3.
38. Khilnani, *Idea of India,* p. 148.
39. Nair, *Promise of the Metropolis,* pp. 90-99, 133-6.
40. Khilnani, *op. cit.*, p. 144.
41. Chatterjee, *Politics of the Governed,* pp. 143-4.
42. Partha Chatterjee, 'On Civil and Political Society in Post-Colonial democracies', in Sudipta Kaviraj and Sunil Khilnani (eds), *Civil Society: History and Possibilities* (Cambridge, 2001).
43. Thomas Blom Hansen, *Violence in Urban India: Identity Politics, 'Mumbai' and the Postcolonial City* (Delhi, 2001); Nair, *Promise of the Metropolis,* pp. 271-98.
44. Fawaz and Bayly (eds), *Modernity and Culture.*
45. Most notably, Morris, *Emergence of an Industrial Labour Force;* and Chandavarkar, *Origins of Industrial Capitalism in India.*
46. Patrick Joyce, *Rule of Freedom: Liberalism and the Modern City* (London and New York, 2003); Mary Poovey, *Making a Social Body:*

British Cultural Formation, 1830-1864 (Baltimore, 1996); Paul Rabinow, *French Modern Norms and Forms of the Social Environment* (Cambridge, Massachusetts, 1989); Brenda S.A. Yeoh, *Contesting Space in Colonial Singapore: Power Relations and the Urban Built Environment* (Singapore, 2003); Joseph W. Esherick (ed.), *Remaking the Chinese City: Modernity and National Identity, 1900-1950* (Honolulu, 1999).

47. Andrew Burton, *African Underclass: Urbanisation, Crime and Colonial Order in Dares Salaam* (Oxford, 2005); Frederick Cooper, 'Urban space, industrial time, and wage labour in Africa', in Frederick Cooper (ed.), *Struggle for the City* (Beverley Hills, 1983); Alan Mayne, *The Imagined Slum: Newspaper Representation in Three Cities, 1870-1914* (Leicester, 1993); Gareth Stedman-Jones, *Outcast London: A Study of the Relationship Between Classes in Victorian Society* (Harmondsworth, 1984).

48. The civic projects that were undertaken prior to the 1890s, insofar as they were implemented, were either designed to bolster the city's commercial infrastructure or provide modern sanitary amenities to the city's elites. For an account of mid-Victorian colonial civic initiatives, see dossal, *Imperial Designs and Indigenous Realities.*

49. The idea of the 'unintended city' was first elaborated in an influential essay by the architect and urban activist Jai Sen. Originally published in April 1975, the essay was subsequently reproduced in a special issue of the Indian journal *Seminar.* See Jai Sen, 'The Unintended City', *Seminar,* 500 (April 2001): 38-47. More recently, Ashis Nandy has deployed the phrase to signify 'the city that was never part of the formal "master plan" but always implicit in it'. Quoted in Prakash, 'Urban Turn', p. 5.

50. James C. Scott, *Seeing like a State: How Certain Schemes to Improve the Human Condition have Failed* (New Haven, 1998).

51. Yeoh, *Contesting Space in Colonial Singapore,* pp. 9-10.

52. Chandavarkar, *Imperial Power and Popular Politics,* pp. 180-233.

53. Timothy Mitchell, 'The Limits of the State: Beyond Statist Approaches and their Critics', *American Political Science Review,* 85 (1991), pp. 77-96; Timothy Mitchell, 'Society, Economy, and the State Effect', in G. Steinmetz (ed.), *State/Culture: State-formation after the Cultural Turn* (Ithaca, 1999), pp. 76-97.

54. For an elaboration of this point in the context of contemporary India, see C.J. Fuller and John Harriss, 'For an Anthropology of the Modern

Indian State', in C.J. Fuller and Véronique Bénéï (eds), *The Everyday State and Society in Modern India* (London, 2001), p. 24.

55. Bayly, *Birth of the Modern World,* pp. 19 3-4.

56. Barbara Daly Metcalf and Thomas Metcalf, *A Concise History of India* (Cambridge, 2002), p. 123.

57. Bayly, 'Evolution of Colonial Cultures', p. 450.

58. As one scholar has noted, 'The discourse of social capital, with its emphasis on cooperation and collaboration, is not sensitive to negative effects in situations of social conflict'. Susanne Hoeber Rudolph, 'Civil Society and the Realm of Freedom', *Economic and Political Weekly* (hereafter *EPW),* 35/20 (2000), p. 1764.

59. Chatterjee, 'On Civil and Political Society in Post-Colonial democracies', pp. 172-4.

60. In this context, see Sandria Freitag, 'Contesting in Public: Colonial Legacies and Contemporary Communalism', in David Ludden (ed.), *Making India Hindu: Community Conflict and the Politics of Democracy* (Delhi, 1996); Aditya Nigam, 'Civil Society and its "Underground": Explorations in the Notion of Political Society', in Rajeev Bhargava and Helmut Reifeld (eds), *Civil Society, Public Sphere and Citizenship: Dialogues and Perceptions* (Delhi, 2005), pp. 236-59.

61. Sudipta Kaviraj, 'In Search of Civil Society', in Sudipta Kaviraj and Sunil Khilnani (eds), *Civil Society: History and Possibilities* (Cambridge, 2001), pp. 310-18; Chatterjee, *Politics of the Governed,* pp. 132-4.

62. Kaviraj, 'In Search of Civil Society', p. 317.

63. C.A. Bayly, *Origins of Nationality in South Asia: Patriotism and Ethical Government in the Making of Modern India* (Delhi, 1998); Carey Anthony Watt, *Serving the Nation: Cultures of Service, Association and Citizenship in Colonial India* (Delhi, 2005).

2

CONTEMPORARY URBAN SOCIOLOGY

City has been locus of all civilisations; the rise and fall of civilisations appear to be integral to the rise and fall of the cities with which they are associated. Not surprisingly, the city, or the urban form, has attracted the attention of scholars from various disciplinary backgrounds, not only social sciences but also natural sciences. Attempts by the social scientists to grapple with the reality of the city have repeatedly highlighted the inherent complexity of the phenomenon and have thrown up many concepts and theorisations. Similarly, attempts by planners and administrators to deal with the urban problems have revealed the limits to planned urban habitat change. It is hardly surprising that the intractability of the urban question in social theory and in urban planning led to cynicism: in 1985, Peter Saunders confidently announced the death of urban sociology.

In retrospect, Saunders's obituary on urban sociology was premature; it even turned out to be unfounded. The rapid unfolding of events since the 1990s—the breakdown of the erstwhile Soviet Union and the disenchantment with communism; the end of the Cold War and the realignment of international economic and political order; the rise of the European Union; the spread of globalisation and the associated ICT (information and communication technology) Revolution with their attendant impact on the movement of human beings, ideas, and capital; the rise of religious fundamentalism and the violence associated with it... has had profound impact on the cities around the world and rejuvenated the academic interest in the urban question.

What globalisation has done is to bring together urban centres, both within individual countries and internationally. This has been greatly facilitated by increased physical connectivity (via improved means of transportation) and efficient electronic connectivity (via television, mobile telephony, and the Internet). Whether it is boom or meltdown in the economy, religious celebrations or racial attacks, democratic elections or military takeovers, no city in the world today can remain unaffected. This internationalisation of the city is both inviting and challenging at the same time: conventional sociologists and post-modernists alike are revisiting the city.

City: Locale and Milieu

In revisiting the city, a distinction needs to be made between the *locale (place)* and the *milieu (space)* dimensions of the urban form. The locale dimension of a city, that is, its physical/territorial boundary, is demarcated, even if arbitrarily, administratively. That is what we see on the map; and that is what administrators define as the jurisdiction of the city. The milieu dimension, on the other hand, is identifiable in terms of the processes around which the city dwellers' life revolves. These processes could be (a) social (involving groupings and intra- and inter-group interactions, with varying degrees of complexity resulting from size and composition of the population), (b) cultural (referring to ways of thinking and acting), and (c) political (having to do with relations of power/control, not necessarily in the formal sense).

Two points need clarification. First, the milieu dimension of the city is embedded in its locale dimension, but the milieu dimension transcends the locale dimension: that is, locale provides the physical context for milieu, but locale does not delimit milieu. The cities are locales in which many milieux interact and new ones emerge. Second, the study of the locale dimension is important in its own right, just as it is in relation to the milieu dimension. But, it calls for a multi-disciplinary, if not interdisciplinary expertise, which conventional sociological training hardly provides in its urban sociology courses.

Thus, the primary focus of revisiting the city in urban sociology would be on people and their culture, rather than on the physical dimensions of the habitat called the city. Focussing on the people and their culture in the cities, the key issues appear to centre around (a) citizenship, local relations and cosmopolitanism, on the one hand, and (b) the articulation and experience of community and identity, on the other. The dialectics of these two foci, namely, community and cosmopolitanism constitutes the contemporary relevance of urban sociology. The scope of the new urban sociology is variegated, just as its thematics are vibrant. In what follows, an attempt is made to discuss these with special reference to India.

Community-Cosmopolitanism Dialectics

There are multiple sources of this dynamics. To start with there has been a *phenomenal growth both in the number of cities and the number of people living in them*. In the developing countries, much of the growth in the urban population is not due to natural reproduction within the cities; it is due to rural-urban migration. What is noteworthy, there have been important changes in the origin and destination of migration. There has been a change in the gender profile of the migrant population: there has been an increase in female migration that is independent of marriage-related relocation. Overall, there has been a greater heterogeneity of the city's population. 'The theme of city life', as Richard Rodrigues observes, 'is the theme of differences'.

The migration of people from rural to urban areas, and the movement of people between these two areas generally, have been facilitated by *communication revolution.* The last two decades have seen a rapid expansion of railway and road networks in India. Far-flung areas of the country have been linked to metropolises and urban centres with direct railway connections. Besides the Government of India's national highways project, called 'the Golden Quadrilateral', the state governments have been improving the state highways linking urban centres. The improved means of transportation has meant increased facilities for movement of people and goods, considerable reduction in journey time, and greater exchange between urban centres and their hinterlands. Contributing further to the last consequence has been the remarkable spread of the electronic medium of communication like television (and also Internet, to some extent) and mobile telephony.

The engine behind these developments is, no doubt, *the nature of and trends in economic development* that has been taking place in the globalisation era, especially after the adoption of the policies of liberalisation and structural adjustment by the Government of India. The traditional industries—for example, jute in Kolkata, textiles in Mumbai, and the public sector in Bengaluru—have declined, and the new ones—the information technology (IT) and the IT-enabled services in Bengaluru, financial services and commercial cinema in Mumbai—have shot into prominence. The changing economy has reinvigorated cities like Chennai, Hyderabad, and Pune, fostered conurbations (as for example, in the case of Gurgaon near Delhi, Hosur near Bengaluru, etc.), and given fillip to many a small town. Not only has the production technology and distribution management have changed, the consumption patterns of urban dwellers have also undergone change: consumerism, consumer society, etc. are the new terms used to designate this change.

The city, which has always been a visible marker of civilisation, has become even more so. *The greater visibility of the city* is seen not only in terms of the extent and variety of assets it possesses (industries and business houses of varying sizes, vast administrative machinery, specialist hospitals and educational institutions, architectural heritage sites and skyscraper buildings, gated colonies and squalid slums, flyovers and metros), but also in the nature and vibrancy of its lifestyles and culture (pubs and malls, performing creative arts and commercial cinema, nightlife and crimes, sport spectacles and mega events). The city has attained heightened observability and become an extraordinary source of dreams, aspirations, and illusions. Naturally, it acts as a magnet not only for public and private investment, but also for rural population as islands of promise in the midst of despair. Interestingly, it is this observability of the city which makes it a site for terrorist attacks. The bomb blasts and terrorist adventurism in Mumbai is a case in point.

Paradoxically, contrary to the analytical prognosis of the classical sociologists and social thinkers (excluding the pessimist like Vilfredo Pareto), with the advancement of science and technology, rationality and law, and the march of industrial capitalism, the bearing of religion on social life has not waned. The consensus mustered by social scientists in the decades following the World War II that modernisation and secularisation would replace religion with faith in science, education, and the rule of law has turned out to be unfounded. Since the 1980s, it became evident that religion was not on the retreat. There have been *aggressive ethnic and religious mobilisations* of various hues, including Buddhism and Hinduism, which were once seen as otherworldly, acquiescent, and docile religions. Globally, cities have become the sites of multiple religious movements, conversions, and cults representing a variety of global evangelism and indigenous traditions. Both new (television and Internet) and conventional (the press) media have been used for this. It is in the context of these developments that the dialectics of community-cosmopolitanism is being played out.

Briefly put, urban modernisation has not engendered secularisation of social life. It appears that equating urbanity with modernity, or urbanism with secularism, has resulted in grave misunderstanding of ethnicity, religion, and identity in urban areas. The paradox under reference cannot be explained either by the essentialist concepts of the ecological school or the deterministic assumptions of the political economy perspective. Understanding and explaining this paradox of urbanism needs new conceptual tools and theoretical forays.

The rapid urbanisation and urban-ward migration of rural population has *aggravated the existing problems* and brought in their train new ones. Overcrowded housing and slums, overloaded transportation services, overstretched medicare facilities, substandard civic amenities, breakdown of urban governance, etc. have been researched at length. Similarly, the governmental and policy initiatives and programmes for addressing them have been reviewed and evaluated. However, the last two decades have witnessed the emergence of new interest groups and initiatives. Citizen groups for developing the city they live in have come into existence. There are many civil society organisations engaged in all activities from garbage collection and disposal to cultural promotion. There are citizen initiatives concerning voter registration, commuting, vigilance against crime, etc. Many of these initiatives and organisations are formally recognised by the government, and some of them are also financially supported by the government. However, there are parallel 'governance' mechanisms in place, which are not recognised, and some are even illegal. For example, the phenomenon of gangs and their warfare in big cities, often dubbed the 'underworld', is least understood. Same is true of the growth of urban violence resulting from gang warfare, communalism, ethnocentric assertions, etc.

Paradoxically, the city appears to be its own undoing: the more it improves, the more attractive it becomes, resulting in greater influx of the population and aggravation of the problems. The urban problems thus would appear to be *sui generis* intractable. One may recall here Henri Lefebvre's observation that 'there can be growth without social development (that is, quantitative growth without qualitative development). Under these conditions, he argues that 'changes in society are more apparent than real. Fetishism and ideology of change (in other words, the ideology of modernity) conceal the stagnation of essential social relations' *(ibid.)*. It is in this context that the scope for a new urban sociology will have to be spelt.

Thematics of Contemporary Urban Sociology

The dialectics of community-cosmopolitanism implies that its constituents, namely, community and cosmopolitanism, constitute two opposing polar tendencies. Apparently, this parallels the dichotomous typologies suggested by early sociologists to grapple with changes that the European society was experiencing due to rapid industrialisation-cum-urbanisation. The conceptualisations propounded by the German sociologist Ferdinand Tönnies and the French sociologist Emile Durkheim readily come to mind. Louis Wirth too alluded to this in implicitly contrasting urbanism as a way of life from the rural way of life. However, what the dialectics of community-cosmopolitanism suggests is something more than the two contrasting types or an evolutionary trajectory (cf. Tönnies and Durkheim). It draws attention to the inevitable contradiction that the juxtaposition of community and cosmopolitanism raises in urban existence.

The concept of cosmopolitanism is premised upon the assumption of what Lefebvre terms the 'homo urbanicus': (a) that city dwellers are atomised individuals with segmented personalities, (b) that urban life recognises the universal human by erasing differences, and (c) that the city offers inclusive citizenship and the 'right to urban life'. As Ernest Gellner notes, 'The individualism inherent in the condition of modular man, if pushed to its logical conclusion, was hostile to the cult of community'.

The concept of community, as used in the urban context, no more refers to a spatio-temporal entity in which face-to-face interaction is by definition important. The definitional criterion of the concept of community now revolves around 'identity', which has to do more with imagined commonalities even among people who may not be personally acquainted, than with face-to-face interactions among people living in physical contiguity. Accordingly, we have such expressions as religious communities, caste communities, linguistic communities, migrant/diasporic communities, etc.—all hinging on 'consciousness of kind' in reference-group terms.

We should hasten to clarify that under certain circumstances face-to-face interaction can solidify and reinforce community identity. Wirth long ago inferred '... the spatial segregation of individuals according to color, ethnic heritage, economic and social status, tastes and preferences...'. He postulated that this is a natural outcome of the larger size of urban population, which involves 'a greater range of individual variation' *(ibid.).* To Wirth, sorting and segregation of the urban population follows a natural ecological principle. He did not consider the forces -economic, political, and social—which can result in voluntary seclusion or forced exclusion of the population on specific identity criteria. The Muslim ghettos in Ahmedabad, Kolkata and Mumbai, the ethnic refugee camps in Chandigarh and Delhi, the linguistic enclaves among slum dwellers in Bengaluru, and the changing composition *of pols* (traditional neighbourhood groupings) in Ahmedabad are cases in point. The point that is emphasised here is that communities come to be constituted; they need not be natural formations. These communities tend to be particularistic in their value orientation, and inclusive in relation to one another.

Viewed in this perspective, it is easy to understand how community (emphasising collectivity, with its narrower and more rigid articulation of identity) and cosmopolitanism (emphasising differences and universal individualism, with its broader and more flexible articulation of multiple identities) are polar tendencies in the city. Their dialectics (a) determines the everyday life of urbanites, (b) shapes their aspirations and facilitates/hinders the realisation of those aspirations, (c) conditions the articulation of their identities, (d) defines the politics of identity and inter-community relations, and (e) constantly redraws the place-space configuration in the city. In the light of this dialectics, in what follows we shall explore the possible areas and issues for empirical investigation.

The Urban Citizen: Contestations over Definition

With reference to a city, one could ask 'Who belongs to the city?' or 'Who are its citizens?' Apparently, this is an easy question to answer: anyone living in that city for a relatively long period (as contrasted from a visitor or a sojourner) is its 'citizen'. A closer examination of the situation in different cities would reveal this answer to be facile; it is, in fact, invariably contested. In law, anyone born in a city or domiciled in it for a defined duration (10 years in Indian cities) is a citizen of that city. The citizenship that so accrues entitles its holder to certain rights, as for instance, in admission to public educational institutions, allotment of public housing or sites (land) for building houses, etc.

However, given the limitation of resources, facilities, and opportunities in any city, and the resulting competition for them, the legal definition of citizenship is challenged in quotidian existence by those who call themselves 'natives' of the city as well as by the migrants. The citizens would like a more *exclusive* definition of the citizenship, restricting it by a rigidly defined 'nativity' in terms of the language of the state in which the city is located. Thus, 'Mumbaikar' (someone belonging to Mumbai) becomes coterminous with being *'Marathi Manus'* (Marathi people), emphasising the idea of *bhumiputra* (the 'sons/daughters of the soil') in linguistic terms. The 'natives' would consciously exclude not only those who have immigrated to the city during the last decade, but even the second and third generation descendents of original migrants. This exclusion has often resulted in aggressive street politics and violence targeting the 'outsiders': the Shiv Sena movement against the South Indians (derisively called Madrassis) in the late 1960s and early 1970s and the Maharashtra Navnirman Sena movement against the North Indians (mostly migrants from Bihar and Uttar Pradesh, derisively called Bhayyas) in Mumbai are illustrative of this.

The migrants, including those who have moved in only recently, would want a more *inclusive* definition of citizenship. After all, the city, by its developmental logic, is a conflux of migrant streams resulting in a unique culture. Most of them are the city's citizens 'by adoption'. Furthermore, it is they who toil for the general prosperity of the city, they would argue. Thus, they are citizens of the city by virtue of being there. It is interesting that violence against migrant communities from Bihar and Uttar Pradesh has produced counter-violence against Maharashtrians and the Marathi-speaking people (not necessarily those hailing from Mumbai) in urban centres in those states. The violence of citizenship politics has drawn the critical attention of the Indian Parliament.

Interestingly, the legal definition of city's citizenship is not a prerequisite for registration for voting in the state assembly or Lok Sabha (the lower house of Parliament) elections or even elections to the civic bodies like city corporation councils or town municipal councils. Obviously, this is a bone of contention: the natives opposing voting rights to the migrants and the migrants pressing for it, as that is the only element of political power that they have, even if it is available to them only once in five years. The emigrants, given their concentration in specific localities, constitute vote banks and they do vote *en bloc;* they have even been successful in getting their candidates elected not only to civic bodies, but also to state legislative assemblies. Given the heterogeneity of the city's population, no political party can afford to lose sight of such vote banks.

The contestations about citizenship are not confined to issues concerning the right to use of facilities, allocation of houses/house-sites, reservation in employment, right to political representation, etc. They spill over into the symbolic space. Many cities in India have been renamed in the last few decades: Bangalore has become

Bengaluru; Baroda, Vadodara; Benaras, Varanasi; Bombay, Mumbai; Calcutta, Kolkata; Madras, Chennai; Trivandrum, Thirvananthapuram; and so on. Within each city there have been demands for renaming the city's landmarks and streets: Crawford Market and Victoria Terminus have become Jyotiba Pule Market and Chatrapathi Shivaji Terminus in Mumbai; Connaught Circus, Rajiv Gandhi Circus in New Delhi; Mount Road, Anna Salai in Chennai; South Parade, Mahatma Gandhi Road in Bengaluru; and so on.

The 'natives' demand priority to be given to the state/regional language both in the public realm—in educational institutions, civic ceremonies, official documents and in private parlance—on nameplates, signboards and hoardings. There have been cases where the native vigilante groups have enforced this through violent methods. There are symbolic contestations about statues, too. In Bengaluru, the statue of Thiruvalluvar (a saint poet) has remained installed but not unveiled in a predominantly Tamil-speaking area of the city. The reason: the native Kannada-speaking activists want a *quid pro quo*—a statue of Sarvajnya (a Kannadiga saint poet) be installed in Chennai, the predominantly Tamil-speaking capital city of Tamil Nadu!

The demand for renaming cities, or their monuments and streets, or for prioritising the use of the local language (as against the official language Hindi, or English, or any other), or for/against installing statues is more than a desire for erasing colonial memories or commemorating the local heroes. It is the dialectics of community-cosmopolitanism at work here. Such demands seem to counter cosmopolitanism; underlying them often are atavistic tendencies glorifying a community or vilifying another, not infrequently based on a mythologised or imagined past, and on frozen memories.

The counter-positioning of nativist movements and cosmopolitanism appears to be more pronounced in cities where a larger section of the population consists of the first, second, or third generation migrants who are 'visibly' different from the natives. In brief, the answer to the question 'Who belongs to the city?' depends on 'Who *defines* citizenship?' The legal and the socio-politically contingent definitions of citizenship seem to vary. As a consequence, the city is the site of myriad articulations of identity and mobilisations of people. The issue of urban citizenship and citizen rights thus throws up a variety of themes and issues for sociological investigation.

Differences, Identities, and Territories

Cities are generally heterogeneous in their composition: the larger the population of a city, the greater the heterogeneity of its population. The identity derived from citizenship of the city would, therefore, be too homogeneous. Except when it is invoked by the 'natives', it is also tenuous and fragile. Only when a citizen performs a feat or conferred an honour, or a team representing the city scores over another in a competitive event is the citizenship identity (for example, 'Mumbaikar') invoked with pride. Similarly, when the city remarkably recovers from a natural disaster (for example, a flood) or human-engineered calamity (for example, a serial bomb-blast) a reference is proudly made about the city's citizenship spirit. The use of citizenship identity with a positive connotation is limited, though not insignificant. However, it is periodically invoked by the 'natives' ('we'/'us') whenever the migrants ('they'/'them') are viewed as a negative reference group. The consequences are negative, and the citizenship identity takes a dent.

Given the heterogeneity of the city's population, we should expect that more non-city-based identities are ascribed or invoked in urban life. There are self-defined and other-defined identities for urban collectivities; correspondingly, there are assumed/ascribed stereotypes and eulogistic/pejorative labels. Apart from region, language and physical features (as in the case of migrants), religion, caste, class, gender, and sexuality may be invoked in identity formation. Thus, as is to be expected, a city dweller has multiple identities; s/he invokes (or responds to an external invocation) an identity or combination of identities depending upon the situation.

The persons invoking identities (of their own or more so of the others) often have limited or no knowledge of the differences: proclivity for prejudices acts as a smokescreen for knowledge. Because of this there is often mistaken invocation of identities. But, once invoked, the identities and the stereotypes that go with them influence the behaviour of people. Even if one is knowledgeable, the process of judgment could be erroneous: judging the behaviour of an individual by reference to the group to which s/he belongs or judging an entire group based on the behaviour of an individual is fraught with danger.

To the extent that identity formation/invocation proceeds on such primordial lines as religion, caste, or linguistic affiliation, there is the inherent danger of essentialising or reifying ethnicities. Categorical distinctions in social situations result in (a) allocating an individual to an ethnic category, (b) behaving towards that person in a particular way, and (c) rationalising/justifying that behaviour. Heightened interaction within the group and avoidance of others is one outcome. The feeling of security within the familiar, on the one hand, and the perception of threat from others results in voluntary or forced exclusion and the formation of ethnic enclaves and ghettos. Violence exacerbates the social distance and hardens the group boundaries. It is in this context that social space gets embedded in physical place.

It is true that territorial demarcation of communities and ethnic enclaves existed earlier too: in almost all traditional Indian cities religious communities and caste groups resided in specific areas of the city, and many of these areas were even known by the names of those communities or castes. Then, the society was more strongly defined by the caste idiom, and the idea of cosmopolitanism was yet to take roots. However, in post-Independence India, caste idiom is officially de-legitimised and discriminations based on religion, caste, and gender are proscribed. Cosmopolitanism is the modern value premise, and the city is expected to be its harbinger. However, not only have the earlier segregated residential areas persisted (with notable exceptions, of course), but also there have been newer articulations of segregation and exclusion. Since open discrimination is violation of law, informal insulation of residential colonies are operative in housing societies, gated communities, etc.

Thus, who belongs to which part/area of the city and why throws up several facets of urban life for sociological inquiry: the formation of urban enclaves, the nature of their interaction with other areas of the city, and the quotidian life of the people living there. The changing geography of class, gentrification of working-class residential areas, and changing composition of slums (the 'shadow cities', as Robert Neuwirth [2005]) need to be understood with locality as the focus.

Social Networks: Negotiating Life in the City

Irrespective of where one lives in the city, negotiating urban life implies establishing social networks. Conventionally, such concepts as 'reachability' (links radiating from a person reaching her/him back), 'multiplexity' (two persons being linked in more than one way, and 'intensity' (individuals being ready to honour obligations) are used in analysing social networks. Cities offer a variety of network possibilities which vary in terms of the scale on which they are organised as also the nature of their organisation: family reunions and kitty parties, clubs and associations, cult groups and secret societies, chit funds and mutual-aid groups, and so on.

These networks aid the urban dwellers in negotiating their everyday life; they are important for them in realising their aspirations. In case of need, they can draw upon resources and social support of their networks. The networks function as resource pools and insurance mechanisms in the urban world characterised by uncertainties and risks. One could postulate that stronger one's social networks in the city, more comfortable would be her/his life; conversely, urban life would be wretched without social networks. We have very little sociological knowledge about the different types of urban social networks, their origin and development, their structure and functioning, and their overall dynamics in urbanism.

Another emergent facet of urban life that calls for sociological attention is the cyberspace. The Information and Communication Technology (ICT) Revolution, which has been an integral part of globalisation, has profoundly affected the city. As Dear has observed, 'No-one can ignore the challenges of the information age, which promises to unseat many of our cherished notions about socio-spatial structuring'. While being predominantly city-centric, the impact of cyberspace is felt widely, even in rural areas. Scholarly attention is now turning to this phenomenon.

In his insightful work on the digitally mediated environment, William J. Mitchell argues that the organisation of the city will undergo profound changes as the cyberspace encompasses its economic, socio-cultural, and political life. In his 'city of bits', Mitchell visualises the ubiquity of networks in an electronically mediated environment. The value of a network connection is determined by bandwidth: 'bandwidth-disadvantaged' (the new have-nots), 'zero bandwidth' (the lack of network communication), 'digital hermit' (the marginalised outcasts of cyberspace) will be the new concepts to work with. Since ICT has been the driver of economic growth in India, scholars are examining its influence on social change. There is urgent need for sociological research on the cyberspace dimension of the city.

City and Civil Society Organisations

Outlining the constituent elements of the 'ideal type' of the city, Max Weber emphasised 'at least partial autonomy and autocephaly, thus also an administration by authorities in the election of whom the burghers participated' and 'a court of its own and at least partially autonomous law'. Both urban administration (executive) and urban courts (judiciary) are formal public institutions; they derive their authority based on legal-rational considerations through legislative enactments. Although, several facets of urban life have traditionally remained outside the public sphere, it can be said with little contradiction today that in all aspects of urban society, directly or indirectly, the presence of governmental authority is apparent.

However, in India, during the last few decades, civil society initiatives have become increasingly prominent in urban areas. Scores of non-governmental organisations are operating in Indian cities. Some of these have sanction under law and are governed by rules and regulations specified under legislative enactments: they must have a constitution, hold periodical elections to offices, conduct general body and other meetings, get their accounts audited, and annually report compliance to the specified authority. However, outside the ambit of law there are several civil society initiatives; not all of them would stand legal scrutiny, and some of them are blatantly illegal (and operate even after they are banned by law).

The civil society initiatives may originate as resistance mechanisms which are opposed to some proposal or programme of the government bodies that would affect the interest of the locality or the community. Some of the resistance initiatives develop into well-organised local interest groups; they may even get co-opted as complementary mechanisms in government's development programmes. A few of them may become oppressive mechanisms indulging in coercion or extortion by using their connections with the administrative machinery or by sheer muscle power. Apparently, the persistence of anachronistic laws, politicisation of policy issues, corruption in politics and administration, and so on have weakened the efficiency of formal governance machinery, opening up the scope for non-formal and non-legitimate governance mechanisms. All this offers scope for research in urban sociology.

A notable development in Indian cities is the large-scale public celebration of religious festivals. Often festivals such as Ganesh Uthsav and Janmashtami in Mumbai or Kali Puja in Kolkata involve meticulous organisation and large-scale mobilisation of money and human resources. The duality of these festivals is noteworthy. On the one hand, there is secularisation of the religious sphere whereby some primordial differences like caste, creed, and linguistic affiliation are temporarily suspended. On the other hand, there is heightened religiosity in secular places during this period. Public display of religiosity and religious symbols, religious processions, etc., whether by a majority or a minority religious community, could be intimidating to the other. This is particularly so in the light of the strained communal relations between, say, the Hindus and the Muslims in some Indian cities.

Another trend in this context is the celebration of birthdays (called *jayathis)* or observance of the death anniversaries of regional heroes (for example, Shivaji in Mumbai and Pune), community leaders (for example, Babasaheb Ambedkar in many cities), nativist politicians (for example, Balasaheb Thackeray in Mumbai), or even charismatic film stars (for example, Rajkumar in Bengaluru). The personalities concerned are venerated as icons; the statues installed in their memory almost assume the status of idols. Considering that these icons and their statues are symbolic representations of sections of the urban population, rather than that of the city as a whole, they also become targets of desecration for sections opposed to them. The cities in India frequently experience violence resulting from such desecration.

While on religion, there is an apparently increased religiosity in Indian cities. Even a cursory glance at the press and the electronic media would show the plethora of cults, *guru/baba* and *mai/amma* traditions outside the brahmanic Hinduism, *sant* (saint) groupings currently prevailing in the cities, and the temples, mosques, churches and shrines dotting its landscape. The migrants from different parts of the country celebrate their own festivals on a scale that such festivals are no more private domestic observances.

Irrespective of whether it is a sectarian/religious festival or the celebration/observance of the birthday/death anniversary of a community icon or a charismatic community/political leader, there are demands for declaration of public holiday to mark the occasion. Facing prolonged agitations, the government has buckled to accede to such demands. For instance, as per the gazette notification of the Government of India, in 2009, there are 17 'closed holidays' and 50 'restricted holidays'. All but three—Republic Day, Independence Day, and Mahatma Gandhi's Birthday—closed holidays are for religious festivals: Buddhist, 1; Christian, 2; Hindu, 5; Jain, 1; Muslim, 4, and Sikh, 1. Similarly, all but 4 restricted holidays are for religious festivals, some of them being festivals of very small sections of the population. The dynamics of religious festivals and celebrations, religious processions, etc. in the civil society sphere thus offer interesting themes for investigation by urban sociologists.

Conclusion

Like the parent discipline sociology, as also all its sub-disciplines, the history of urban sociology has witnessed the rise and fall and reincarnation of paradigms. The urban ecology propounded by the Chicago School and the political economy perspective of the Marxist scholars both enriched the development of the subject by their delineation of the key concepts, theoretical premises, and methodologies. Both also betrayed their incapability to explain the significant turn of events from their respective theoretical perspectives. In revisiting the city, it is important to realise that theories and methodologies are not an end by themselves; they are basically analytical frameworks for understanding social realities. Globalisation has not only resulted in unprecedented changes, it also appears to have debunked many an axiomatic notion about the city and the changes therein. Thus, critical eclecticism appears to be the viable option for urban sociology now.

Sociology is not the only discipline interested in the city or the urban form; anthropology, architecture, economics, geography, etc. have been enriching our knowledge of the city. It is time that urban sociology looks outward, consciously crossing the disciplinary boundaries, though being firmly located in the fundamentals of the parent discipline. This implies a willingness to work with practitioners of other disciplines, and openness to the methods, tools and techniques that they deploy in their approach to the city. Perhaps this will also help urban sociology to overcome the blinkers of its former dominant paradigms.

Focusing on a single city, or a detailed study on one aspect of the city, has been the dominant tradition in urban sociology. Such studies no doubt add to the substantive body of knowledge about a given city or some aspects of that city. It does not take our theoretical understanding of the processes and patterns of the city under globalisation *per se.* For that, we need comparative analysis. As Dear bemoans, 'Unfortunately, the empirical, methodological and theoretical bases for such analysis are weak', and 'Our methodological and theoretical apparatuses for cross-cultural urban analyses are also under-developed'. We lack an adequate sample of national and international cities, of big cities and small towns.

Speaking of comparative analysis, conventionally, the nature and problems of the city have been sought to be explained in terms of the overall development of the country: the cities in the developed countries as contrasted with their counterparts in the developing countries. While there appears to be a correlation between development and urbanisation, for understanding the cities in the globalisation era, the extent of urbanisation of a country has special nuances. Thus, first, we need to make a distinction between the city in countries (a) in which the majority of the population lives in cities/towns and their immediate surroundings (USA, for instance), and (b) in which the majority of the population lives in rural areas (China or India, for instance), but are profoundly influenced by urban areas. Cities such as Singapore (which is a modern city-state) and Hong Kong (which was a British urban colony since returned to

China) are of a different genre. We could conclude our discussion on revisiting the city by recalling what Lefebvre had to say about the city and its future:

> To think about the city is to hold and maintain its conflictual aspects: constraints and possibilities, peacefulness and violence, meetings and solitude, gatherings and separation, the trivial and the poetic, brutal functionalism and surprising improvisation. The dialectic of the urban cannot be limited to the opposition centre-periphery, although it implies and contains it... Thinking the city moves towards thinking the world (thought as a relationship to the world)... globality as totality... the universe, space-time, energies, information, but without valuing one rather than another... One can hope that it will turn out well but the urban can become the centre of barbarity, domination, dependence and exploitation... In thinking about these perspectives, let us leave a place for events, initiatives, decisions. All the hands have not been played. The sense of history does not suppose any historic determinism, any destiny.

NOTES AND REFERENCES

Castells, Manuel. 1977. *The urban question: A Marxist approach* (translated by Alan Sheridan). London: Edward Arnold.

— 1996. *The rise of network society.* Cambridge, Mass.: Blackwell.

Chaplin, Susan E. 2007. 'Partnerships of hope: New ways of providing Sanitation services in India', in Annapurna Shaw (ed.): *Indian cities in transition* (83-103). Chennai: Orient Longman.

Childe, V. Gordon. 1957. 'Civilisation, cities, and towns', *Antiquity* (March): 210-13.

Dear, Michael J. 2000. *The postmodern urban condition.* Oxford: Blackwell.

Dubey, Bharati. 2009. 'Hindu soc [housing society] slams door on actor' and 'No ban on Muslims, says society secy [secretary]', *The times of India,* Mumbai, 31 July 2009: 1 and 9.

Durkheim, Emile. 1964/1893. *The division of labour in society.* New York: The Free Press. Dürrschmidt, Jörg. 2000. *Everyday lives in the global city: The delinking of locale and milieu.* London: Routledge.

Eckert, J.M. 2003. *The charisma of direction action: Power, politics, and the Shiv Sena.* New Delhi: Oxford University Press.

Ellin, Nan. 2006. *Integral urbanism.* New York: Routledge.

Flanagan, William G. 1993. *Contemporary urban sociology.* Cambridge: Cambridge University Press.

Gohain, Manash Pratim and Dipak Dash. 2009. 'Muslims in Delhi too find doors slammed on them', *The times of India,* Mumbai, 3 August, 2009: 13.

Graham, S. and S. Marvin. *Telecommunications and the city: Electronic spaces, urban places.* London: Routledge.

Gupta, Dipankar. 1982. *Nativism in a metropolis: the Shiv Sena in Bombay.* New Delhi: Manohar.

Harvey, David. 1985. *The urbanisation of capital: Studies in the history and theory of capitalist urbanisation.* Baltimore: Johns Hopkins University Press.

Jayaram, N. 1989. 'Sanguine plans and stark realities: Limits to planned urban habitat change (The case of Bangalore)', *Nagarlok,* 21 (3): 36-52.

——2008. 'Why read Marx now?' (Dr Debiprasad Chattopadhyaya Memorial Lecture, Bangalore, 20 May 2007). Bengaluru: Ma-Le Prakashana.

Kaur, Ravinder. 2001. 'The eclipse or the renaissance of "community"? The career of the concept', in Surinder S. Jodhka (ed.): *Community and identities: Contemporary discourses on culture and politics in India* (80-94). New Delhi: Sage Publications in association with The Book Review Literary Trust, New Delhi.

Kofman, Eleonore and Elizabeth Lebas. 1996. 'Lost in transposition: Time, space and the city', Introduction to Henri Lefebvre: *Writings on cities* (translated and edited by Eleonore Kofman and Elizabeth Lebas) (3-60). Oxford: Blackwell Publishers.

Lefebvre, Henri. 1996. *Writings on cities* (Selected, translated and introduced by Eleonore Kofman and Elizabeth Lebas). Oxford: Blackwell Publishers.

Maciver, R.M. and Charles H. Page. 1962/1950. *Society: An introductory analysis.* London: Macmillan. Mahadevia, Darshini. 2007. 'A city with many borders: Beyond ghettoisation in Ahmedabad', in Annapurna Shaw (ed.): *Indian cities in transition* (341-389). Chennai: Orient Longman.

Mehta, Suketu. 2004. *Maximum city: Bombay lost and found.* New Delhi: Penguin Books. Mitchell, William J. 1995. *City of bits: Space, place, and the infobahn.* Cambridge, Mass.: Massachusetts Institute of Technology.

Neuwirth, Robert. 2005. *Shadow cities: A billion squatters, a new urban world.* New York: Routledge.

Park, Robert Erza. 1915. 'The city: Suggestions for the investigation of human behaviour in the city', *American journal of sociology,* 20: 577-612.

—1926. 'The urban community as a spatial pattern and a moral order', in Ernest W. Burgess (Ed.): *The urban community: Selected papers from the proceedings of the American Sociological Society, 1925* (3-20). Chicago: University Chicago Press.

Patel, Sujata. 2006. 'Bombay and Mumbai: Identities, politics, and populism', in Sujata Patel and Kushal Deb (eds.): *Urban studies* (249-273). New Delhi: Oxford University Press.

Ray, C.N. 2008. 'The traditional neighbourhoods in a walled city: *Pols* in Ahmedabad', *Sociological bulletin,* 57 (3): 337-52.

Saith, Ashwani; M. Vijayabaskar and V. Gayathri (eds.). *ICTs and Indian social change: Diffusion, poverty, governance.* New Delhi: Sage Publications.

Saunders, Peter. 1985. *Social theory and the urban question* (2nd edition). London: Hutchinson & Co.

Sawers, Larry. 1984. 'New perspectives on the urban political economy', in William K. Tabb and Larry Sawers (eds.): *Marxism and the metropolis: New perspectives in urban political economy* (3-17). New York: Oxford University Press.

Short, John Rennie and Yeong-Hyun Kim. 1999. *Globalisation and the city.* Harlow, Essex: Addison Wesley Longman Limited.

Spengler, Oswald. 1928/1922. *The decline of the West* (2 volumes) New York: Alfred A. Knopf.

Times News Network. 2009a. 'Don't allow shrines in public places: SC [The Supreme Court of India]', *The times of India,* Mumbai, 1 August 2009: 9.

— 2009b. 'No shrines in public places, SC [The Supreme Court of India] tells government', *The times of India,* Mumbai, 1 August 2009: 1.

Times News Network and Agencies. 2009. 'HC [High Court] okays Tamil poet statue in Karnataka', *The times of India,* Mumbai, 8 August 2009.

Tönnies, Ferdinand. 1957/1887. *Community and association.* Michigan: Michigan State University.

Upadhya, Carol and A.R. Vasavi (eds.). 2008. *In an outpost of the global economy: Work and workers in India's information technology industry.* New Delhi: Routledge.

Weber, Max. 1958/1908. *The city* (translated and edited by Don Martindale and Gertrud Neuwirth). New York: The Free Press.

Wirth, Louis. 1964/1938. 'Urbanism as a way of life', in Paul K. Hatt and Albert J. Reiss Jr. (eds.): *Cities and society: The revised reader in urban sociology* (46-63). New York: The Free Press of Glencoe, 1964.

3

URBANISATION AND SOCIAL CHANGE

It is often said that change is the only unchanging aspect of society. Anyone living in modern society does not need to be reminded that constant change is among the most permanent features of our society. In fact, the discipline of sociology itself emerged as an effort to make sense of the rapid changes that Western European society had experienced between the seventeenth and nineteenth centuries. But, though social change seems such a common and obvious fact about modern life, it is -comparatively speaking—a very new and recent fact. It is estimated that human beings have existed on planet earth for approximately 500,000 (five lakh) years, but they have has a civilised existence for only about 6,000 years. Of these civilised years, it is only in the last 400 years that we have seen constant and rapid change; even within these years of change, the pace has accelerated only in the last 100 years. Because the speed with which change happens has been increasing steadily, it is probably true that in the last hundred years, change has been faster in the last fifty years than in the first fifty. And within the last fifty years, the world may have changed more in the last twenty years than in the first thirty...

Social Change

'Social change' is such a general term that it can be, and often is, used to refer to almost any kind of change not qualified by some other term, such as economic or political change. Sociologists have had to work hard to limit this broad meaning in order to make the term more specific and hence useful for social theory. At the most basic level, social change refers to changes that are significant—that is, changes which alter the 'underlying structure of an object or situation over a period of time' (Giddens 2005:42). Thus, social change does not include any and all changes, but only big ones, changes which transform things fundamentally. The 'bigness' of change is measured not only by how much change it brings about, but also by the scale of the change, that is, by how large a section of society it affects. In other words, changes have to be both intensive and extensive—have a big impact spread over a large sector of society—in order to qualify as social change.

Even after this kind of specification, social change still remains a very broad term. Attempts to further qualify it usually try to classify it by its sources or causes; by its nature, or the kind of impact it has on society; and by its pace or speed. For example, evolution is the name given to a kind of change that takes place slowly over a long period of time. This term was made famous by the natural scientist Charles Darwin, who proposed a theory of how living organisms evolve—or change slowly over several centuries or even millenia, by adapting themselves to natural circumstances.

Darwin's theory emphasized the idea of 'the survival of the fittest'—only those life forms manage to survive who are best adapted to their environment; those that are unable to adapt or are too slow to do so die out in the long run. Darwin suggested that human beings evolved from sea-borne life forms (or varieties of fish) to land-based mammals, passing through various stages the highest of which were the various varieties of monkeys and chimpanzees until finally the homo sapiens or human form was evolved. Although, Darwin's theory referred to natural processes, it was soon adapted to the social world and was termed 'social Darwinism', a theory that emphasised the importance of adaptive change. In contrast to evolutionary change, change that occurs comparatively quickly, even suddenly, is sometimes called 'revolutionary change'. It is used mainly in the political context, when the power structure of society changes very rapidly through the overthrow of a former ruling class or group by its challengers. Examples include the French revolution (1789-93) and the Soviet or Russian revolution of 1917. But, the term has also been used more generally to refer to sharp, sudden and total transformations of other kinds as well, such as in the phrase 'industrial revolution' or 'telecommunications revolution', and so on. Types of change that are identified by their nature or impact include structural change and changes in ideas, values and beliefs. Structural change refers to transformations in the structure of society, to its institutions or the rules by which these institutions are run. For example, the emergence of study money as currency marked a major change in the organisation of financial markets and transactions. Until this change came about, most forms of currency involved precious metals like gold and silver. The value of the coin was directly linked to the value of the gold or silver it contained. In contrast, the value of a study currency note has no relationship to the value of the paper it is printed on, or the cost of its printing. The idea behind paper money was that a medium or means for facilitating the exchange of goods and services need not itself be intrinsically valuable. As long as it represents values convincingly—i.e., as long as it inspires trust—almost anything can function as money. This idea was the foundation for the credit market and helped change the structure of banking and finance. These changes in turn produced further changes in the organisation of economic life.

Changes in values and beliefs can also lead to social change. For example, changes in the ideas and beliefs about children and childhood have brought about very important kinds of social change, there was a time when children were simply considered small adults — there was no special concept of childhood as such, with its associated notions of what was right or wrong for children to do. As late as the 19th century for example, it was considered good and proper that children start to work as soon as they were able to. Children were often helping their families at work from the age of five or six; the early factory system depended on the labour of children. It was during the 19th and early 20th centuries that ideas about childhood as a special stage of life gained influence. It then became unthinkable for small children to be at work, and many countries passed laws banning child labour. At the same time, there emerged ideas about compulsory education, and children were supposed to be in school rather than at work, and many laws were passed for this as well. Although, there are some industries in our country that even today depend on child labour at least partially (such as carpet weaving, small tea shops or restaurants, match-stick making, and so on), child labour is illegal and employers can be punished as criminals.

But, by far the most common way of classifying social change is by its causes or sources. Sometimes, the causes are pre-classified into internal (or endogenous) and external (or exogenous) causes. There are five broad types of sources or causes of social change: environmental, technological, economic, political and cultural.

Environment

Nature, ecology and the physical environment have always had a significant influence on the structure and shape of society. This was particularly true in the past when human beings were unable to control or overcome the effects of nature. For example, people living in a desert environment were unable to practise settled agriculture of the sort that was possible in the plains, near rivers and so on. So, the kind of food they ate or the clothes they wore, the way they earned their livelyhood, and their patterns of social interaction were all determined to a large extent by the physical and climatic conditions of their environment. The same was true for people living in very cold climates, or in port towns, along major trade routes or mountain passes, or in fertile river valleys.

But, the extent to which the environment influences society has been decreasing over time with the increase in technological resources. Technology allows us to overcome or adapt to the problems posed by nature, thus reducing the differences between societies living in different sorts of environments. On the other hand, technology also alters nature and our relationship to it in new ways. So it is perhaps more accurate to say that the effect of nature on society is changing rather than simply declining.

But, how, you might ask, does this affect social change? The environment may have shaped societies, but how did it play any role in social change? The easiest and most powerful answer to this question can be found in natural disasters. Sudden and catastrophic events such as earthquakes, volcanic eruptions, floods, or tidal waves (like the tsunami that hit Indonesia, Sri Lanka, the Andaman Islands and parts of Tamil Nadu in December 2004) can change societies quite drastically. These changes are often irreversible, that is, they are permanent and don't allow a return to the way things were. For example, it is quite possible that many of those whose livelihoods were destroyed by the tsunami will never be able to return to them again, and that many of the coastal villages will have their social structure completely altered. There are numerous instances of natural disasters leading to a total transformation and sometimes total destruction of societies in history. Environmental or ecological factors need not only be destructive to cause change, they can be constructive as well. A good example is the discovery of oil in the desert regions of West Asia (also called the Middle East). Like the discovery of gold in California in the 19th century, oil reserves in the Middle East have completely transformed the societies in which they were found. Countries like Saudi Arabia, Kuwait or the United Arab Emirates would be very different today without their oil wealth.

Technology and Economy

The combination of technological and economic change has been responsible for immense social changes, specially in the modern period. Technology affects society in a wide variety of ways. As seen above, it can help us to resist, control, adapt to or harness nature in different ways. In combination with the very powerful institution of the market, technological change can be as impressive in its social impact as natural factors like a tsunami or the discovery of oil. The most famous instance of massive and immediately visible social change brought about by technological change is the Industrial Revolution itself, which you have already read about.

You will surely have heard of the massive social impact made by the steam engine. The discovery of steam power allowed emerging forms of large scale industry to use of a source of energy that was not only far stronger than animals or human beings, but was also capable of continuous operation without the need for rest. When harnessed to modes of transport like the steam ship and the railway, it transformed the economy and social geography of the world. The railroad enabled the westward expansion of industry and trade on the American continent and in Asia. In India too, the railways have played a very important role in shaping the economy, specially in the first century after their introduction in 1853. Steamships made ocean voyages much faster and much more reliable, thereby changing the dynamics of international trade and migration. Both these developments created gigantic ripples of change which affected not only the economy but also the social, cultural and demographic dimensions of world society.

The importance and impact of steam power became visible relatively quickly; however, sometimes, the social impact of technological changes becomes visible only retrospectively. A technological invention or discovery may produce limited immediate effects, as though it were lying dormant. Some later change in the economic context may suddenly change the social significance of the same invention and give it recognition as a historic event. Examples of this are the discovery of gunpowder and writing paper in China, which had only limited impact for centuries until they were inserted into the context of modernising Western Europe. From that vantage point, given the advantage of enabling circumstances, gunpowder helped to transform the technology of warfare and the paper-print revolution changed society forever. Another example closer home is the case of technological innovations in the textile industry in Britain. In combination with market forces and imperial power, the new spinning and weaving machines destroyed the handloom industry of the Indian subcontinent which was, until then, the largest and most advanced in the world.

Sometimes changes in economic organisation that are not directly technological can also change society. In a well-known historical example, plantation agriculture—that is, the growing of single cash crops like sugarcane, tea or cotton on a large scale—created a heavy demand for labour. This demand helped to establish the institution of slavery and the slave trade between Africa, Europe and the

Americas between the 17th and 19th centuries. In India, too, the tea plantations of Assam involved the forced migration of labour from Eastern India (specially the Adivasi areas of Jharkhand and Chattisgarh). Today, in many parts of the world, changes in customs duties or tariffs brought about by international agreements and institutions like the World Trade Organisation, can lead to entire industries and occupations being wiped out or (less often) sudden booms or periods of prosperity for other industries or occupations.

Politics

In the old ways of writing and recounting history, the actions of kings and queens seemed to be the most important forces of social change. But as we know now, kings and queens were the representatives of larger political, social and economic trends. Individuals may indeed have had roles to play, but they were part of a larger context. In this sense, political forces have surely been among the most important causes of social change. The clearest examples are found in the history of warfare. When one society waged war on another and conquered or was conquered, social change was usually an immediate consequence. Sometimes, conquerors brought the seeds of change and planted them wherever they went. At other times, the conquered were actually successful in planting seeds of change among the conquerors and transformed their societies. Although, there are many such examples in history, it is interesting to consider a modern instance—that of the United States and Japan.

The United States won a famous victory over Japan in the Second World War, partly through the use of a weapon of mass destruction never seen before in human history, the nuclear bomb. After the Japanese surrender, the United States occupied and ruled over Japan for several years, bringing about lots of changes, including land reform in Japan. Japanese industry, at that time, was trying very hard to copy American industry and learn from it. By the 1970s, however, Japanese industrial techniques, specially in fields like car manufacturing, had gone far ahead of the Americans. Between the 1970s and 1990s, Japanese industry dominated the world and forced changes in the industrial organisation of Europe and specially the United States. The industrial landscape of the United States in particular was decisively altered by the impact of Japanese industrial technology and production organisation. Large, traditionally dominant industries like steel, automobiles and heavy engineering suffered major setbacks and had to restructure themselves according to Japanese technological and management principles. Emerging fields like electronics were also pioneered by the Japanese. In short, within the space of four decades, Japan had turned the tables on the United States, but through economic and technological means rather than warfare.

Political changes need not only be international—they can have enormous social impact even at home. Although, you may not have thought of it this way, the Indian independence movement did not only bring about political change in the form of the end of British rule, it also decisively changed Indian society. A more recent instance is to be found in the Nepali people's rejection of monarchy in 2006. More generally, political changes bring about social change through the redistribution of power across different social groups and classes.

Considered from this viewpoint, universal adult franchise—or the 'one person, one vote' principle—is probably the single biggest political change in history. Until modern democracies formally empowered the people with the vote, and until elections became mandatory for exercising legitimate power, society was structured very differently. Kings and queens claimed to rule by divine right, and they were not really answerable to the common people. Even when democratic principles of voting were first introduced, they did not include the whole population—in fact only a small minority could vote, or had any say in the formation of the government. In the beginning, the vote was restricted to those who were born into high status social groups of a particular race or ethnicity, or to wealthy men who owned property. All women, men of lower classes or subordinated ethnicities, and the poor and working people in general were not allowed to vote.

It is only through long struggles that universal adult franchise came to be established as a norm. Of course, this did not abolish all the inequalities of previous eras. Even today, not all countries follow democratic forms of rule; even where elections are held, they can be manipulated; and people can continue to be powerless to influence the decisions of their government. But, despite all this, it cannot be denied that universal adult franchise serves as a powerful norm that exerts pressure on every society and every government. Governments must now at least appear to seek the approval of the people in order to be considered legitimate. This has brought massive social changes in its wake.

Culture

Culture is used here as a short label for a very wide field of ideas, values, beliefs, that are important to people and help shape their lives. Changes in such ideas and beliefs lead naturally to changes in social life. The commonest example of a socio-cultural institution that has had enormous social impact is religion. Religious beliefs and norms have helped organise society and it is hardly surprising that changes in these beliefs have helped transform society. So important has religion been, that some scholars have tended to define civilisations in religious terms and to see history as the process of interaction between religions. However, as with other important factors of social change, religion too is contextual—it is able to produce effects in some contexts but not in others. Max Weber's study 'The Protestant Ethic and the Spirit of Capitalism' showed how the religious beliefs of some Christian Protestant sects helped to establish the capitalist social system. It remains one of the most famous examples of the impact of cultural values on economic and social change. In India too we find many examples of religion bringing about social change. Among the best known are the impact of Buddhism on social and political life in ancient India, and the widespread influence of the Bhakti Movement on medieval social structure including the caste system. A different example of cultural change leading to social change can be seen in the evolution of ideas about the place of women in society. In the modern era, as women have struggled for equality, they have helped change society in many ways. Women's struggles have also been helped or hindered by other historical circumstances. For example, during the Second World War, women in western countries started to work in factories doing jobs that they had never done before, jobs which had always been done by men. The fact that women were able to build ships, operate heavy machinery, manufacture armaments and so on, helped establish their claims to equality. But, it is equally true that, had it not been for the war, they would have had to struggle for much longer. A very different instance of change produced by the position of women can be seen in consumer advertising. In most urban societies, it is women who take most of the everyday decisions about what to buy for their households. This has made advertisers very sensitive to the views and perspectives of women as consumers. Significant proportions of advertising expenditure are now directed at women, and this in turn has effects on the media. In short, the economic role of women starts a chain of changes which can have a larger social impact.

For example, advertisements may tend to show women as decision-makers and as important people in ways that would not have been considered or encouraged before. More generally, most advertisements used to be addressed to men; now they are addressed as much to women, or, in some sectors like household appliances and consumer goods, mainly to women. So it is now economically important for advertisers and manufacturers to pay attention to what women think and feel.

Yet, another instance of cultural change bringing about social change can be found in the history of sports. Games and sports have always been expressions of popular culture that sometimes acquire a lot of importance. The game of cricket began as a British aristocratic pastime, spread to the middle and working classes of Britain, and from there to British colonies across the world. As the game acquired roots outside Britain, it often turned into a symbol of national or racial pride. The very different history of intense rivalry in cricket shows the social importance of sport in a very telling manner. The England-Australia rivalry expressed the resentment of the socially subordinated colony against the dominant upper class centre of authority (England). Similarly, the complete world dominance of the West Indies cricket team during the 1970s and 1980s, was also an expression of racial pride on the part of a colonised people. In India, too, beating England at cricket was always seen as something special, particularly before independence. At another level, the immense popularity of cricket in the Indian sub-continent has altered the commercial profile of the game which is now driven by the interests of South Asian fans, specially Indians.

As will be clear from the above discussion, no single factor or theory can account for social change. The causes of social change may be internal or external, the result of deliberate actions or accidental events. Moreover, the causes of social change are often interrelated. Economic and technological causes may also have a cultural component, politics may be influenced by environment... It is important to be aware of the many dimensions of social change and its varied forms. Change is an important subject for us because the pace of change in modern and specially contemporary times is much faster than what it used to be before. Although, social change is better understood retrospectively—after it has already occurred —we also need to be aware of it as it happens, and to prepare for it in whatever ways we can.

Social Order

The meaning of social events or processes often becomes clear through contrasts, just as the letters on the page that you are reading become legible because they contrast against the background. In the same way, social change as a process acquires meaning against the backdrop of continuity or lack of change. It may sound odd, but change makes sense as a concept only if there are also some things that are not changing, so that they offer the possibility of comparison or contrast. In other words, social change has to be understood together with social order, which is the tendency within established social systems that resists and regulates change.

Another way of looking at the relationship between social change and social order is to think about the possible reasons why society needs to prevent, discourage, or at least control change. In order to establish itself as a strong and viable social system, every society must be able to reproduce itself over time and maintain its stability. Stability requires that things continue more or less as they are — that people continue to follow the same rules, that similar actions produce similar results, and more generally, that individuals and institutions behave in a fairly predictable manner.

The above argument was an abstract and general one about the possible reasons why societies may need to resist change. But, there are usually more concrete and specific reasons why societies do in fact resist change. Most societies most of the time are stratified in unequal ways, that is, the different strata are differently positioned with respect to command over economic resources, social status and political power. It is not surprising that those who are favourably placed wish for things to continue as they are, while those who are suffering disadvantages are anxious for change. So, the ruling or dominant groups in society generally resist any social changes that may alter their status, because they have a vested interest in stability. On the other hand, the subordinated or oppressed groups have a vested interest in change. 'Normal' conditions usually favour the rich and powerful, and they are able to resist change. This is another broad reason why societies are generally stable.

However, the notion of social order is not restricted to the idea of resistance to change, it also has a more positive meaning. It refers to the active maintenance and reproduction of particular pattern of social relations and of values and norms. Broadly speaking, social order can be achieved in one of two ways — when people spontaneously wish to abide by a set of rules and norms; or when people are compelled in various ways to obey such norms. Every society employs a combination of these methods to sustain social order.

Spontaneous consent to social order derives ultimately from shared values and norms which are internalised by people through the process of socialisation. (Revisit the discussion of socialisation in Introducing Sociology). Socialisation may be more or less efficient in different contexts, but however efficient it is, it can never completely erase the will of the individual. In other words, socialisation cannot turn people into programmed robots — it cannot produce complete and permanent consent for all norms at all times. You may have experienced this in your own lives: rules or beliefs which seem very natural and right at one point of time, don't seem so obviously correct at other times. We question things we believed in the past, and change our minds about what we regard as right or wrong. Sometimes, we may even return to beliefs we once held and then abandoned, only to rediscover them afresh at some later stage of life or in different circumstances. So, while socialisation does take on much of the burden of producing social order, it is never enough by itself.

Thus, most modern societies must also depend on some form of power or coercion to ensure that institutions and individuals conform to established social norms. Power is usually defined as the ability to make others do what you want regardless of what they themselves want. When a relationship of power is stable and settled, and the parties involved have become accustomed to their relative positions, we have a situation of domination. If a social entity (a person, institution or group) is routinely or habitually in a position of power, it is said to be dominant. In normal times, dominant institutions, groups or individuals exercise a decisive influence on society. It is not as though they are never challenged, but this happens only in abnormal or extraordinary times. Even though it implies that people are being forced to do things they don't necessarily want to do, domination in normal times can be quite 'smooth', in the sense of appearing to be without friction or tension. Why, for example, did women not want to claim their rights in their families of birth? Why did they 'consent' to the patriarchal norm).

Domination, Authority and Law How is it that domination can be non-confrontational even when it clearly involves unequal relationships where costs and benefits are unevenly distributed? But, why does this power work? Does it work purely because of the threat of the use of force? This is where we come to an important concept in sociology, that of legitimation.

In social terms, legitimacy refers to the degree of acceptance that is involved in power relations. Something that is legitimate is accepted as proper, just and fitting. In the broadest sense, it is acknowledged to be part of the social contract that is currently prevailing. In short, legitimacy implies conformity to existing norms of right, propriety and justice. We have already seen how power is defined in society; power in itself is simply a fact—it can be either legitimate or not. Authority is defined by Max Weber as legitimate power—that is, power considered to be justified or proper. For example, a police officer, a judge, or a school teacher all exercise different kinds of authority as part of their jobs. This authority is explicitly provided to them by their official job description—there are written documents specifying their authority, and what they may and may not do.

The fact that they have authority automatically implies that other members of society — who have agreed to abide by its rules and regulations — must obey this authority within its proper domain. The domain of the judge is the court room, and when citizens are in the court, they are supposed to obey the judge or defer to her/his authority. Outside the courtroom, the judge is supposed to be like any other citizen. So, on the street, She must obey the lawful authority of the police officer. When on duty, the policeman or woman has authority over the public actions of all citizens except her/his superior officers. But, police officers do not have jurisdiction over the private activities of citizens as long as they are not suspected of being unlawful. In different way — different because the nature of the authority involved is less strictly or explicitly defined — the teacher has authority over her/his pupils in the classroom. The authority of the teacher does not extend into the home of the pupil where parents or guardians have primary responsibility and authority over their children.

There may be other forms of authority that are not so strictly defined, but are nevertheless effective in eliciting consent and cooperation. A good example is the authority wielded by a religious leader. Although, some institutionalised religions may have partly formalised this authority, but the leader of a sect or other less-institutionalised minor religious group may wield enormous authority without it being formalised. Similarly reputed scholars, artists, writers and other intellectuals may wield a lot of authority in their respective fields without it being formalised. The same is true of a criminal gang leader — he or she may exercise absolute authority but without any formal specifications.

The difference between explicitly codified and more informal authority is relevant to the notion of the law. A law is an explicitly codified norm or rule. It is usually written down, and there are laws that specify how laws are to be made or changed, or what is to be done if someone violates them. A modern democratic society has a given body of laws created through its legislature, which consist of elected representatives. The laws of the land are enacted in the name of the people of that land by the people's representatives. This law forms the formal body of rules according to which society will be governed. Laws apply to all citizens. Whether or not I as an individual agree with a particular law, it has binding force on me as a citizen, and on all other citizens similarly regardless of their beliefs.

So, domination works through power, but much of this power is actually legitimate power or authority, a large part of which is codified in law. Consent and cooperation are obtained on a regular and reliable basis because of the backing of this structure of legitimation and formal institutional support. This does not exhaust the domain of power or domination — there are many kinds power that are effective in society even though they are illegitimate, or if legitimate are not codified in law. It is the mix of legitimate, lawful authority and other kinds of power that determines the nature of a social system and also its dynamics.

Contestation, Crime and Violence

The existence of domination, power, legitimate authority and law does not imply that they always meet with obedience and conformity. You have already read about the presence of conflict and competition in society. In a similar way, we need to recognise more general forms of contestation in society. Contestation is used here as simply a word for broad forms of insistent disagreement. Competition and conflict are more specific than this, and leave out other forms of dissent that may not be well described by such terms.

One example is that of 'counter cultures' among youth or 'youth rebellion'. These are protests against or refusal to conform to prevalent social norms. The content of these protests may involve anything from hairstyles and clothing fashions to language or lifestyle. More standard or conventional forms of contestation include elections —which are a form of political competition. Contestations also include dissent or protest against laws or lawful authorities. Open and democratic societies allow this kind of dissent to different degrees. There are both explicit and implicit boundaries defined for such dissent; crossing these boundaries invites some form of reaction from society, usually from the law enforcement authorities.

As you know very well, being united as Indians does not prevent us from disagreeing with each other. Different political parties may have very different agendas even though they may respect the same

Constitution. Belief in or knowledge of the same set of traffic rules does not prevent heated arguments on the road. In other words, social order need not mean sameness or unanimity. On the other hand, how much difference or dissent is tolerated in society is an important question. The answer to this question depends on social and historical circumstances but it always marks an important boundary in society, the boundary between the legitimate and the illegitimate, the legal and the illegal, and the acceptable and the unacceptable.

Although, it generally carries a strong moral charge, the notion of crime is strictly derived from the law. A crime is an act that violates an existing law, nothing more, nothing less. The moral worth of the act is not determined solely by the fact that it violates existing law. If the existing law is believed to be unjust, for example, a person may claim to be breaking it for the highest moral reasons. This is exactly what the leaders of the Freedom Movement in India were doing as part of their 'Civil Disobedience' campaign. When Mahatma Gandhi broke the salt law of the British government at Dandi, he was committing a crime, and he was arrested for it. But, he committed this crime deliberately and proudly, and the Indian people were also proud of him and what he stood for. Of course, these are not the only kinds of crime that are committed! There are many other kinds of crime that cannot claim any great moral virtue. But, the important point is that a crime is the breaking of the law — going beyond the boundary of legitimate dissent as defined by the law.

The question of violence relates at the broadest level to the basic definition of the state. One of the defining features of the modern state is that it is supposed to have a monopoly over the use of legitimate violence within its jurisdiction. In other words, only the state through its authorised functionaries may lawfully use violence—all other instances of violence are by definition illegal. There are exceptions like self defense meant for extraordinary and rare situations. Thus, technically, every act of violence is seen as being directed against the state. Even if I assault or murder some other individual, it is the state that prosecutes me for violating its monopoly over the legitimate use of violence.

It is obvious that violence is the enemy of social order, and an extreme form of contestation that transgresses not only the law, but important social norms. Violence in society is the product of social tensions and indicates the presence of serious problems. It is also a challenge to the authority of the state. In this sense it also marks the failure of the regime of legitimation and consent and the open outbreak of conflicts.

Social Order and Change in Village, Town and City

Most societies can be divided into rural and urban sectors. The conditions of life and, therefore, the forms of social organisation in these sectors are very different from each other. So also, therefore, are the forms of social order that prevail in these sectors, and the kinds of social change that are most significant in each.

We all think we know what is meant by a village and by a town or city. But, how exactly do we differentiate between them? From a sociological point of view, villages emerged as part of the major changes in social structure brought about by the transition from nomadic ways of life based on hunting, gathering food and transient agriculture to a more settled form of life. With the development of sedentary forms of agriculture — or forms that did not involve moving from place to place — social structure also changed. Investment in land and technological innovations in agriculture created the possibility of producing a surplus—something over and above what was needed for survival. Thus, settled agriculture meant that wealth could be accumulated and this also brought with it social differences. The more advanced division of labour also created the need for occupational specialisation. All of these changes together shaped the emergence of the village as a population settlement based on a particular form of social organisation.

In economic and administrative terms, the distinction between rural and urban settlements is usually made on the basis of two major factors: population density and the proportion of agriculture related economic activities. Contrary to appearances, size is not always decisive; it becomes difficult to separate large villages and small towns on the basis of population size alone. Thus, cities and towns have a much higher density of population—or the number of persons per unit area, such as a square km—than villages. Although, they are smaller in terms of absolute numbers of people, villages are spread out over a relatively larger area. Villages are also distinguished from towns and cities by the larger share of agricultural activities in their economic profile. In other words, villages will have a significant proportion of its population engaged in agriculture linked occupations, much of what is produced there will be agricultural products, and most of its income will be from agriculture.

The distinction between a town and city is much more a matter of administrative definition. A town and city are basically the same sort of settlement, differentiated by size. An 'urban agglomeration' (a term used in Censuses and official reports) refers to a city along with its surrounding sub-urban areas and satellite settlements. A 'metropolitan area' includes more than one city, or a continuous urban settlement many times the size of a single city.

Given the directions in which modern societies have developed, the process of urbanisation has been experienced in most countries. This is the process by which a progressively larger and larger proportion of the country's population lives in urban rather than rural areas. Most developed countries are now overwhelmingly urban. Urbanisation is also the trend in developing countries; it can be faster or slower, but unless there are special reasons blocking it, the process does seem to occur in most contexts. In fact, the United Nations reports that by 2007, for the first time in human history, the world's urban population will outnumber its rural population. Indian society is also experiencing urbanisation: the percentage of the population living in urban areas has increased from a little less than 11 per cent in 1901 to a little more than 17 per cent in 1951, soon after independence. The 2001 Census shows that almost 28 per cent of the population now lives in urban areas.

Social Order and Social Change in Rural Areas

Because of the objective conditions in villages being different, we can expect the nature of social order and social change to be different as well. Villages are small in size so they usually permit more personalised relationships; it is not unusual for members of a village to know all or most other members by sight. Moreover, the social structure in villages tends to follow a more traditional pattern: institutions like caste, religion, and other forms of customary or traditional social practice are stronger here. For these reasons, unless there are special circumstances that make for an exception, change is slower to arrive in villages than in towns.

There are also other reasons for this. A variety of factors ensure that the subordinate sections of society have much less scope for expressing themselves in rural areas than their counterparts in cities. The lack of anonymity and distance in the village makes it difficult for people to dissent because they can be easily identified and 'taught a lesson' by the dominant sections. Moreover, the relative power of the dominant sections is much more because they control most avenues of employment, and most resources of all kinds. So, the poor have to depend on the dominant sections since there are no alternative sources of employment or support. Given the small population, it is also very difficult to gather large numbers, particularly since efforts towards this cannot be hidden from the powerful and are very quickly suppressed. So, in short, if there is a strong power structure already in place in a village, it is very difficult to dislodge it. Change in the sense of shifts in power are thus slow and late to arrive in rural areas because the social order is stronger and more resilient.

Change of other sorts is also slow to come because villages are scattered and not as well connected to the rest of the world as cities and towns are. Of course, new modes of communication, particularly the telephone and the television have changed this. So the cultural 'lag' between villages and towns is now much shorter or non-existent. Communication links of other sorts (road, rail) have also generally improved over time so that few villages can really claim to be 'isolated' or 'remote', words often unthinkingly attached to villages in the past. This has also accelerated the pace of change somewhat.

For obvious reasons changes associated with agriculture or with agrarian social relations have a very major impact on rural societies. Thus, measures like land reform which alter the structure of land ownership have an immediate impact. In India, the first phase of land reforms after independence took away proprietary rights from absentee landlords and gave them to the groups that were actually managing the land and its cultivation in the village. Most of these groups belonged to intermediate castes, and though they were often not themselves the cultivators, they acquired rights over land. In combination with their number, this factor increased their social status and political power, because their votes mattered for winning elections. M.N. Srinivas has named these groups as the 'dominant castes'. In many regional contexts, the dominant castes became very powerful in economic terms and dominated the countryside and hence also electoral politics. In more recent times, these dominant castes are themselves facing opposition from the assertive uprisings of castes further below them, the lowest and the most backward castes. This has led to major social upheavals in many states like Andhra Pradesh, Bihar, Uttar Pradesh and Tamil Nadu.

In the same way, changes in the technological organisation of agriculture also has a large and immediate impact on rural society. The introduction of new labour saving machinery or new cropping patterns may alter the demand for labour and thus change the relative bargaining strength of different social groups like landlords and labourers. Even if they don't directly affect labour demand, technological or economic changes can change the economic power of different groups and thus set in motion a chain of changes. Sudden fluctuations in agricultural prices, droughts or floods can cause havoc in rural society. The recent spate of farmer suicides in India is an example of this. On the other hand, large scale development programmes aimed at the rural poor can also have an enormous impact. A good example of this is the National Rural Employment Guarantee Act of 2005.

Social Order and Social Change in Urban Areas

It is well-known that though the city itself is very old—even ancient societies had them—urbanism as a way of life for large segments of the population is a modern phenomenon. Before the modern era, trade, religion and warfare were some of the major factors that decided the location and importance of cities. Cities that were located on major trade routes, or had suitable harbours and ports had a natural advantage. So did cities that were well located from the point of view of military strategy. Finally, religious places attracted large numbers of pilgrims and thus supported an urban economy. In India too we have examples of such old cities, including the well known medieval trading towns of Tezpur on the Brahmaputra river in Assam or Kozhikode (formerly known as Calicut) on the Arabian Sea in northern Kerala. We also have many examples of temple towns and places of religious pilgrimage, such as Ajmer in Rajasthan, Varanasi (also known as Benaras or Kashi) in Uttar Pradesh, or Madurai in Tamil Nadu.

As sociologists have pointed out, city life and modernity go very well together; in fact, each may be considered an intimate expression of the other. Though it houses large and very dense populations, and though it has been known throughout history as the site for mass politics, the city is also the domain of the modern individual. In its combination of anonymity and the amenities and institutions that only large numbers can support, the city offers the individual boundless possibilities for fulfillment. Unlike the village, which discourages individuality and cannot offer much, the city nurtures the individual.

But, while the many artists, writers, and scholars who have celebrated the city as the haven of the individual are not wrong, it is also true that freedom and opportunity are available only to some individuals. More accurately, only a socially and economically privileged minority can have the luxury of a predominantly free and fulfilling life. Most people who live in cities have only limited and relative freedoms within larger constraints. These are the familiar economic and social constraints imposed by membership in social groups of various kinds, already known to you from the previous chapter. The city, too, fosters the development of group identities — based on factors like race, religion, ethnicity, caste, region, and of course class — which are all well represented in urban life. In fact, the concentration of large numbers in a relatively small space intensifies identities and makes them integral to strategies of survival, resistance and assertion.

Most of the important issues and problems of social order in towns and cities are related to the question of space. High population density places a great premium on space and creates very complex problems of logistics. It is the primary task of the urban social order to ensure the spatial viability of the city. This means the organisation and management of things like: housing and residential patterns; mass transit systems for transporting large numbers of workers to and from work; arranging for the coexistence of residential, public and industrial land-use zones; and finally all the public health, sanitation, policing, public safety and monitoring needs of urban governance. Each of these functions is a huge undertaking in itself and presents formidable challenges of planning, implementation and maintenance. What adds to the complexity is that all of these tasks have to be performed in a context where the divisions and tensions of class, ethnicity, religion, caste and so on are also present and active.

For example, the question of urban housing brings with it a whole host of problems. Shortage of housing for the poor leads to homelessness, and the phenomenon of 'street people' — those who live and survive on the streets and footpaths, under bridges and flyovers, abandoned buildings and other empty spaces. It is also the leading cause for the emergence of slums. Though official definitions vary, a slum is a congested, overcrowded neighbourhood with no proper civic facilities (sanitation, water supply, electricity and so on) and homes made of all kinds of building materials ranging from plastic sheets and cardboard to multi-storeyed concrete structures. Because of the absence of 'settled' property rights of the kind seen elsewhere, slums are the natural breeding ground for 'dadas' and strongmen who impose their authority on the people who live there. Control over slum territory becomes the natural stepping stone to other kinds of extra-legal activities, including criminal and real estate-related gangs. Where and how people will live in cities is a question that is also filtered through socio-cultural identities. Residential areas in cities all over the world are almost always segregated by class, and often also by race, ethnicity, religion and other such variables. Tensions between such identities both cause these segregation patterns and are also a consequence. For example, in India, communal tensions between religious communities, most commonly Hindus and Muslims, results in the conversion of mixed neighbourhoods into single-community ones. This, in turn, gives a specific spatial pattern to communal violence whenever it erupts, which again furthers the 'ghettoisation' process. This has happened in many cities in India, most recently in Gujarat following the riots of 2002. The worldwide phenomenon of 'gated communities' is also found in Indian cities. This refers to the creation of affluent neighbourhoods that are separated from their surroundings by walls and gates, with controlled entry and exit. Most such communities also have their own parallel civic facilities, such as water and electricity supply, policing and security.

Finally, housing patterns are linked to the economy of the city in crucial ways. The urban transport system is directly and severely affected by the location of residential areas relative to industrial and commercial workplaces. If these are far apart, as is often the case, an elaborate mass transit system must be created and maintained. Commuting becomes a way of life and an ever present source of possible disruption. The transport system has a direct impact on the 'quality of life' of working people in the city. Reliance on road transport and specially on private rather than public modes (i.e., cars rather than buses) creates problems of traffic congestion and vehicular pollution. As will be clear to you from the above discussion, the apparently simple issue of distribution of living space is actually a very complex and multi-dimensional aspect of urban society.

The form and content of social change in urban areas is also best understood in relation to the central question of space. One very visible element of change is the ups and downs experienced by particular neighbourhoods and localities. Across the world, the city centre—or the core area of the original city—has had many changes of fortune. After being the power centre of the city in the 19th and early 20th century, the city centre went through a period of decline in the latter half of the 20th century. This was also the period of the growth of suburbs as the affluent classes deserted the inner city for the suburbs for a variety of reasons. City centres are experiencing a revival now in many major western cities as attempts to regenerate community life and the arts bear fruit. A related phenomenon is 'gentrification', which refers to the conversion of a previously lower class neighbourhood into a middle and upper class one. As real estate prices rise, it becomes more and more profitable for developers to try and effect such a conversion. At some point, the campaign becomes self-fulfilling as rental values increase and the locality acquires a critical minimum of prosperous businesses and residents. But, sometimes the effort may fail and the neighbourhood goes back down the class scale and returns to its previous status.

Changes in modes of mass transport may also bring about significant social change in cities. Affordable, efficient and safe public transport makes a huge difference to city life and can shape the social character of a city apart from influencing its economic fortunes. Many scholars have written on the difference between cities based on public transport like London or New York and cities that depend mainly on individualised car-based transport like Los Angeles. It remains to be seen, for example, whether the new Metro Rail in Delhi will significantly change social life in that city. But, the main issue regarding social change in cities, specially in rapidly urbanising countries like India, is how the city will cope with constant increase in population as migrants keep streaming in to add to its natural growth.

NOTES AND REFERENCES

Khilnani, Sunil. 2002. *The Idea of India* , Penguin Books, New Delhi.

Patel, Sujata and Kushal Deb (eds). 2006. *Urban Sociology* (Oxford in India) Readings in Sociology and Social Anthropology series). Oxford University Press, New Delhi.

4

ISSUES AND CHALLENGES FOR THE URBAN FAMILY

Disability is a universal human condition; however, it has received scant attention in the social sciences in India. According to the Census of India, 2001, there are 2.19 crore persons with disability in India which amounts to 2.13 per cent of the total population. The National Sample Survey of India in its 2002 July to December round put the figure at 19 million, of which the mentally disabled accounted for 17 per cent of the total disabled population, of which mental retardation accounted for 5.37 per cent, and Cerebral Palsy and Multiple Disabilities 1.48 and 10.63 per cent respectively.

However, it is widely acknowledged by activists and researchers that these figures are grossly inadequate. Due to inadequate information and social stigma, many disabled persons remain 'uncounted'. Those who are destitute or have been cast away by their families remain outside the pale of official recognition. This is particularly true of persons with mental or intellectual disabilities and mental illnesses.

This study relates to Autism Spectrum Disorder, a disability whose occurrence does not find mention in the official disability statistics of the country. Autism is the third most common developmental disability whose incidence is greater than that of Down's Syndrome and Cerebral Palsy. According to Cohen and Volkmar, no other childhood disability has such clearly defined and consistent diagnostic criteria; indeed, the manifestations of autistic symptoms are remarkably consistent across nations and cultures. Daley speculates that the reason why autism is such a misunderstood and misdiagnosed condition is because it frequently falls between the cracks of mental retardation and mental illness. Indeed, many of its behavioural manifestations are seen as indicative of "madness'; hence it carries immense stigma.

According to WHO estimates, approximately 1.7 million persons in India alone are likely to be autistic. This figure is based on the prevalence rates believed to exist in the Western countries like the UK and the USA, where considerable research on Autism has been conducted ever since it was recognised as a disorder in the 1940's. In this context it would be in place to examine some recent research findings. According to the findings of the National Foundation for Autism Research, San Diego, USA the prevalence rate of Autism in the USA is 1 in 150. Rate of autism was also found to be consistent across all race classifications, according to a recent research study undertaken in Atlanta, whose results were published in 2003. It is disturbing to note that the study revealed that only 50 per cent of autistic children received a diagnosis before they entered Kindergarten. In the UK, Prof. Simon Baron Cohen and his team at Cambridge University found that for every 3 children who receive a diagnosis of autism, 2 remain undiagnosed formally. Detailed assessments suggest that the prevalence rate among school children in Cambridge could be as high as 1 in 64.

Extrapolating from these figures, we may estimate that anywhere between 2 to 4 million persons in India alone are on the Autism Spectrum. Unfortunately, in the absence of any large scale epidemiological study, figures quoted can only be speculative. It is an unfortunate reality that are no specific community linked studies on the prevalence and incidence of Autism in India. Autism came to be recognised as a disability by the Government of India in 1999, after intense lobbying by Non Government Organisations and Parent Support Organisations. Due to lack of awareness and information amongst lay persons and professionals alike, the study of autism has virtually been uncharted territory in India.

This study attempts a sociological understanding of the issues and challenges of grappling with this much misunderstood disorder. It specifically focuses on families of children diagnosed with autism, as it is usually the family that is solely responsible for obtaining a diagnosis, accessing facilities and services and the life-long care and maintenance of the autistic person. The onus of care assumes added salience in the context of rapid industrialisation, urbanisation and the dissolution of traditional circles of support exemplified by the extended family and kinship obligation. The uneven availability of appropriate educational, rehabilitation and other facilities exacerbates the difficult situation families find themselves in. However, we also note the proactive steps taken by the state and civil society initiatives to enable persons with disability and their families live with dignity.

Aims and Objectives

The aims and objectives of the study are as follows;

1. To delve into the lived experiences of families and present a nuanced picture of everyday life with an autistic child.
2. To examine the changes taking place in the urban Indian family through the prism of a child's autism, by examining the patterns of coping and care, differential roles of mothers and fathers and family dynamics.
3. To explore the interface between family ,community and State in the context of Disability management.
4. To briefly highlight some of the proactive steps taken by the State and chart out a roadmap for the future.

As autism impacts the faculties that are essential for social interaction and reciprocity viz., language, imagination and social skills, parenting and living with such a child is difficult and challenging. In the context of a social structure where conformity is emphasised and differences are often viewed with suspicion and hostility, there are limited social spaces available for such families and their children. At the same time, discourses pertaining to disability, and the responsibility of society and state towards its disabled citizens are gaining ground, largely on account of the global emphasis on human rights, and grass-roots activism and advocacy by voluntary agencies, self-help groups and associations of affected individuals.

There has as yet been no large-scale epidemiological study on the prevalence and manner of manifestation of autism in India. (Daley, 2004). Awareness of the condition although gradually increasing on account of the work of non-governmental organisations and the impact of mass media, is confined to select urban pockets. The metropolis of Delhi with its large public and private hospitals, and well developed and active NGO sector has become as it were, the 'autism hub' of India. Indeed, the availability of diagnostic and other facilities in Delhi prompts many families from all over the country to come to Delhi to "show" their child and find answers to their questions about his/her developmental deviancies.

A difficult circumstance like a child's disability acts as a 'critical event' or a breach in the fabric of 'normalcy' challenging existing rules and regulations and bringing to light the weaknesses in the social fabric. (Grinker, 2007). It is in a sense a natural laboratory in which to view the changes supposedly taking place in the urban family.

Busy urban life-styles, the time spent commuting and the pressures at increasingly competitive work-places result in reduced interaction with relatives who may live in the same city, but may find it hard to make time for each other. Family get together are often restricted to special occasions like weddings or festivals. The help of relatives and extended kin in times of crisis, notably sickness, hospitalisation etc. is solicited hesitantly due to the pressures on people's time and the physical distances between homes. The family, as a site of nurture and support, of sharing and caring, is seemingly becoming confined to the nuclear unit.

Under these circumstances, how is disability managed by the family? To what limits can kin support be stretched? Are there emerging institutions or opportunities that 'take over' where the family has left off? What is the role of support groups and friendship circles in this context? The changes taking place among the urban professional classes, as outlined above, rarely attract sociological attention, perhaps because it is the very group to which sociologists belong, and therefore too close to home. Yet, it is felt that the study of this group is particularly interesting because it is precisely here that shifts and changes in social patterns may be clearly seen.

Methodology

Twenty families were identified for the purpose of the study. The Delhi based NGO Action For Autism enabled the researcher to gain access to families. The sample was generated through snowballing and personal contacts. The researcher's own position as a parent of a disabled child enabled access to families and facilitated the process of building up rapport. Owing to the sensitive nature of the subject, identities and biographical details were anonymised and confidentiality respected scrupulously.

The main tools for data collection were the long, narrative interview and participant observation. The twenty families were predominantly middle class and upper middle class (revealing the difficulty in accessing diagnosis by all but the educated and well-to-do) and represented various linguistic and regional orientations. All but one family were Hindu; one was Roman Catholic. The children (14 boys and 6 girls) displayed symptoms of varying severity. All were in receipt of some form of schooling (2 mainstream and the rest in special schools).

An attempt was made to spend time observing the day to day routine as well as special occasions and activities in the life of the child and his/her family. The data thus generated were noted and common issues and themes identified and discussed.

Core Themes and Research Questions

The first of the research concerns taken up in the study pertained to cultural conceptions of intellectual disability with special reference to autism. The findings indicate that there is growing awareness and information about Western bio-medical conceptions of child development, 'normalcy' and of developmental deviances. This growing awareness amongst young parents sits rather uneasily with more relaxed parenting styles of earlier generations, and 'folk wisdom' like boys being late talkers etc. We link this anxiety regarding 'normal development' with the skewed, in egalitarian educational system, the competition for scarce resources like 'good' and 'reputed' schools job prospects etc. and dwindling family supports. Under these circumstances, we find that the 'mind-body' dualism, characteristic of Western culture and the emphasis on intellectual capacities and capabilities as the markers of 'normal' personhood is gaining salience. In a culture where familism and respect for hierarchies has strong roots, the recent trends towards mobility co-exist with the need for conformity. (Sinha 1988). The 'law-breaking' or rule defying aspects of autism thus make it a difficult condition to fathom and come to terms with (Shaked, 2005).

How then do families make sense of their child's disability? Through their narratives, we culled certain metaphors or images that represent their understandings of the disability. These include the conceptualisation of autism as curse, as a product of *'karma'* an enigma that is hard to explain, understand and predict, a state of permanent childhood and therefore also a sign of divinity. These metaphors clearly indicate the difficulties families face in dealing with the child's symptoms and the manner in which cultural referents are drawn upon to 'make sense' of the disability and come to terms with it.

The second research concern pertained to identification of the disability, help-seeking behaviour and the process of arriving at diagnosis. We noted that the salient symptom reported by families was the child's lack of social relatedness (Daley, 2004). The notion of the child's autism as a breach, a rupture of order and regularity, was highlighted. The various factors, social, cultural, economic which comprised a 'health belief model (Mechanic, 1978) according to which families assessed their children's symptoms was analysed. We traced the interface of the family with a medical system that views disability within a 'disease-cure' framework that has little meaning in the context of developmental disabilities like autism.

A significant finding that emerges is that the onus for identifying the child's problem rests squarely on the family. As a result, only those families that have the material and educational background to consult a variety of specialists and sometimes travel long distances, can hope to secure an appropriate diagnosis. Due to the middle and upper middle-class profile of such families, the notion that autism is a Western disorder, the product of family fission and disengaged parenting, is further exacerbated. This has serious implications at the macro level, in terms of policy planning, welfare provisions, state sponsored intervention.

Moving to the impact of the disorder on family relationships, patterns of coping and care and factors promoting and impeding resilience, we noted that families find themselves isolated and pushed into a corner when confronted with a complex disability like autism. The child's bizarre, sometimes disruptive behaviours make it socially awkward, embarrassing and difficult for contact to be sustained with kin and community. (Gray, 1993)

The immense cultural weight given to the mother-child bond, the valourisation of selfless 'mother's love' and the expectations, internalised by mothers, that they must become 'more than mothers' was explored through their narratives, and the entrapping and empowering dimensions of 'mothering ideology' (Ruddick, 1983). Fathers' experiences, the expectations of masculinity and 'responsibility', the conflicts that sometimes arose between their breadwinning and nurturing roles was also highlighted. We also discussed the role of competitive work environments and the emphasis on appearances and self-presentation in promoting attitudes that were intolerant of difference and deviance. The impaired body and impaired mind thus become markers of shame and stigma.

The impact of the child's autism on the marital relationship we noted strengthened the marital bond through a common suffering and a shared concern for the best interests of the child in some cases, and leads to complete divergence of goals and interests in others. The consistent pattern that emerged was that couples felt compelled to maintain intact the family unit for the sake of the child, even in the face of irreconcilable differences. At the structural level, we see the reinforcement of family values and the assertion of the primacy of the family in coping with a circumstance like disability. At the same time, parents' concern for their children over and above other relationships, the willingness to take difficult decisions like migrating and setting up independent conjugal units, reflects a child-centric trend in urban families. Adult identities are also contingent upon parenting performances. Decision making about children is also done by the conjugal unit, sometimes in contradiction, even defiance of elders and other authority figures. Thus, while there is nostalgia for the 'lost' joint or extended family and the support it is supposed to give, the conjugal unit has become critical. The belief that 'only the family can look after the child' also translated into the way sibling bonds were conceptualised.

The experiences and feelings of grandparents reflected the generational change in the conception of intellectual disabilities and brought out the politics of family life particularly with regard to the vexed question of 'who is to blame?' The issues of maternal responsibility, decline of 'family-like atmosphere' and the pressure of urban lifestyles were seen by some as the reason for the child's difficulties. This aptly brought out the difficulty experienced by the family in conceptualising the child's behaviour as a neurological disorder, rather than evidence of poor upbringing.

Observing Daily Life and Activities was the underlying and unifying research concern which reflected in the qualitative methodology employed. The fieldwork strategy which relied upon unstructured narrative interviews and participant observation, elicited data on everyday routines pertaining to feeding, dressing, recreation, commuting, shopping, schooling, in other words, the activities and practices that form the bedrock of domestic life, in and through which families constructed the disability of the child and negotiated with it. We observed that families built up and modified their routines around those of the disabled child and, over time, the special efforts and adjustments they made became absorbed into the family routine.

Examining the Interface between Family and Community with Special Reference to Parent Support Organisations, it was noted that the interactions between families and the wider community were fraught with tensions; neighbours were, on the whole concerned but cautions, and strangers often reacted with curiosity, amusement or ridicule to odd behaviours exhibited by the child. While children with severe symptoms were regarded as deranged or mad, the mildly affected or high functioning ones managed to "pass", usually with difficulty.

A case study of 'Action for Autism', a Delhi-based parent directed Non-Governmental Organisation was undertaken. We traced its genesis from the efforts of a handful of motivated parents to a multi-pronged and dynamic organisation at the vanguard of autism rehabilitation and disability activism. Interestingly, the NGO is conceptualised by some families as a sort of extended family, and its leaders the figures of strength and solace that are called upon or consulted during crisis. This transfer of dependency has become problematic, now that the organisation has expanded its activities and reach and is changing from a small, intimate group of parents to an organisation staffed by experts and professionals.

At the same time, we observe that the role of NGOs is necessarily limited; ultimately, it is the state and society that has to own responsibility for its disadvantaged citizens, and must, in concert with other stake-holders, put in place systemic changes and safeguards. While the changes in legal frameworks covering the intellectually disabled are welcomed, their implementation and monitoring require commitment to welfare goals and the creation of a humane society.

There is, therefore, a need to foster an ethical community in which primary support roles are taken up by family, friends and extended support networks rather than professionals alone. (Parmenter, 2001). The 'de-institutionalisation' of the intellectually disabled currently underway in the West is based on the premise that community care is better and cheaper than institutional care. Within the urban Indian context, we note that traditional patterns of support are disappearing and have yet to be replaced by viable alternatives.

We make a case for the reinterpretation and revitalisation of values of community care such that people with disabilities are able to assume their place within the community as fully participating members. At this juncture, it would be in place to briefly review some of the specific disabled-friendly measures undertaken by the Government in concert with civil society initiatives in order to chart out the way forward for persons with disabilities and their families.

Proactive Steps Taken by the State and Civil Society Initiatives

The decade of the 1990s was one of change and this reflected in the area of disability as well. Three important Acts of Parliament- The Rehabilitation Council Act of 1992, The Persons With Disabilities Act of 1995 and the National Trust Act of 1999 were promulgated. The Ministry of Social Justice and Empowerment of the Government of India is vested with the responsibility of working towards the economic, social and educational development and ensuring the welfare and rights of the disabled population. It has launched various programmes of study in the field of disability. In the period 2004 to 2008, the Ministry introduced new courses of study including a Masters in Disability Rehabilitation Administration, MPhil in Special Education and a Bachelors degree in Special Education.

Autism was given recognition as a disability in its own right due to the efforts of disability related NGOs and parent support organisations. The umbrella organisation 'Parivaar', a National Federation of Parents' Associations for Persons with Mental Retardation, Autism, Cerebral Palsy and Multiple Disabilities which is an 'organisation of organisations', has played a key role in this context. Nearly 150 NGOs and Parents' associations in 27 states of India are included under the 'Parivaar' banner. Disability organisations are now lobbying hard to ensure the inclusion of Autism Spectrum Disorder in the Persons with Disabilities Act (1995) which is the benchmark legislation mandated to secure entitlements like education, employment and equal opportunities to persons with disabilities. The availability of Government sponsored as well as private NGOs has brought disability, including autism out of the four walls of the domestic sphere and into the public realm and public consciousness.

Recognising that persons with autism and other mental disabilities have certain specific issues that need redress, the National Trust Act for the Welfare of persons with Autism, Cerebral Palsy, Mental Retardation and Multiple Disabilities was brought into force in 1999. The Act (NTA) has recognised the need to put in place a system of guardianship for persons with these disabilities who may be in need of life-long care and has instituted a rigorous procedure for appointment of legal guardians (individuals as well as institutions) and most importantly, provisions for monitoring the quality of guardianship, and if necessary withdrawing it in case of abuse or neglect. The Trust has also launched innovative schemes like 'Nirmaya', an insurance scheme that provides insurance over upto Rs. 1 lakh for PWD, 'Gyan Prabha', a post schooling and scholarship scheme, and 'Udyam Prabha', a scheme for self-employment ,to name a few. The various State Governments also provide Disability Pensions and allowances to persons with disability registered under these schemes, which differ from state to state. The amount of pension varies between Rs 500 to Rs 1000 per registered individual.

One of the greatest difficulties faced by families in India is the limited availability of trained personnel in the areas of education and rehabilitation of PWD. The Rehabilitation Council of India (RCI) is mandated to regulate and monitor services given to persons with disability, train school teachers and professionals in early intervention, rehabilitation and special education, standardise syllabi and maintain a Central rehabilitation register of all qualified personnel in rehabilitation and special education. It is also empowered to take punitive action against unauthorised personnel, thereby protecting vulnerable families and children from unscrupulous practitioners who promise expensive or quick-fix 'cures'. In 2003, the RCI launched a Diploma in Special Education (Autism) to train a cadre of educators to work with Autistic children.

The NSSO 2002 survey, cited previously reveals that 55 per cent of India's disabled population is illiterate. The Government is taking several steps towards inclusion of disabled children through its literacy programmes, most notably the 'Sarva Shiksha Abhiyan' which aims at ensuring at least 8 years of elementary schooling for all children in the age group of 6 to 14 years including children with disability by the year 2010. It aims to promote the use of educational options like alternative schooling, home based education, vocational education, open learning ,etc. It also provides an additional amount of Rs. 1200 per disabled child enrolled in school which can be utilised for various activities such as early detection, aids and appliances ,formal and functional assessments etc. The philosophy of inclusion is also gaining ground in privately run schools and there is more receptivity towards children with special needs. However, it must be pointed out that those children with autism who receive placements in mainstream schools tend to be on the high-functioning end of the Spectrum. Children with more serious difficulties are rarely or reluctantly accommodated.

A recent and very heartening development in February, 2009 is the decision by the Central Board for secondary Education to permit students with autism certain accommodations like the use of an amanuensis, additional time to complete the exam and only one language instead of the compulsory two. This will surely enable many more children with autism to obtain the educational certification that will improve their employment chances and self-esteem.

Conclusion

The various initiatives highlighted above certainly indicate that disability has emerged as a significant issue in human resource policy and planning. While it may be argued that these policies are yet to percolate down to the persons who most need them, the fact of their recognition and incorporation into national agendas and public discourse is of significance. The very fact that 'Autism' is being spoken about, written about, discussed in various fora, covered by the media and increasingly depicted in popular culture like television serials and films, reveals that the intense lobbying and grass roots work of parent organisations and NGOs has started to bear fruit.

NOTES AND REFERENCES

Cohen, D.J. and Volkmar, F. (1997). *Handbook of Autism and Pervasive Developmental Disorders.* New York: Wiley

Daley, T.C. (2004). "From Symptom Recognition to diagnosis: Children with Autism in urban India," *Social Science and Medicine,* 58:1323-1335.

Daley, T.C. (2002). The need for cross-cultural research on Pervasive developmental disorder, *Transcultural Psychiatry,* 39(4): 531-551.

Goffman, E. (1963). *Stigma: Notes on the management of Spoiled Identity.* Englewood Cliffs, N.J: Prentice Hall. Gray, D. (1993).

Shaked, M. (2005). 'The Social Trajectory of Illness: Autism in the ultra-orthodox community in Israel', *Social science and medicine,* 61: 2190-2200.

Sharan, P. (2006). 'Need for epidemiological Work on Autism in India', *Journal of the Indian association of Child and Adolescent Mental Health* 2(3): 700-701.

Sinha, D. (1988). 'The family scenario of a developing country and its implications for mental health: The case of India', in Dasen, P.R. Et al (eds), *Health and Cross Cultural Psychology: Towards applications.* Newbury Park: Sage Publications.

5

CHALLENGES FOR SUSTAINABLE URBANISATION

Government intervention is often required to guide urban development for achieving an orderly development of the different areas of the city so as to improve the quality of the city and the standard of life of the people. 'Various proposals for arresting urban sprawl and encouraging the planned and orderly development of the fringes of our metropolitan areas are receiving public attention. The current practice, generally, involve spatial planning to ensure the best land use, distribution of necessary urban infrastructure and services judiciously, proper implementation of the plan and smooth management of urban functioning of the services.

In practice, all these matters are not achieved as they should have been. Consequently, the concept of urban sprawl-emergence of a situation of unauthorised and unplanned development, normally at the fringe areas of cities especially haphazard and piecemeal construction of homesteads, commercial areas, industrial areas and other non-conforming land uses, generally along the major lines of communications or roads adjacent to specified city limits, is observed which is often termed as the Urban Sprawl. The area of urban sprawl is characterised by a situation where urban development adversely interferes with urban environment which is neither an acceptable urban situation nor suitable for an agricultural rural environment.

Aruna Saxena describes the situation in her paper as follows: The process of urbanisation operating in the fringe has given rise to typical land use associations where the contemporary and dynamic land use pattern is developing side by side in the contemporary context, the various land uses. Old villages, new residential extensions, commerce and industry , city service and farming are not neatly sorted out into homogenous areas but are intermingled in a random fashion which gives a distinctive quality to the land use pattern of rural urban fringe. The haphazard development of slums, unauthorised colonies, piecemeal commercial development, intermixes of conforming and non-conforming uses of land coupled with inadequate services and facilities have become common features in the fringe. The dynamic change from rural to urban land use is so fast that the resultant need and complex uses coupled with shortage of land have led to the speculation and increase in land values."

Main Focus

Many individuals preferred to live in or near the urban areas because of availability of different means of earning livelihood in a more or less compact area and availability of necessary facilities for comfortable living in a consolidated area including utilities and services, shopping, recreational and cultural facilities, educational facilities, means of communications and movement. Urban areas developed either through objectively planned areas, guided and regulated by deliberate regulation and control systems or spontaneous growth through unplanned isolated constructions especially on the city fringes.

Ideally, the growth that takes place around urban areas should be channeled in an orderly manner that will produce an economically efficient, socially and personally satisfying living environment. In practice, ideal growth can hardly be achieved due to many practical reasons and difficulties including inefficiency and lack of timely funding of development projects, inefficient management systems, weak legal support etc.

Definition of the Term Urban Sprawl

The term urban sprawl coined by William Whyte has developed through much deliberation and now can be given a reasonably precise definition:

'Urban sprawl is the growth of a metropolitan area through the process of scattered development of miscellaneous types of land use in isolated locations on the fringe, followed by the gradual filling-in of the intervening spaces with similar uses'.

' Urban sprawl, and the economic and regulatory systems which create it, not only produce an inefficient and unpleasant environment on the urban fringe, but adversely affect the inner city and the rural areas as well.

Methodology

Methodology covers following a planning process of in-depth investigation of the causes and nature of the urban sprawl, its good and bad effects on the urban environment and the efficiency with which the remedial efforts that are managed. The process is likely to lead to guidelines for the actions to be taken to achieve sustainable development as alternative to harmful urban sprawl.

Creation of Urban Sprawl

Identification of the Causes of Urban Sprawl

Conditions favorable to urban sprawl can be identified as follows:

- lower land price compared to developed areas of the main city
- availability of un-built agricultural land
- high rate of urbanisation and rapid development activities
- availability of some municipal services in mixed development without paying for it
- less control on urban development being located outside the urban limit
- lower taxes on industries
- influence of speculators on the agricultural land owners for selling land to developers
- high rate of urbanisation
- results of failure to match demand of urban infrastructure and services

Creation of Urban Sprawl along the Main Lines of Communication

The more outlying areas contiguous to the city area going to be urbanised spontaneously in an unplanned way tend to grow very slowly. As a result the costly infrastructure facilities and services that have to be provided are under used and even lay idle for a long period.

Harmful Effects on the Fringe Agricultural Land and on the Life of the Residents

Encroachment of built up areas on the agricultural land rendering agricultural worker jobless or displaced to move to other areas for different occupation. The unplanned metropolitan growth has a number of serious adverse effects. Large areas become characterised by the initial scattered land uses so that balanced planning of the areas become impossible. The lack of planning is also reflected in the high cost and poor quality of public facilities serving the urban fringe areas. 'Land resources are also wasted because the land is divided in small parcels which are difficult to utilise efficiently'.

Effective Measures of Avoiding Urban Sprawl for Attaining Sustainable Urban Environment

Need for Use of New Techniques

In order to deal with the chaotic conditions of unplanned development of the urban sprawl instead of using the traditional methods of management, new techniques of urban planning and management are required to be applied for effective actions to tackle the urban sprawl in the fringe areas of the metropolitan cities.

The problem of urban sprawl has been under serious investigation over time since the early decades of the nineteenth century. 'Beginning with Peter Kropotkin and Ebenezer Howard, a line of utoplans, reformers and revolutionaries that included Lewis Mumford, Frank Lloyd Wright and Mao Ze Dong had visions of a city in the countryside' In pursuance of finding a new technique devised a model termed as a 'modular urbanisation'. His, Golam Rahman, Deanna Alam and Sirajul Islam, City Growth with urban Sprawl and Problems of Management, 44th ISOCARP Congress 2008 model basically included units of self- governed city units planned with integration of provision of necessary urban services.

The model includes almost all aspects of the ingredients of functioning of the modular urbanisation technique such as area, size of optimum population, necessary urban infrastructures and services, all whether network of road connections, solar power, small manufacturing industries, trade and commerce and a regional framework for a balanced economy. The model more or less conformed to well known 'New Town' concept but is lack in number of considerations which had doubts of success. For instance, unplanned isolated spots of development in an elongated spatial form along the main roads emanating from and depending upon the main city have difficulty in dealing with under the self-governed modular city. The working relationship with the main city may also be unmanageable.

Once, restrictions on haphazard development is imposed under the pre-prepared physical development plans, rate of construction within the particular area of urban sprawl will be significantly reduced, and the migrants and opportunist developers will move to different areas for their operation. Therefore, the Friedman model is likely to face enormous obstacles in practice and as such limitations may make the model is less preferable technique applicable for successful management of the urban sprawl but as a non-traditional technique it may be useful in a modified form.

Another important technique which may be helpful to efficient urban planning and management of the areas under urban sprawl is the GIS information gathering and feed back system. Utilisation of one such system was studied by Nigam, R.K. in the study "Application of Remote Sensing and Geographical Information system for land use/land cover mapping and change detection in the rural urban fringe area of Enschede city, The Netherlands".

The study states, 'Management and planning of urban space requires spatially accurate and timely information on land use and changing pattern. Monitoring provide the planners and the decision-makers with required information about the current state of development and the nature of changes that have occurred. Remote sensing and Geographical information system (GIS) provides vital tools which can be applied in the analysis at the district as well as the city level. The system provides detailed land use and spatial changes regularly which may assist the planner to effectively regulate and guide development in the urban management process.

Properly Planned and Developed Compact City Provide Alternative to Urban Sprawl

There is little doubt that unplanned development must be replaced with planned development of the area concerned with orderly location and relocation of urban infrastructures and services. It should be noted that only proper planning will not solve the problems, efficient management including efficient regulation and control are essential for tackling the adverse effects of urban sprawl.

- administratively, regulation of the ever growing difference between the demand and supply of urban services worsens the situation unauthorised development in favour of acceleration of the process of increased formation of urban sprawl.
- environmental degradation due unplanned development: Unplanned development of the fringe areas leads to the lack of public facilities such as educational institutions, playgrounds, public open spaces, health centers, water supply, sanitation and drainage facilities.
- Golam Rahman, Deanna Alam and Sirajul Islam, City Growth with urban Sprawl and Problems of Management, 44th ISOCARP Congress 2008

Measures to Prevent Urban Sprawl

Urban sprawl can be stopped only if scattered small scale development is replaced by the planning and development of large tracts of land on a comprehensive basis (Bosselman, 1968).

Problems and policy measures as identified by Saxena, 2008 are:

- protection of prime agricultural land
- control of sub-urban sprawl
- control of growth
- provision of adequate services
- maintenance of life style in the face of growth
- jurisdictional, legal and financial limitations
- maintenance of environmental quality

- planned greenbelt but these can hardly be maintained. The controlling authorities have inadequate legal provision, skilled manpower, and priority action by the authorities stand on the way.

Bosselmam in the Report—Foreword and Introduction,' Alternatives to Urban Sprawl' observed during 1960's that 'solutions to the growing problems of guiding urban land use in American cities may have to be sought through bold departures from the past practices'. He studied three approaches for the solution of the problem, namely

- Planned Development Zones, which call for intensive development at a prescribed minimum scale
- Compensative Regulations, which involve payments to owners whose property is subjected to highly restrictive regulations
- Public Land Assembly, in which the power of eminent domain would be used as a means of assuring orderly private development.

Planned Development Zoning

The concept of Planned Development Zoning is a substantial extension of the increasingly common use of special regulations for planned unit development, i.e., large tracts of land planned as a single unit. A Planned Development Zone would permit no intensive use of land except as part of a large-scale planned development. Development of small tracts would be permitted only if they were planned as an integral part of the overall development of a larger area. The zoning would be reviewed every few years and the land placed in traditional zoning categories at such time as the desirable trend of development becomes clear. Planned Development Zoning constitutes a major departure from traditional zoning techniques. But, traditional zoning theories requiring a pre-mapped plan are based on existing statutes; these requirements can be eliminated by new state legislation.

Compensative Regulation

If any land use regulation is so restrictive that it would be held invalid by the courts as a taking of property without compensation, the Compensative Regulation technique would enable the authority of the governmental unit which established the regulation the opportunity to pay the landowner the difference between the value of his property subject to the over-restrictive regulation and the value of his property under some regulation which meets constitutional standards. If the governmental unit chose not to pay it could remove the over-restrictive aspect of the regulation. This system would allow the enforcement of the type of restrictive regulations that are necessary to prevent urban sprawl effectively.'

Public Land Assembly

Large-scale Public Land Assembly technique can be used as a means of arresting urban sprawl and promoting balanced development on the fringe of metropolitan areas. The power Golam Rahman, Deanna Alam and Sirajul Islam, City Growth with urban Sprawl and Problems of Management, 44th ISOCARP Congress 2008 of eminent domain for Public Land Assembly may be exercised either by a public agency or by private developers under certain conditions. The expansion of the constitutional doctrine of "public purpose" indicates that the prevention of urban sprawl and planning of balanced development would constitute valid basis for the exercise of the power of eminent domain.

Major conclusions drawn were that the bad effects of to-day's poorly controlled urban growth provide the justification for the adoption of various techniques which, in different circumstances, may have been unacceptable (with respect to the existing laws). The conclusions with respect to the three approaches were as follows:

- the advantages of subdivisions and new communities which are planned and developed on a large scale justify making sharp distinctions in permitted land uses according to the scale at which development will take place.
- regulations about the use that may be made of property which, standing alone, might be overly restrictive, can become a proper exercise of government power when accompanied by fair payments to the landowner,
- governments can properly use the power of eminent domain to assist in private land assembly, to more fully control areas around the public facilities, to prevent undesirable or premature development.

Planned Urban Development for Sustainable Urbanisation

One of the most important independent variables of globally required sustainable urbanisation is planned urban development. In the broad sense and long run, sustainable urbanisation should take the following indicators into significant concern:

- process of urban planning
- components of sustainable urban environment
- definition and expected size of the city
- survey and assessment of the existing features of the city area
- development plan to serve national goals
- spatial planning and distribution of urban infrastructure and services

Case Studies—Dhaka, the Capital City of Bangladesh

Location

The Metropolitan City of Dhaka is located in the District of Dhaka in Bangladesh. Its central location in the country has considerable importance in the overall planning and development of the city. The initial city was established on a loop of land bounded by a perennial main river on the south, the river Buriganga and a branch of the river surrounding the other sides. The area in 1610 A. D, was five to seven square miles and total population was about thirteen thousand.

Nature of Growth of the City

The Metropolitan city of Dhaka is nearly four hundred years old. During the last four hundred years of growth of the city of Dhaka witnessed spectacular epoch-making changes. It is said that in 1700 A.D., population of Dhaka was more than that of London. Table 5.1 shows the changes of the population of Dhaka, increasing at certain period and decreasing in another although the areas kept on increasing with time.

At the birth of East Pakistan urban fringe areas in Dhaka started to grow rather slowly, but its impetus has been increased tremendously after the creation of Bangladesh. An initial study has been incorporated in the Dhaka Metropolitan Development Plan (DMDP), 1995-2015. The post established area from the year 1983 was treated the urbanising fringe area in the DMDP plan. This is the area of land which was converted to urban use in the 1980s. It is widely scattered around most of Dhaka's established urban area. It comprises one tenth of the 1991 urban area which supports almost 0.54 million people. However the developed area has taken place in a spontaneous, but haphazard way, leaving little way neither for an appropriate road network nor for basic infrastructure facilities and services. But, haphazard development is undesirable for sustainable development.

The policy proposed in the DMDP Plan appears to be not in line with the policy of urban development without urban sprawl. But, however this has been in practice in the framework of planning due to lack of planners and regulatory issues in plan administrations.

Observation of Urban Sprawl and its Nature

The Metropolitan city of Dhaka provides a unique example to indicate how efficient spatial planning and development control regulation and management can regulate the urban sprawl to ensure sustainable urbanisation without sprawl. It is found to be a representative example of the developing countries of the Southeast Asia.

It will be observed that at the early stage of the city growth under their Mughal Subedar, 120 Golam Rahman, Deanna Alam and Sirajul Islam, City Growth with urban Sprawl and Problems of Management, 44th ISOCARP Congress 2008.

Provincial governor under the Mughal Empire in India' during the seventeenth century, population started increasing fast from nearly 13,000 in 1610 and rose to 200,000 in 1640 A.D. The reason behind the dramatic growth was supposed to be facilitated by the prosperity in trade, commerce and industry due to increased activities of the Europeans and added efficiency in administration by the ruler. But, the trend of progress did not last long. In 1700 A.D. population decreased to 100,000 persons and after shifting of the capital to Murshidabad, a place over 150 miles towards the north-west in India. In 1710 A. D. the population of the city started falling sharply. After taking over of the province of Bengal by the British East India Company in 1757, importance of Dhaka further reduced. After the Sepoy Mutiny (Solder's Mutiny) 1857 and taking over the country by the British Government, population of Dhaka city further declined.

Situation changed for the better after 1947 when the British left India and Dhaka became the Capital of East Pakistan. Mass migration took place. The population of Dhaka became 0.3 million within the area of 28 square miles. When in 1971, East Pakistan became the independent state of Bangladesh, the population of Dhaka started to sharply rise again. According to population census, in 1981, area of the Dhaka city was 289.3 square miles with a population of 3.45 million, in 1991 with an area of 350 square mile with a population 69.50 million and in the 2001 population census population of greater Dhaka city was shown as 9.912 million in an area of 590 sq. miles.

Looking at the urban sprawl situation, the different time picture of Dhaka shows that up to 1850, growth of population appears to be absorbed within the boundaries of the existing city area. After that date urban sprawl started gaining ground and after the mass migration to city after (1947) partition of India and establishment of Bangladesh in 1971, population of Dhaka could not be accommodated within the boundaries of the planned city area. The urban sprawl has taken unacceptable proportions. The detailed land use of the city of 2001 shows that urban sprawl along the main spinal road towards the north and along the road to the south east, was widespread. Besides unauthorised isolated settlements at he fringe areas adjacent to the border lines of the city created slum areas with all the harmful consequences of urban sprawl.

The satellite towns of Tongi (14 miles in the north) and Narayangonj (16 miles in the south-east) were in the process of development which was expected to absorb additional migrants to the city and contend urbanisation and urban sprawl. Considerable gap between the main city and the satellite towns with rural agricultural land were expected to check urban sprawl of a continuously elongated pattern. Unfortunately, inappropriate urban planning and inefficient urban management failed to bring about success.

Causes

In-migration towards cities, due to lack of employment in the agricultural sector and displacement of people due to river erosion and frequent natural disasters produce high rate of urbanisation. People desperately looking for shelter, job and urban services, tend to grab opportunities whatever they get. They look for the assistance of the government and public agencies for meeting their needs and demands. The Public agencies, on the other hand, hopelessly lag behind to rise to the occasion. Planned areas of the main city can hardly provide them space to settle except in the vacant land under the ownership of the government where they take shelter without authorisation. Slum areas created. But, most of them move to the urban fringe and settle down on the vacant agricultural land, mostly under the ownership of the government or under private ownership. Sometimes, vacant land which is relatively cheap, are purchased for the purpose of settlements. These settlements are found to be located near the main roads of the main city to take the advantage of the public services and utilities and adjacent to the border line of the city to take advantage of the natural source of water which may be available in the rural agricultural land. Such isolated Golam Rahman, Deanna Alam and Sirajul Islam, City Growth with urban Sprawl and Problems of Management, 44th ISOCARP Congress 2008 and unplanned settlements along the road in an elongated pattern form the urban sprawl in the city of Dhaka as well.

The process of formation of the urban sprawl encourage the establishment of housing mostly in the form of isolated homesteads and different sizes of various industries in an admixture of other land uses in the middle of agricultural land without necessary infrastructural base. 'As no single authority is responsible for overall planning and management of the metropolis, an extended metropolitan area with mixed urban and rural characteristics is a complex phenomenon'.

Pradhan and Parera (2008) in their research paper "Socio-economic impacts and natural resources management conflicts in the urban fringe areas," with respect to the Mega-city of Bangkok, Thailand, probes into the conflict between development and the environment in an extended metropolitan area. The studies, the relationship between urbanisation, industrialisation and the continuous exploitation of natural resources such as land and water resources, for non-agricultural use. Expanding human requirements and economic activities are placing ever-increasing pressures on natural resources, creating competition and conflicts. If in the future, human resources are to be met in a sustainable manner, it is now essential to resolve these conflicts and move towards more effective and efficient use of existing natural resources.

The research study comes to the conclusion that land use planning and proper development management is the key instrument for effectively dealing with the urban sprawl. Two elements were suggested to be essential in the planning and management process. One is involvement of the stakeholders or public participation and the second is regular monitoring and feedback of data related information and efficiency of the regulation and control mechanism.

Similar situation arose in case of the city of Dhaka and similar steps may be helpful in efficiently dealing with the urban sprawl. The important implications of the unacceptable urban sprawl can be enumerated as follows:

- loss of agricultural land due encroachment of urban sprawl
- sub-standard urban development under urban sprawl
- lack of public utility services and little incentive for provision
- sustainable development is difficult once unplanned built up areas are proliferated irreversible changes taking place

Remedial Measures

Remedial measures involve three distinct areas of endeavors. Proper urban planning to be informed, new techniques to be devised for efficient development management and new methods to be applied in stead of the ineffective traditional methods along with strong monitoring and feedback systems. The three distinct areas are mentioned below:

(1) appropriate urban planning to ensure planned development to prevent isolated spot developments

(2) appropriate and effective institutional arrangement to ensure proper regulation and control of planned urban development

(3) appropriate legal support to ensure proper guidance and control of development of the city and its fringe areas.

Past Performance and Proposed Solutions

Preparation of Appropriate Urban Development Plans

Spatial development plans were prepared for Dhaka metropolitan area in 1953, 1981 and in 1995 for Dhaka metropolitan area to deal with proper development of the city and ensure sustainable urbanisation without sprawl. They were not effective. There were no mentions of Golam Rahman, Deanna Alam and Sirajul Islam, City Growth with urban Sprawl and Problems of Management, 44th ISOCARP Congress 2008 special conditions of the fringe areas in the first two development plans. In the third plan, unplanned development with deficiency of urban infrastructure and facilities were mentioned but in stead of suggesting measures to stop harmful urban sprawl, proposals were made for speedy provision of necessary infrastructures and services. The decision helped to expand the unauthorised urban sprawl further. There attention should be given to appropriate urban planning of the fringe areas.

Reducing encroachment of agricultural land by expansion of urban sprawl. It is generally accepted that the rich agricultural land around should be protected against urban development as far as possible. In the case of Dhaka city, urban sprawl has been grabbing the agricultural land around the city especially in the fringe areas. Effective urban planning and its implementation is the answer to such problems.

Institutional Arrangements to ensure Effective Management of Fringe Areas

The traditional executive agencies for management of urban development failed to stop urban sprawl in the case of Dhaka. The following important causes and their remedies may be suggested as follows:

- Non-planners as head of the executing agencies relating to urban development cannot generally conceive of the appropriate policies to be adopted and as such problems cannot be properly handled. The remedy lies in placing the appropriate persons to the appropriate place.

- There are often disagreements among the relevant parallel agencies such among different administrative ministries of the government on policy matters relating to the development of the city and delays and disruptions in the development process ensues. This problem of management can be removed through placing the development agency such as the development authority directly under the office of the Prime Minister.
- Even under the autonomous agency for development, if created, should have a separate unit to look after the affairs of the urban fringe so that constant monitoring and feedback is ensured and unauthorised development in the fringe areas are checked and actions taken to deal with them. An effective system of co-ordination in development is essential for success.

Regulation and Control of the Development

Planning as well as regulations and control are required. Simply preparation of a development plan leaves it in a normal process of execution has been found to be unworkable in dealing with the urban sprawl effectively. Therefore, innovative techniques of regulation and control should be devised and applied.

Legal Aid in Support of Effective City Planning and Management

Innovative Rules and Regulations are very much essential for fringe Area management. The problems occurring on the fringe areas due to urban sprawl, if analysed in-depth, guidelines for adoption of appropriate legislative measures can be obtained.

Conclusion

Policy towards urban sprawl should include two things: (i) stream lining the existing condition aimed at removing harmfull effects and (ii) taking steps for stopping urban sprawl process occuring in future.

Urban Sprawl is not Checked by Urban Plans Alone

One of the most important elements which provide opportunities for proliferation of urban sprawl is unplanned urban development.

But, urban sprawl cannot be checked by a pre-Golam Rahman, Deanna Alam and Sirajul Islam, City Growth with urban Sprawl and Problems of Management, 44th ISOCARP Congress 2008 prepared plan alone. Efficient guidance, development control and regulation must be ensured for the success.

Management of Development is the Critical element for Success

Land use control and regulation are important tools and instruments for planning of the cities and towns and to regulate growth and associated sprawl (Saxena, 2008). According to the author, to stop land speculation, especially on vacant land on the fringe of the city the following suggestions deserve attention:

- restrictions on premature conversion of agricultural land
- taxes on land transfer to check speculation
- the need for generation of digital topographical data base for various towns
- use of high resolution data for planning and urban information generation
- needs on the utility of high resolution data/GIS techniques in the preparation of District planning
- satellite based information system has flexibility to accommodate any new data and provides integration as well as updating
- training of manpower essential to adopt new technology of Remote Sensing and GIS in urban/regional planning
- digital database generation for cadastral applications
- promote use of remote sensing and GIS in urban authorities
- generation of data base for macro, mesa, micro levels tasks pertaining to regional, Urban and Zoning planning

NOTES AND REFERENCES

Aguilar, A. G. and Ward, P.W. (2003): "Globalisation, Regional Development, and Mega-city Expansion in Latin America: Analysing Mexico City's Peri-urban Hinterland", *Cities,* 20(1), 3-21.

Bosselman, Fred P. (1968): Alternatives to Urban Sprawl: Legal Guidelines for Governmental Action, The National Commission on Urban Problems, Research Report No 15, Washington, D.C. 1968.

Government of the Peoples republic of Bangladesh, "Dhaka Metropolitan Development Plan (1995-2015)", Volume I, pp. 57-63

Government of East Pakistan (1948); "The East Bengal (Emergency) Requisition of Property Act, 1948 (East Bengal Act XIII of 1948", The Government of East Pakistan, Dhaka.

Pradhan, P., Perera, R. (1998), "Socio-economic Impacts and Natural Resources Management conflicts in the Urban Fringe Areas", Asian Institute of Technology, Bangkok, Thailand.

Prodhan, Pravakar & Perera, Rangith (2008): Socio-economic impacts and natural resources management conflicts in the urban fringe areas, Research Paper, Asian Institute of Technology, Bangkok, Thailand, 2008

Rabinson, I. M. (1995): 'Emerging Spatial Patterns in ASEAN Mega-Urban Regions: Alternative Strategies", in McGee, T. G. and Robinson, I. W. (eds), The Mega-Urban Regions of Southeast Asia, UBC Press, pp 78-108, Canada

Saxena , Aruna (2008): Monitoring of urban fringe using Remote Sensing and GIS techniques, Research Paper, 2008

Friedmann, John (1993): Modular cities: beyond the rural-urban divide, Department of Urban Planning, School of Public Policy and Social Research, UCLA, Golam Rahman, Deanna Alam and Sirajul Islam, City Growth with urban Sprawl and Problems of Management, 44th ISOCARP Congress 2008.

Ministry of Housing and Public Works (1995), "Dhaka Metropolitan Development Plan (DMDP) 1995-215", Ministry of Housing and Public Works vol. I, Dhaka Master Plan p. 63.

Ministry of Law and Parliamentary Department (1953), "The Town Improvement Act, 1953", Ministry of Law and Parliamentary Affairs, Government of the Peoples' Republic of Bangladesh, Dhaka, Bangladesh.

6

CULTURE, POLITICS, AND DISCOURSES ON SEXUALITY

This study investigates the political context of recent debates on sexuality in India, with a special focus on the sexual and citizenship rights of people of alternative sexualities. The historical moment in focus is the expanding HIV/AIDS epidemic in the country. The study argues that HIV/AIDS has been one of the most significant factors in breaching Indian society's powerful taboo on public discussion about sexuality, in the process creating an unprecedented opportunity for multiple sexuality discourses. This new dialogue challenges narrow constructions of patriarchal gender relations and heteronormativity.

A striking illustration of this opportunity is the new visibility of formerly marginalised sexual and transgender communities, and the current debate over Section 377 of the Indian Penal Code—inherited from British rule in 1860—that criminalises them. However, this very opportunity is being complicated by the tendency to sanitise the new openings through a public health discourse, that is, "men who have sex with men" (MSM) as a "risk group" for HIV transmission, and, the persistence of cultural nationalism that essentialises both sexuality and gender.

Using the lens of the most visible symbol of the struggle for sexuality rights in India today—the movement for legal reform focusing on Section 377 of the Indian Penal Code—the study charts the construction of sexual rights, the key players in these debates and struggles, the positions and strategies of these players, and the strategic dilemmas confronting the sexual rights movement today. The analysis takes place within a framework of various interwoven strands: historical precedents and contradictions; convergences and disjunctions within the rights struggles; the impact of the globalisation process, which constitutes a key element in the overarching economic, cultural, and political environment within which the rights struggle is taking place; and the comparative efficacy of the mechanisms available to the struggling actors.

Section 377 I PC: Historical Background

Entitled, Of Unnatural Offences, the anti-sodomy law, Section 377 of the Indian Penal Code, states, "Whoever voluntarily has carnal intercourse against the order of nature with any man, woman or animal, shall be punished with imprisonment for life or with imprisonment of either description for a term that may extend to 10 years and shall also be liable to fine. Explanation: Penetration is sufficient to constitute the carnal intercourse necessary to the offence described in this section." The British enactment of Section 377 was in deference to the existence of similar laws in Britain at the time that criminalised all non-pro-creative sexual behaviour, whether homosexual or heterosexual, in keeping with Victorian values relating to family and sexuality. Additionally, colonial jurists justified Section 377 as a protective measure against what they described as "the Oriental disease." In their unflattering descriptions of Indian society — "culturally degenerate" social institutions like matriliny, polyandry and polygamy, child marriage, female infanticide and widow immolation; weak, effeminate, lascivious Hindu men; oppressed women; a barbaric religion consisting of hundreds of licentious gods — English social reformers also made direct and indirect references to Indian men's proclivity for seeking out the company of young boys, and deplored the corrupting effects of such tendencies.

The combined impact of nineteenth-century Western homophobia, and the sense of cultural inferiority evoked by colonial servitude, resulted in a complex historical process of modernisation. Along with laws that abolished practices such as child marriage and widow immolation, systems of marriage like matriliny and polygamy, and sexual sub-cultures such as temple prostitution and "third sex" communities also underwent legal and social change. The cultural landscape, particularly relating to sexuality, was steadily divested of some of its diverse "little traditions" that had risen and ebbed through history (for example, the country's ancient and medieval mythic, artistic and social traditions that had accorded spaces—albeit marginal, but not criminalised nor labeled deviant for explicit representations of various forms of non-pro-creative heterosexual and non-heterosexual sexuality and erotic pleasure). Indian culture came to be reconstructed as unilinear and co-terminus with Hinduism, and Hinduism, in turn, as narrowly "pure" and norm driven.

Section 377 remained unchallenged in independent India until the advent of HIV/AIDS towards the close of the twentieth-century, nearly 50 years after the British left the country. It remains on the statute books nearly 40 years after the anti-sodomy law was abolished in Britain itself. The paradox is that an archaic and outmoded law of colonial origin embedded in nineteenth-century Victorian norms of morality, and what some sexual rights activists describe as culturally alien Judaeo-Christian values is being defended by the independent, modern Indian state, not to mention large sections of civil society that perceive such sexual practices as violating Indian culture. Widespread "nŏrms" of universal marriage, monogamy, and procreative heterosexuality involving chaste women and masculine men and enforced by the triumvirate institutions of patriarchal family, caste and community, contribute to a consensual societal framework of silence about sexuality.

Admittedly, the direct reach of Section 377 is limited; an individual is only eligible for conviction if he is found committing said sexual act, while those who merely profess same-sex attraction are not. Only 46 cases were brought before the courts in the 150 years between 1860 and 2000, resulting in 29 convictions. Of these, only six prosecuted male-to-male adult anal intercourse and only one involved consensual anal sex, thus exposing the redundancy of the law. Section 377 has been useful in convicting cases of child sexual abuse; 30 cases and 19 convictions a fact used by the courts and the government to argue that Section 377 ought to remain on the statute books as a benign provision. As if in confirmation of this, 1990 to 2000 — the decade of growing visibility of the AIDS epidemic and of people of alternative sexualities—saw the largest number of convictions under Section 377 in 150 years.

Section 377 IPC: Issues of Sexual Rights

Evidence has been mounting in recent decades showing that the real "strength" of Section 377 lies in the manner in which it attracts police corruption and abuse of power. Being a cognisable (or high intensity) offence, Section 377 does not require a court order or warrant for making an arrest. This gives the police the power to threaten arrests and extort money, or to keep victims in jail indefinitely before letting them go in exchange for bribes. Often victims, particularly those who are unable to pay up, are also subjected to physical, verbal and sexual abuse while in police custody, the latter being the very crime for which they were arrested. Thus, most arrests are not pursued in the courts.

Section 377 opens opportunities for the abuse of other criminal laws. There are cases of 377 being read in conjunction with other penal code provisions such as Section 116 (abetment, defined as intention to commit the crime), or Section 109 (interpreted as instigating or encouraging "unnatural sex"), in order to make arrests. Police also make arrests under a variety of criminal laws relating to loitering, soliciting, or indecency, all of which are open to ambiguous interpretations. Examples include various Public Nuisance Acts: Section 268 (any conduct in a public place that causes injury/danger/ annoyance to the public); sections 292, 93, and 94 (the obscenity act and its provisions, which proscribes "obscene" literature, paintings, and other objects, and "obscene" acts); Section 375 (sexual assault); the Dramatic Performances Act of 1876, whereby any play may be banned as "depraved"; the Indecent Representation of Women (Prohibition) Act of 1986 (empowering the state to define any representation of women as "corrupting of public morality"); the Juvenile Justice Act of 1980 (empowering the State to take away a child from parents deemed "immoral or unfit"); the National Security Act No. 65 of 1980 (acting in any manner prejudicial to the maintenance of public order); and even the Customs Act of 1962 (empowering the state to ban the import of any goods which affect the "standards of decency or morality").

In addition to these national laws, several state and city/municipal acts contain provisions that could give police inordinate powers. Among the most notorious are sections under the Bombay Police Act—110, 111 (annoying passengers in the street), and 112 (misbehaving with intent to breach the peace)—and sections 92 and 93 (public nuisance) under the Delhi Police Act. All these laws become excuses for harassment and blackmail by both police and members of the public, and for making arrests. This harassment is all the more effective because most victims have little knowledge of the law and fear the social repercussions of public knowledge about their sexual identity.

While the law may not in itself generate homophobia, its very existence moulds beliefs and attitudes, and drives the demeaning and abusive treatment meted out to people of alternative sexualities and those who work with them. NGOs conducting research or outreach work that involves counseling and distribution of health/rights literature and condoms risk becoming victims of human-rights abuses by police who use penal code provisions of "abetting unnatural sex," "obscenity," and even "threats to national security," to get them to stop their work. The state also sanctions and promotes medical educational literature supporting the myth that homosexuality is a mental health problem. Mental health professionals thus maintain the outmoded position that same-sex attraction is an unnatural phenomenon, and resort to potent drugs and/or electric shock therapy when counseling fails to change the preferences of young people brought in by parents. The absence of a rational discourse within the medical profession on sexuality and alternative sexualities—even after the advent of the HIV/AIDS epidemic—makes for doctors who are insensitive or hostile to the medical needs and health rights of people of alternative sexualities and HIV-positive people in general. Shunned by the medical system these people stay away and early signs of (anal) infections and other sexual transmitted diseases (STDs) go untreated.

The greatest mental abuse takes place in the private sphere of the family. Families seek out mental health professionals, threaten children who refuse compulsory marriage, or enforce mental "cures" through temporary confinement in religious institutions. There is also physical battering, formal or informal imprisonment, or citing "family honor" to induce guilt, shame, anxiety and depression. Those whose physical appearance does not conform to gender prescriptions and who do not have the economic and social support to undergo sex change treatments have little choice but to leave home. Suicidal impulses, public stigma, loss of primary relationships of family and friends, and loss of economic support through the inability to hold down jobs or dismissal from employment, are all real dangers for those who do not reconcile themselves to marriage and parenthood or who are unable to conform to prescribed gender roles.

Community and family honor still constitute the most important anchors of individual identity in Indian society. And that community, caste, and family relentlessly enforce cultural norms prescribing early and universal marriage and the birth of sons as an individual's primary duty, leading many people of alternative sexualities to submit to heterosexual marriage and to raise families. Many men lead double lives plagued by secrecy and insecurity. The lack of safe private spaces forces them to seek out furtive unprotected sex in public places, a behaviour that militates against long-term relationships. If they contract HIV they may pass it on to their wives and unborn children. Vulnerable in public spaces, they become victims of persecution and blackmail by the unscrupulous and police who use the penal code provisions to mete out violence, including sexual violence, further adding to the risk of HIV transmission.

The first salvo against Section 377 of the Indian penal Code was fired in 1992, six years after the first HIV case was identified in the country. It came from a Delhi-based group, *AIDS Bhedbhav Virodhi Andolan* (ABVA)—translated as Movement Against AIDS Discrimination — and followed the first-ever demonstration outside the police headquarters in New Delhi. The protest was against police harassment and arrests of suspected homosexuals in public parks under the nuisance clauses of the Delhi Police Act. The ABVA petitioned the national parliament for repeal of Section 377 on grounds that the law violated several articles of the Indian Constitution: 14 and 15 (protection against discrimination); 19 (right to freedom of speech and expression); and 21 (right to life and liberty, encompassing the right to privacy). The attempt was unsuccessful as the organisation was unable to enlist the support of even one Member of Parliament to argue the petition.

In 1994, ABVA again mounted a challenge to Section 377, this time in the form of a public interest litigation (PIL) filed in the Delhi High Court. The action was prompted by a survey finding that several male prisoners in Tihar Jail in New Delhi, reputedly the largest jail in the country, had tested HIV-positive. When ABVA raised the issue of condom distribution with the jail's superintendent, she refused permission claiming it would be tantamount to legalising homosexuality. The ABVA turned to the law demanding that Section 377 be repealed on the basis that it is unconstitutional, illegal and void. ABVA also asked that steps be taken to prevent the segregation, isolation, and stigmatisation of prisoners identified as homosexual and/or suffering from HIV or suspected to have participated in consensual intercourse; that condoms be freely distributed to prisoners and disposable syringes be used in the jail dispensary; and that jail officials regularly consult with the government's National AIDS Control Organisation (NACO). The legal case went the way of the parliamentary petition; it languished in the Delhi High Court and was eventually lost for lack of follow-up by the ABVA. It would be another few years before a fresh petition was filed.

The silence surrounding homosexuality at the time was also the silence surrounding sexuality in general and HIV/AIDS in particular. For nearly a decade following the identification of the first HIV-positive case in the country in 1986, both the Indian state and civil society were in denial apparently convinced that a sexually transmitted disease like AIDS could not possibly spread in a country that had the protective effect of Indian culture. The initial evidence that the virus was carried by sex workers—and in Western countries, by homosexual men — was seised upon as confirmation of HIV's links with all that was criminal and socially deviant (and of "non-Indian" origin). Such "depravity" therefore deserved marginalisation. NACO, set up in the late 1980s but hamstrung by this tunnel vision, was unable to give the enlightened and effective policy leadership that the epidemic required. Not only were sexuality issues invisible within the HIV/AIDS sector, including the special vulnerability of people of alternative sexualities, HIV/AIDS itself remained isolated from the mainstream health sector and its family planning programme (within which condom use had only a marginal legitimacy), and from any other related areas of development planning. The new human rights issues that HIV/AIDS raised did not yet figure in the concerns of women's or human rights organisations, and mainstream media coverage of HIV/AIDS-related issues tended to be scanty, disjointed and sensationalised.

Struggle for Sexual Rights

The successor to the ABVA legal petition came six years later in 2001. In 1994, a newly-registered NGO in New Delhi, Naz Foundation India Trust, explicitly adopted the objective of addressing the health problems of gay men and "men who have sex with men" in the context of the HIV/AIDS epidemic. The Naz strategy was to nurture the emergence of distinct class and sexual orientation self-help groups—English-speaking and Hindi-speaking gays, lesbians, *hijras,* and *kothis*—by allowing them to find their feet as discrete entities under its organisational umbrella until they felt confident enough to network across class and linguistic barriers and, perhaps, become registered organisations in their own right. When Naz outreach workers graduated from identifying major cruising areas and building rapport, to disseminating educational materials and condoms, they attracted regular police harassment. In the general climate of police persecution against people of alternative sexualities, carrying condoms and sexuality-related literature was itself becoming "evidence" of culpability under Section 377. Added to this were repeated attacks by local hoodlums on visitors to the Naz drop-in center and clinic. The fact that the visibility of its HIV/AIDS work was acting as a roadblock to its attempts at building a stable community for self-care, led Naz to approach the HIV/AIDS unit of the Lawyers Collective, a legal aid NGO committed to fighting for the civil rights of HIV/AIDS-affected persons, to challenge the constitutional validity of Section 377.

The Delhi High Court admitted the resulting petition in December 2001. The petition challenged the constitutional validity of 377 on the following grounds: that the prohibition of private, consensual relations violated the right to privacy guaranteed in the constitution "within the ambit of the right to liberty;" that a distinction between procreative and non-procreative sex was unreasonable and arbitrary and undermined the equal protection provision of the constitution; that the punishments prescribed in the section were grossly disproportionate to the prohibited activity; that 377 violated the prohibition of discrimination on the grounds of sex because it criminalised predominantly homosexual activity; and, that the right to life guaranteed in the constitution was violated by the jeopardising of HIV/AIDS prevention, by the denial that sexual preferences were an inalienable component of the right to life, and by the social stigma and police abuse that was being perpetuated.

The petition emphasised the larger context of HIV/AIDS and the threat that 377 posed to individuals and NGOs attempting outreach to "men who have sex with men." It cited evidence from the report of the first National Consultation on Human Rights and HIV/AIDS, held in November 2000 in New Delhi and organised by the National Human Rights Commission, that MSM continued to be driven underground by Section 377 despite NACO's professed policy of including them in its intervention programmes. The petition also named the government of Delhi, the Delhi Commissioner of Police, Delhi State AIDS Control Society, and NACO, as well as the ministries of Home, Health, and Social Welfare. It did not ask for the repeal of 377, but rather the exemption of private consensual adult sex from its purview. In doing so, both Naz and the Lawyers Collective were deferring to the concerns of child rights groups who were against the repeal of the law given the absence of sound laws that protected child rights.

The prospects looked hopeful. The Lawyers Collective felt it had done its homework well. It had studied judgments from around the world and it had framed the petition within a description of the Indian cultural tradition of tolerance and inclusion of sexual diversity drawn from recent re-interpretations of Indian myths and ancient texts. It was also relying on synergy with the report of the 172nd Law Commission, which was prompted by a public interest litigation asking for a review of rape laws. Filed by Sakshi, a women's rights organisation in Delhi, the report recommended a redefinition of sexual assault to make it gender-neutral and inclusive of oral, anal, vaginal, and other forms of penetrative intercourse, including insertion of objects without consent. The report also recommended more effective laws governing sexual abuse of children, thus rendering Section 377 redundant.

Constructions of Sexual Citizenship and Mobilisation Strategies in the Alternative Sexualities Spectrum

Close to the time the petition was to be filed, however, Naz came in for severe criticism from a new generation of alternative sexualities activist groups, who were beginning to develop their positions on the question of sexual rights. These groups—located mainly in metropolitan cities across the country- had been formed in the 1990s. Several were self-support *gay/MSM/hijra/kothi* groups dedicated to HIV/AIDS work. There were also lesbian groups that had organised in the wake of the violence and controversy surrounding the release in 1999 of the Hindi film, *Fire,* which portrayed a lesbian relationship between two middle-class women.

In 2000, the groups held their first National Conference of Sexual Minorities, which resulted in the formation of the Coalition for Sexual Minorities Rights. The groups accused Naz of failing to engage with them in a countrywide consultative process on the petition. They also felt that public spaces ought to have been specified in the petition, and that by privileging private consensual sex Naz had left out in the cold the lower social classes for whom public spaces were the only recourse (poor gay men, and most acutely transgendered persons/ hijras/ *kothis* whose appearance, violative of gender-normativity itself, attracted the most violent abuse). *Transgender/hijra/kothi* and lesbian groups did not feel adequately represented given the emphasis on MSM in the petition, since many transgendered *persons/hijras/kothis* have complex gender identities and do not necessarily see themselves as MSM. Lesbian groups felt further marginalised by the preoccupation with sexual minorities within the context of AIDS infection. For them the absence of a clearer focus on sexual rights within the framework of patriarchy was a serious gap.

Naz countered these criticisms by arguing that the identification of private consensual sex was the first strategic step in what was, essentially, a long battle on the issue of homosexuality and rights. Both Naz and the Lawyers Collective reminded their critics that they had made consistent attempts to keep interested groups informed about progress on the petition. Regular updates on the petition had appeared in the Lawyers Collective newsletter, *The Lawyers.* The lawyers concerned had also held discussions with individual groups of stakeholders who had taken the initiative to voice their concerns, such as child-rights groups, and they had even discussed the petition at a special session of the National Sexual Minorities Conference in 2000. Finally, Naz had found in the course of its work that gay men and MSM were almost universally married. The importance of reaching out to them as a first priority lay in the fact that their considerable numbers and invisible alternative sexual behaviours made for the violation of women's sexual rights and their right to safety from infection, and fuelled the spread of HIV/AIDS. The fact that MSM had been identified as a target group for AIDS intervention by NACO and its international donors accorded them a certain measure of legitimacy for purposes of the petition.

Some of the polarisation described above, came about because there was as yet no community of people of alternative sexualities. Many of the activist groups were still at an embryonic stage of development having arrived on the scene after Naz initiated its work on the petition. Localised, small, still engaged in self-exploration, such groups were attempting to expand through networking activities including: organising conferences and cultural programmes on sexuality; building links with international groups working on broader platforms, notably forums on alternative sexualities in Asia (the NGO Naz International based in London, and *Trikone* magazine published in the U.S., both catering to South Asian gays, and the Asian Lesbian Network, were among the earliest contacts) and the International Gay and Lesbian Human Rights Commission; and participating in international AIDS and lesbian, gay, bisexual, transgender/transsexual (LGBT) conferences.

At this stage enthusiasm for legal reform was generally weak—or, at least, not a priority—particularly among gay and *hijra/kothi* groups. Some gay groups with more pronounced left-wing leanings had little faith in the capacity of the legal process to bring about social change. Several groups, particularly *kothis* and *hijras,* were severely economically disadvantaged and had yet to develop the ideological and organisational capability to participate actively in the largely English language debates around law, social change, and human rights.

The lesbian activist groups—middle class, small in scale and mainly located in metropolitan cities—had a somewhat different character, and, besides, were still in the process of working out their level of equality with other groups in the alternative sexualities spectrum. Several had first found their political feet within the autonomous feminist groups that had burgeoned in the 1980s, when the women's movement had undergone a growth spurt following the debates around rape and the campaign for reform of rape laws. Catapulted into political visibility by the turbulence following the release of the film, *Fire,* they continued to identify with feminist agendas and were struggling to gain legitimacy for their identity within the women's movement even while they worked to build their own local lesbian groups, rights agendas and networks.

Locating themselves within a critique of patriarchy and viewing lesbian sexual rights within the larger framework of women's sexual rights, they saw legal reform as a positive force for social change. For them, the repeal of Section 377 was as vital for women's empowerment, as was the reform of rape laws to include both men and women and homosexual and heterosexual rape. They framed their political agenda for sexuality rights as one of working for the sanction of alternative sexuality as a private and inalienable right, but demanding state intervention on issues that under patriarchy were considered private, namely domestic violence, incest and marital rape. To this end, they had taken the independent initiative, under the aegis of the Campaign for Lesbian Rights (CALERI) launched in 1999, to demand the repeal of Section 377 in a memorandum submitted to the Committee on Empowerment of Women: Appraisal of laws Relating to Women.

Impact of Global and Local Processes on the Struggle for Sexual Rights

Despite the incipient constructions of sexual citizenship, differing positions, fledgling organisational character, and absence of a cohesive strategy, the voices of Indian activists had been raised, due in large part to the growing momentum through the 1990s of major and complex changes in the national and international political and economic climate. One of the most important changes was undoubtedly the international movement of ideas stimulated by the interrelated actions of the global women's health movement and the global HIV/AIDS epidemic, and aided by a host of bilateral and multilateral donors. Another was the accelerated liberalisation of the Indian economy and the sexual revolution that it was inspiring.

The global women's health movement brought to the table a new set of discourses around the interrelated issues of population, gender, reproductive health, and sexuality. The discourse critiqued states-led demographic agendas that focused on controlling women's fertility to the exclusion of their health and it articulated the rights of women and men to reproductive health and a safe and enjoyable sexuality. In so doing it de-linked sexual and reproductive health from procreation, highlighting the sexual and reproductive health concerns of unmarried youth, widows and post-menopausal women, women in sex work and non-heterosexual men and women. By challenging the structures of patriarchy the discourse also provided an overarching framework for critically reviewing prevailing sexual behaviours and all forms of sexual violence. It drew its strength from the unfolding global HIV/AIDS epidemic, which necessitated an unprecedented re-examination of ideologies and practices relating to sexuality and gender in individual societies and cultures.

Through advocacy and networking at both local and global levels, this global movement of ideas played a critical role in building consensus for national policies that reflected these concerns, as seen in the outcome of the 1994 International Conference on Population and Development (ICPD). International funding agencies that had previously supported states-led demographic agendas now made funds available to NGOs and grassroots pressure groups for research and interventions in women's reproductive health, sexuality, and HIV/AIDS.

Population control had been a major theme in Indian developmental planning since the late 1950s and the Indian family-planning programme, initiated in the early 1960s and the largest of its kind in the world, had, from the start, focused exclusively on targeting women's bodies for fertility control. The policy never looked at men's responsibilities for sex and procreation, and generally left unquestioned the social arrangement of the patriarchal family with its gender-sexuality equations. The only brief threat to men's sexual hegemony came between 1975 and 1977 in the form of compulsory vasectomy drives during a state of emergency imposed by the then Prime Minister, Indira Gandhi. The political repercussions proved too severe, and the drives were hastily withdrawn; thereafter, any reference, however oblique, to male contraception of any kind, including condoms, receded into obscurity.

The combined manipulation of women's bodies by the patriarchal family (the duty to produce sons rather than daughters) and by the interventionist state (the duty to terminate fertility after two or three children) has left a history of severe abuse to women's bodily integrity, including the use of sex-selection tests to abort female fetuses, unsafe (albeit legal) abortion services, and sub-standard maternal health services. The result has been widespread reproductive ill health for women arising out of pregnancy, childbirth, and fertility control methods such as abortion, IUDs and sterilisation. The debates and struggles led by Indian women's groups and health NGOs around these policies also fed into the global movement of ideas leading to the ICPD accord.

The country's mainstream HIV/AIDS discourse began its slow emergence from the stranglehold of the conservative medical community in the latter half of the 1990s under persistent pressure from global debates. Evidence from exploratory field-based social science research—often conducted by, or in collaboration with, community-based health NGOs—suggested that widespread poverty and silence around sexuality stimulated the rapid spread of the virus. The research also highlighted, for the first time, the fact that a very wide range of sexual behaviours existed in the country that did not all conform to the idealised set of norms labeled "Indian culture." Further, the combination of poverty, men's tacit freedom from sexual controls, and women's duty to unquestioningly submit to the sexual demands of their husbands, seemed a potent factor in women's enhanced vulnerability to STDs and HIV. There were pressures on

NACO from foreign funding agencies to include MSM in policy-making bodies as critical stakeholders, both in their own interests and in their role as a "bridge population" in infecting women. LGBT activism in Western Europe and the U.S., with its new language of rights, was another crucial influence. Finally, patient activism in those countries pushing for access to generic antiretroviral drugs threw into sharp relief the contradictions in India's new identity as a major global producer of generic antiretroviral drugs; the country's increasing engagement with the world economy, and the concomitant pressures to adhere to the World Trade Organisation (WTO) and other trade agreements, compromised the ability of its own citizens to access those very drugs.

The Indian state, as a signatory to the ICPD consensus, renamed the national family-planning programme the Reproductive and Child Health Programme in 1998; the old demographic agenda was uneasily linked with some elements of the new discourse, notably the reproductive health of married women. But, issues of reproductive and sexual health of unmarried and non-heterosexual groups, and of sexuality rights in general and the rights of sexual minorities in particular—raised by the ICPD and predicated by the HIV/AIDS epidemic—remained invisible, both in state policies and in the women's and human rights movements. For both the state and women's groups, the hierarchy of concerns in relation to women had always been weighted in favour of economic equity issues within the developmental agenda of the state. Both sides viewed female sexual minorities, like women in sex work, as victims requiring paternalistic state intervention for their rehabilitation rather than as groups deserving of citizenship rights.

For women's groups, sexual rights outside of heterosexual rape remained a silent issue; lesbian crises were merely "lesbian issues" rather than "women's issues," and discourses on sex worker's rights were seen as aiding women's exploitation. In an environment where women's issues and struggles were just beginning to gain societal acceptability, women's groups feared jeopardising their own hard-won legitimacy by permitting open discussions about sexuality, sexual rights, or lesbianism. For human rights organisations in the country homosexuality, if not seen as explicitly criminal, was still perceived as deviant. And, for all these progressive groups, as indeed for the established left-wing parties, sexuality was of little concern and homosexuality was a "capitalist aberration," an elitist and imperialist import (Human. Post-ICPD, AIDS intervention projects for the two criminalised groups of MSM and sex workers did begin to proliferate under NACO aegis. But, without changes in the criminal law the new visibility of these groups only increased their victimisation by the police, and this repression went unchallenged by NACO. Moreover they were without social movement allies, since there was no political support from civil society.

Even while alternative sexuality groups were undergoing birthing pangs, their rights to sexual citizenship still mere cries in the political wilderness, the sexuality landscape of the country had begun to change under the impact of an unexpected source—the globalisation of markets and lifestyles. India has been witnessing an unprecedented increase in employment opportunities and disposable income (and with it, economic autonomy) among educated youth due to the rapid pace of urbanisation, with its attendant loosening of social controls, opportunities for exposure to multiple cultural influences, revolutionary changes in communications technologies, and a burgeoning domestic market for global material and cultural consumption. One feature of the country's new global capitalist culture is a growing tendency to commodify sexuality. Print and electronic mass media, films and theatre, fashion, advertising, and the Internet bristle with globalised images of heterosexual desire with a price tag. Couched as a public discourse on personal freedom and the right to sexual pleasure, these media messages entitle the country's youth to this pleasure, and nurture the emergence of a new, young adult sexual culture. (Young people constitute more than a quarter of the country's population, are increasingly mobile in the search for material opportunities, and tend to delay the age at marriage.)

Repressive reactions from patriarchal forces have not been slow in coming. The new market-led openings are setting off a crescendo of anxieties among a wide spectrum of political and civil society groups. These groups talk about preserving the "purity" of Indian culture and/or specific regional culture(s), as reflected in the virtue of women, and seek to reinforce orthodox moral codes relating to women's sexuality. The general concern of the entire spectrum is to control the sexuality of mainstream, unmarried heterosexual youth in the face of unprecedented change. Actions include: discouraging "Western" symbols like Valentine's Day; laying down strictures, like dress codes for college students that are disproportionately directed at young women; harassment of young couples in public parks; and public interest litigations demanding censorship of television programme content. The most vocal and often violent protests have come from religious fundamentalists of all hues—notably right-wing Hindu fundamentalist political parties and their allies — whose actions are often in concert with instruments of the state, such as the police, and with lumpen elements.

Nevertheless, these social controls are quite unlike the plethora of criminal laws or the cries that "the Indian nation is at stake" when AIDS activists call for public debate on serious issues. It is important to note that the market-driven sexuality of the increasingly affluent urban middle classes runs parallel to the AIDS crisis and the multiple discourses on sexuality that it has generated. It reinforces heteronormativity and has little in common with the aspirations for citizenship, freedom and pleasure of those from the margins who question the prevailing constrictive constructions of patriarchal gender relations. In so doing, its trajectory actually runs counter to the larger and vital political import of the social justice issues raised by the nascent sexual rights movement.

It must be conceded, however, that the globalisation of lifestyles opened possibilities, at least in the large metropolises, for persons who were simply part of gay groups seeking a space for social interaction. Whereas railway stations and parks had been the main areas for sexual activity—even for relatively well-off, English-speaking, middle-class gay men in big cities like Mumbai—now smart city clubs and discotheques, spotting an excellent business opportunity, were becoming available for partying, discussion, viewing films, and other recreational activities. Electronic mailing lists opened up communication within groups like Gay Bombay. Gay magazines such as the Mumbai-based *Bombay Dost*—begun in 1990 as India's first English language gay and lesbian magazine, with both gays and lesbians on its Board—offered a platform for sharing ideas. A 1993 festival of films with gay and lesbian themes became an annual event. Members of this relatively affluent group are usually married and in the closet but their activities have fostered a certain level of comfort regarding gay sexuality in large urban centers and greater openness from the mainstream English-language press. However, social interactions within groups like Gay Bombay don't extend to economically disadvantaged gay men, *hijras,* and kothis who don't speak English. For them, public spaces such as parks—with the lurking danger of police brutality—are still the only recourse.

A dramatic change occurred in December 1999 that introduced a new and contentious political visibility into sexuality issues. *Fire,* the first-ever Hindi film about a lesbian relationship, was released in cinema houses in metropolitan cities. Set in India and made by Deepa Mehta, a woman of Indian origin based in Canada, *Fire's* central characters are two middle-class women. The film, which had been passed by India's National Film Censor Board, was well-received by the public and theatres were even offering women-only shows. But, within a few days of the film's release the *Shiv Sena,* a right-wing Hindu fundamentalist party, and its political allies, set off a chain of riots and protests that included the vandalising of cinemas in Mumbai and Delhi and demands that the film be banned. The protests were led by the women's wing of *Shiv Sena.* The protesters questioned the right of a foreign-resident filmmaker to violate the norms of "Indian culture"—that is, importing alien ideas about women and their sexual desires into a culture that looked upon women as chaste, self-abnegating wives and devoted mothers, and worshipped them as goddesses. They denounced the film on grounds of obscenity insisting that the Hindu community had been hurt by the portrayal of "immoral" behaviour "demeaning" of women, and the use of the name of a goddess symbolising chastity for one of the two lesbian protagonists.

The ensuing debate over women's sexuality took on national proportions, engaging the national and regional media and both houses of parliament. The government-appointed National Commission for Women condemned the violence. Some liberal political parties and groups would only go so far as to declare that they were not against the film. Large sections of the metropolitan intelligentsia and the film community ranged themselves against the conservative forces, predominantly on grounds of freedom of artistic expression as guaranteed by the country's constitution. Progressive groups (including women's and human rights groups, as well as lesbian groups who now found themselves suddenly exposed) volunteered for counter-protests such as picketing cinemas in Mumbai and Delhi where the film was being shown. But, they too limited their demands to freedom of expression and opposition to the forces of communalism, sidelining the lesbians' primary plea for freedom of sexual choice.

Lesbian activists who were already part of women's groups mustered a coalition of 31 women-oriented civil society organisations. It was from this group that the most cogent critique was mounted: the constitutional right to freedom of artistic expression and public debate, particularly on the "hypocrisy and tyranny of the patriarchal family... women's sexuality and... the silence around alternative emotional/sexual relationships." A separate statement by lesbian groups highlighted issues of forced marriages, forced heterosexuality, women's exploitation through domestic violence, and mainstream cinema's celebration of physical and sexual violence against women.

Very early in the struggle the lesbian groups realised that they were on their own. The film community simply wanted the film back in theatres. The filmmaker quickly distanced herself from her lesbian supporters, declaring that *Fire* was not about lesbians at all but about women's "loneliness and lack of choice" — despite the fact that she had marketed the film in the West through lesbian/gay and university networks. For most women's groups, the *Fire* controversy was simply an issue of democratic rights; in the hierarchy of legitimate women's concerns, economic and social rights stood high, and sexuality tended to be seen as a lower-order issue, a matter of "personal choice." Some solidarity came from gay individuals and MSM support groups/help-lines/social-action organisations that were now active in urban centers. But, they were unable to empathise entirely with the lesbians; the fledgling gay men's liberation movement lacked a gender perspective, so what analysis it did conduct remained firmly patriarchal. The film itself was sent back to the Censor Board and soon returned to the cinema halls after a few minor cuts. Future screenings took place uneventfully.

Fire marked a political watershed of sorts. It was the first significant moral panic by right-wing political forces that targeted alternative sexualities. It was the turning point for the emergence of lesbians as a political group with its own manifesto, though they remained committed to participation in forums like the annual National Conference on Women's Movements, and to using sexuality issues to push the women's movement to expand its critiques of patriarchy. Eventually, the experience of confronting the diverse political constructions of sexual citizenships moved the lesbians in the direction of making common cause with other alternative sexualities groups, and working towards a consensus on opposition to Section 377.

Struggle for Sexual Rights

There was one more flashpoint that was decisive in changing the state of fragmentation on the Naz petition within the alternative sexualities spectrum, and that acted as a tool for mobilising consensus. It came in July 2001, just a few months before the Naz petition was filed in the Delhi High Court, in the form of state repression of gay activist organisations in Lucknow, the capital city of Uttar Pradesh, one of the largest states in the country and a culturally conservative region in terms of the status of women.

Four activists from two organisations working on HIV/AIDS prevention in Lucknow, Bharosa Trust and Naz Foundation International, were arrested and imprisoned for 47 days following a police raid on their offices. They were accused of running a gay "sex racket" and the educational materials seised from their offices were declared legally "obscene." They were charged under several sections of the Indian Penal Code: 377 (unnatural offences); 120B (criminal conspiracy to commit a serious offence); 107 and 109 (aiding and abetting a crime); 292 (sale of obscene materials); and the Indecent Representation of Women Act of 1986. Although, both organisations were accredited NGOs, recognised by the Uttar Pradesh State AIDS Control Society (UPSACS) and working within NACO guidelines, the judicial magistrate declared they were "polluting the entire society by encouraging young persons and abating [sic] them to committing the offence of sodomy." The prosecution pronounced that by abetting homosexuality, the accused were going "against Indian culture," a remark that was repeated by the senior superintendent of police in Lucknow.

The arrests sparked protests across the country by alternative sexualities groups. In the months that followed, it became clear that the work of Bharosa Trust and Naz Foundation had been severely compromised; indeed the Bharosa Trust never recovered from the assault. The sense of foreboding among sexuality activist groups was palpable. It was a group of lawyers that played the most constructive role in the incident; members of the Lawyers Collective, so severely criticised by the sexual minority groups over the Naz petition, represented the accused and eventually got them released. The fact that Naz's involvement had been immediate and direct through open, active support and advocacy now generated a minimal willingness among the groups to come together to support its legal petition.

The incident highlighted the vulnerability of people in centers of social and political conservatism outside the big metropolises. It also provided further evidence that major infringements on civil rights followed close on the heels of new visibility, in this case AIDS interventionists with declared group identities, office premises, and funding, all enviable symbols of material progress in a status-ridden society. The police, accustomed to viewing people of alternative sexualities as criminals, were unable to come to terms with this new social legitimacy, which, in their eyes, had no legal sanction, and they looked for opportunities to provoke individuals and groups. The incident also confirmed that the government's AIDS policy leadership—whether at national or state levels—was in silent collusion with the police and the law; UPSACS had not responded to calls for help, and NACO had responded all too feebly and ineffectively.

In terms of the media, the Lucknow case marked a watershed in coverage of sexuality issues. Even in big metropolises, such as Delhi, media attention was mostly prurient and derogatory, prompting even greater police surveillance of cruising areas. Following every media expose, levels of extortion and blackmail of gay men, *kothis* and *hijras,* on pain of arrest under Section 377, rose dramatically, as observed by a gay rights lawyer from the Lawyers Collective who worked on the Lucknow case:

> "Policemen take advantage of this fear of the judicial process to threaten sexual minorities with Section 377. They employ such threats to blackmail, extort, rape and physically abuse their victims. And because obtaining rapid redress is a virtual impossibility, members of sexual minorities usually pay up or accede to the abuse. This also means that the police records never reflect the fact that the threat of 377 was used, for no case is ever registered. The lack of a paper trail—of records of the prosecution of consensual sexual acts between adult males—is in turn used by the police to claim that Section 377 is a benign provision chiefly enforced, as they falsely claim, to deal with cases of male rape... Today the issue of Section 377... is a question of corruption, simply because it is one of the lucrative and easy sources of supplemental income for a venal police. Their real objection to its repeal is the fear of losing this easy money."

In the ensuing period *hijras* and *kothis* were subjected to increased brutalisation. In 2002 Sangama, a two-year-old NGO working for the rights of *hijras* and *kothis,* faced police repression in its office in Bangalore. Claiming to act on complaints of other residents in the neighbourhood who were objecting to the presence of *hijras* and *kothis* accessing Sangama's drop-in center and other resources, the police prohibited these groups from coming to the office, and ordered that their meetings be held outside the city limits. The fact that this level of discrimination occurred in metropolitan Bangalore—a global information technology hub and cultural icon of India's rapid economic growth—highlights the coexistence of multiple dualisms; not only a hiatus between metropolitan cities and smaller towns/more conservative areas of the country, but also within metropolitan cities between the cultures of metropolitan enclaves and the rest.

Intensified police repression of sexually marginalised groups was becoming evident across the country. In 2002, VAMP, a sex workers collective in Nipani, Maharashtra, had bought a piece of land and built an office where it held its meetings and conducted its condom-distribution activities under the National AIDS Control Programme. Local elites, abetted by the police, ordered the collective to desist from using these premises on the grounds that it was an affront to the "decent" people who lived in the area. The women were ordered to conduct their meetings outside the town, and to refrain from "provoking" the townspeople with their new-found identity and legitimacy as AIDS workers. When the women refused, their premises were attacked and they themselves were threatened with violence, including rape. In 2004 a subsequent attack on VAMP and its parent organisation SANGRAM, under the guise of implementing the "prostitution pledge", in which NGOs applying for U.S. government AIDS-control funds must promise not to support prostitution, was sanctioned by PEPFAR, the U.S. government's programme for foreign assistance against HIV/AIDS, illustrating how externally imposed neocolonial "laws" could be used to echo the hangover of colonial forms of repression in the name of cultural/ political "security."

The parallels between the women sex workers of Nipani and the *hijras* and *kothis* of Karna-taka, also sex workers, are striking. Both groups are seen as defying the invisibility imposed on them by the institutions of patriarchy, marriage, family and the law, and by lower-class status. In the case of *hijras* and *kothis,* gender non-conformity puts them at additional risk of entrapment by the police in public spaces, and abuse and rape in police stations and jails. While sex workers are criminalised under the Immoral Trafficking Prevention Act, *hijras* and *kothis* are triply criminalised; they can be arrested without warrants under the Immoral Trafficking Prevention Act (1986), Section 377, and the still-surviving vestiges of the colonial Criminal Tribes Act (1871). The sexual violence faced by *hijras* and *kothis* at the hands of police and civilians alike — so effectively documented by Karnataka People's Union for Civil Liberties— illustrates what makes them the most exploited group within the LGBT spectrum.

In September 2003, the government of India filed its affidavit in response to the Naz petition. In stating its position rejecting the plea for the repeal of 377, the government as one of the respondents in the petition argued that, "The purpose of Section 377 is to provide a healthy environment in society by criminalising unnatural sexual activities... By and large, Indian society disapproves of homosexuality... This disapproval is strong enough to justify it being treated as a criminal offence." Most of the judges involved were of the opinion that the matter required detailed consideration and accordingly issued a Rule—a step that courts take when they consider a matter serious enough to be decided in a full hearing. They also issued notice to the Attorney General of India since the constitutional validity of a law was being challenged. However when the petition came up before the Division Bench, headed by the then chief justice, it was dismissed on a minor technicality; that the petition could not be maintained since Naz was not personally aggrieved in that no case under Section 377 had been filed against the group.

Legally, Naz now had two options before it, to file a review or to file an appeal in the Supreme Court. The alternative sexualities groups, hitherto on the fringes of the Naz/Lawyers Collective efforts around the petition and maintaining a critical stance even while grudgingly agreeing to a consensus, were alarmed by the government's response and what they saw as the prospect of the law remaining effective in perpetuity. They now approached the Lawyers Collective with a request to be educated on the meaning of the government's position and the options ahead. What resulted was a national meeting, in September 2003, of a spectrum of NGOs representing alternative sexualities (including the lesbian groups referred to earlier), intravenous drug users, sex workers and child rights advocates. The meeting, led by the Lawyers Collective, discussed the Naz petition and resolved to bury differences and form a coalition called Voices Against 377 to carry the campaign forward. The consensus was that a review petition be filed, and that public awareness activities be conducted around the country on the issue of Section 377 to mobilise social support for the petition and to culminate in a million signatures voicing protest.

During this period, another crisis occurred that cast a pall but also pushed Voices Against 377 into taking its case to the Supreme Court of India. On August 14, 2004, Pushkin Chandra, an affluent gay man, resident of New Delhi and employee of USAID, was brutally murdered in his home along with a friend who was with him at the time. The criminal investigations, widely covered in the national media, revealed his homosexual background, and highlighted his habit of picking up young men, generally poor and unknown to him, for sex. The media's prurient coverage of the homosexual aspects of the case, evoking the "dark underbelly" of Delhi and the "economic and sexual exploitation" of poor young men by the gay community, were accorded an inordinate amount of column inches. Articles deplored the "new gay evangelism," the "growing climate of moral laxity," "gay criminality," and "assault on family values," as well as the "fear" of "ordinary, decent people about speaking out against the perversions in the gay community lest it be construed as intolerance".

Articles in alternative forums pointed out the bias of the mainstream press in equating gay issues with criminality, especially when compared to its silence on the high incidence of rape and rampant trafficking in girl children in the country. The state's position on homosexuality was described as a case of double standards since it did not question the legality of heterosexuality in the face of rape of women and girl children by men a criticism that could well have been applied to the civil society response to Pushkin Chandra's murder. The very public debate, however, was evidence that the visibility of people of alternative sexualities, and their determination to carve out their own niche, was coming of age, at least in the metropolitan cities and among the better off, English-speaking classes.

The Lawyers Collective and Naz, with the weight of the alternative sexualities community behind them, filed the review petition. It cited 14 reasons that justified Naz's legal intervention on behalf of a section of the population, whose criminalisation made it dangerous for them to access the courts. The review petition was dismissed by the Delhi High Court just 19 days later. The question now was whether Naz should pursue an appeal in the Delhi High Court or, alternatively, file a petition in the High Court of another state of the country. Another round of consultations within the coalition elicited a range of different opinions. There was concern about going before the Supreme Court because once it decided the case there could be no further appeal. After a third round of consultations, despite many lingering differences, the coalition was able to take an informed and collective decision to file an appeal to the Supreme Court on a single issue; whether the Delhi High Court was correct in finding that Naz Foundation India did not have the locus standi to file and maintain a public interest litigation, and thereby dismissing the petition.

Between December 2003 when the Voices Coalition was formed and January 2005 when the final consensus was reached, the Lawyers Collective continued to take the lead in consolidating the opposition to Section 377, organising meetings in Delhi, Mumbai, Calcutta and Bangalore in association with local groups. Soon there were some 70 groups across the country—predictably concentrated in the metropolitan cities of Mumbai (11), New Delhi (10), Bangalore (11) and Calcutta (8)—discussing the petition and building consensus on the next steps.

In January 2005, the Voices Coalition stepped up its public outreach efforts, staging peaceful demonstrations and holding press conferences in major cities to keep alive the opposition to 377, and collecting signatures in support of the petition as proof that civil society in the broadest sense, with Naz as the tip of the iceberg, had the *locus standi* to protest against a socially unjust law. The evolving consensus among the alternative sexualities groups had come to rest on a composite construction of sexual citizenship: "We state that our struggle against control of sexuality is a matter of social justice and linked to our struggle for women's rights, our fight against fundamentalism, and our vision of a just world where people have the freedom to be different and yet be treated as equals".

The Million Voices Campaign, as the petition drive was called, is the apex of a broader set of decentralised actions, with each group negotiating challenges at the local level and working, to the extent possible, with police, media, politicians, academia, bureaucrats, and medical institutions and professionals. Individual streams in the coalition are seeking to grow according to their own imperatives and to build their own coalitions with allies, such as lesbians who are out, for whom public sanction of their sexuality is critical, and transgender groups, which are examining their commonalities with sex workers.

On September 26, 2005, the Ministry of Home Affairs submitted its response to the Naz petition. The state's position remained unchanged. The Ministry held that the Naz petition was merely "academic" in nature and did not call for any "substantial question of law of public importance;" that there was no evidence HIV-prevention work was being hampered due to Section 377; that "public opinion and the current societal context in India does not favour the deletion of the said offence from the statute book;" that "the right to privacy cannot be extended to defeat public morality;" and that it was for the legislature to decide whether homosexuality should remain an offence.

Nevertheless, the years of advocacy had begun to yield some returns, made easier, perhaps, after the 2004 general elections when the government changed from a right-wing coalition to a centrist/left-of-center coalition. The cultural government's Planning Commission appointed a task force to re-examine the laws criminalising homosexuality and sex work in the light of the spreading HIV/AIDS epidemic. An HIV/AIDS Bill now before the parliament addresses the civil rights of persons of alternative sexualities among other significant rights relating to HIV-positive people. A government-appointed group is already deliberating on the recommendations of the 172nd Law Commission. On World AIDS Day in December 2005, the Prime Minister appealed to the country for a freer social climate for public discussion of sexuality related issues in the interests of the safety of youth who are falling prey to HIV/AIDS. It was the first significant position on HIV/AIDS taken by an Indian prime minister and, certainly, the most liberal public statement on sexuality by a political leader. Most recently, in October 2006, NACO, under new leadership and in a major position shift, filed its response to the Naz petition — its first publicly stated position on the matter—in which it supported the decriminalising of alternative sexualities. The other responses are awaited.

In the midst of these hopeful initiatives, again in Lucknow, on January 3, 2006, police entrapped four closeted and married homosexual men in their homes and in restaurants, apparently as an outcome of monitoring gay website chat rooms. Falsely charged under Section 377 on grounds of having been caught having sex in a public park, the men were effectively tried by the media and publicly stripped of all dignity, in violation of all journalistic ethics. Thirteen others were publicly named and their personal and professional profiles broadcast.Around the same time, two young women in Meerut, a town in the vicinity of Delhi, declared themselves married to each other in a local temple. They were separated and thrashed by their respective families, resulting in one of them attempting suicide.

As the time nears for the Supreme Court judgment, the Voices Coalition has made its final thrust in building public opinion in favour of the petition. In September 2006, English language metropolitan newspapers published an open letter on their front pages titled, Same Sex Love in India: Open Letter Against Section 377. The letter was addressed to the Government of India, members of the judiciary, and all citizens of India, and signed by several prominent Indian citizens, metropolitan and overseas-based professionals from the arts, media and academia headed by Amartya Sen, the Nobel laureate, and Vikram Seth, the internationally acclaimed author. Sen also issued another statement explaining the reasons for his support. The letter and the issues that it raised received wide media coverage.

Conclusion

The politics of Section 377 of the Indian Penal Code, with its multiple actors, positions and contradictions, affords a glimpse of the layered and discontinuous nature of the politics of sexuality in India. The foregoing analysis has examined the process of bringing disparate alternative sexualities groups across the country into a national-level community. The various actions taken by these groups in response to repression, in concert with civil society organisations engaged in HIV/AIDS prevention and legal aid, proved instrumental in diminishing conflict around the comparative efficacy of available mechanisms. Their objective was to mount a social movement for countering state instruments of control. For most groups in the Voices Against 377 movement, the significance of the decision to support the Naz petition all the way to the highest court in the land is in its usefulness as a mobilising tool. Opposition to a law that was itself acting as an instrument of illegality brought them together as no other single principle could, and the legal reform campaign, while serving to develop a common ideology and strategy, relied on this organised movement for strength and legitimacy as it engaged with the state.

The movement offers significant lessons on the strategic dilemmas that social activists face when determining how to act instrumentally and effectively; in this case, taking advantage of the spaces created by members of the middle class and the public health discourse prompted by the AIDS epidemic, even as they run the risk of becoming distracted by these discourses.

The inevitable tension between calibrating arguments according to the narrow assumptions of the law and the ideal trajectory of the movement toward broadening rights is one source of ambivalence activist groups experienced in using legal mechanisms. At the broadest level, working through the legal system may result in laws becoming further entrenched, and a change in the law does not necessarily translate into social change. At a more practical level, many activist groups lack the knowledge and literacy necessary to participate in complex legal processes, particularly those who are economically and socially disadvantaged.

Paradoxically, criminalisation makes it dangerous for affected groups to access the courts on their own behalf, but working through intermediaries may bring with it a sense of opacity and alienation. One of the fallouts in the struggle against Section 377 is that the campaign leadership has remained in the hands of metropolitan-based, educated activists, and the movement itself is still limited to functioning in the relatively more liberal, English-speaking environment of the metropolises.

The "legalisation" of the struggle for LGBT rights also throws into sharp relief other problematic implications of class, such as the exclusion of the majority of transgendered persons, *hijras,* and *kothis,* who, on account of their poverty, engage in sex in public spaces. Backed neither by legal reform nor by benefits arising from the globalising economy, the continuing plight of these groups—further accentuated by their non-normative gender behaviour—highlights the perpetuation of the pre-existing dualisms of private and public, metropolitan and non-metropolitan, upwardly mobile and poor, and gendered and transgendered, with little end in sight. Although, they are strategic constituents of the current legal reform movement, these grassroots groups are seeking to build their own independent bridges with other potential and real allies for long-term change in social attitudes towards their demand for citizenship rights. These groups, which feel the greatest urgency to publicly advocate their cause, also seek cultural legitimacy by their claim to a historically sanctioned place in pre-colonial, quintessentially "Indian" regimes of sexuality that celebrated diversity. This claim, already infused with new life from recent and ongoing scholarly work, exposes the instability of es-sentialist assumptions about the meaning of the past, and how that past justifies the present. But, it also runs the risk of a backlash (the reassertion of hyper-masculinity) from dominant fundamentalist political groups, and by accentuating an Indian/non-Indian dualism might further distance these vulnerable groups from the modernist vision of their more affluent and educated metropolitan allies in the alternative sexualities spectrum.

The public health formulation of "men who have sex with men" has its own contradictions. The acceptance of the sanitised identity of MSM may have gained for the movement a shift to the center from the margins. But, it highlights the problematic role of gender, self-identities, and multiple sexualities in influencing political balances within the incipient LGBT community, the relative legitimacy of different groups in relation to the state, and the movement forward of a broad-based rights agenda. Here again, it is the gender-ambivalent trans-gendered persons, *hijras,* and *kothis* who are at a distinct disadvantage. The MSM approach also carries with it the potential loss of some aspects of women's sexual rights, most notably lesbian rights. By virtue of the fact that the MSM concept does not engage with the patriarchal organisation of gender, which is at the root of the current crises around sexuality, it precludes LGBT alliances with other significant social movements such as feminist groups, whose own emancipation is contingent on overturning this same gender organisation.

One of the strengths of the consensus that built up around the Naz petition was that it did not allow the strategic use of the MSM concept to get in the way of collective mobilisation for the limited objective of legal reform. The recently changed stance of NACO, the deliberations of the 172nd Planning Commission, the open letter of social support signed by metropolitan citizens, and the progress of globalisation with its concomitant opening up of spaces for freer sexual expression (albeit commodified and confined to metropolitan cities) may, together, make for a supportive external environment for the final push for the reading down of Section 377. But, the reassertion of normative sexuality and stigma is always a possibility as are changes in the external environment, both national and international, such as the "routinisation" of national AIDS policies, conservative shifts in international AIDS funding, the political resurgence of fundamentalist forces, or a widening chasm between those regions of the country witnessing a faster pace of globalisation and those undergoing a much slower process of social change. The only bulwark against these possibilities is the development of a theoretical and political agenda for sexual rights that includes the entire spectrum of people of alternative sexualities, that draws its strength from the debates and struggles generated by the HIV/AIDS epidemic, and that goes beyond the freedoms held out by the market. In other words, a willingness to critique patriarchy, dominant masculinity, and sexual violence, which govern both the subordination of women and repression of marginalised sexual and transgender communities, and recast sexual rights in terms that go beyond market definitions of heterosexual pleasure, to social justice for all sexualities.

NOTES AND REFERENCES

Aggarwal, S. (2002). ABVA writ petition for repeal of Section 377. In B. Fernandez (Ed.) *Humjinsi: A resource book on lesbian, gay and bisexual rights in India.* Mumbai: India Center for Human Rights and Law.

Bandhopadhyay, A. (2002). Where saving lives is a crime: the Lucknow story! In B. Fernandez (Ed.) *Humjinsi: A resource book on lesbian, gay and bisexual rights in India.* Mumbai: India Center for Human Rights and Law.

CALERI (Campaign For Lesbian Rights). (1999). Lesbian Emergence: A Citizens' Report. New Delhi.

Chakravarty, U. (1993, April 3). Conceptualising Brahmin Patriarchy. *Economic and Political Weekly.*

Counsel Club. (2002). A self-help story. In B. Fernandez (Ed.) *Humjinsi: A resource book on lesbian, gay and bisexual rights in India.* Mumbai: India Center for Human Rights and Law.

Desai, M. (2002). Civil laws affecting gay men and lesbians. In B. Fernandez (Ed.) *Humjinsi: A resource book on lesbian, gay and bisexual rights in India.* Mumbai: India Center for Human Rights and Law.

Doniger, W. (2000). *Splitting the difference: Gender and myth in ancient Greece and India.* New Delhi: Oxford University Press.

Dutta, A. (2004, August 9). Homosexual victim exposes the Delhi press. *Media South Asia.* http://www.thehoot.org.

Fernandez, B. (Ed.) (2002). *Humjinsi: A resource book on lesbian, gay and bisexual rights in India.* Mumbai: India Center for Human Rights and Law.

Gopalan, A. (2005). Client advocacy and service provision: the Naz Foundation's mission. In R. Ramasubban & B. Rishyasringa (Eds.) *AIDS and civil society: India's learning curve.* Jaipur and Delhi: Rawat Publications.

Grover, A. (2005). Meeting the unmet legal needs of positive people: The Lawyers Collective HIV/AIDS Unit. In R. Ramasubban & B. Rishyasringa (Eds.) *AIDS and civil society: India's learning curve.* Jaipur and Delhi: Rawat Publications.

Gupta, A. (2002). Trends in the application of Section 377. In B. Fernandez (Ed.) *Humjinsi: A resource book on lesbian, gay and bisexual rights in India.* Mumbai: India Center for Human Rights and Law.

Human Rights Law Network. (2002). Perspectives on gay and lesbian rights. In B. Fernandez (Ed.) *Humjinsi: A resource book on lesbian, gay and bisexual rights in India.* Mumbai: India Center for Human Rights and Law.

Human Rights Watch. (2002). Epidemic of abuse: Police Harassment of HIV/AIDS outreach workers in India, 14(5).

Jaffrey, Z. (1996). *The invisibles: A tale of the eunuchs of India.* New York: Vintage Books.

Law Commission of India. (2000). *One hundred and seventy-second report: Review of rape laws.* New Delhi: Government of India.

Lawyers Collective. (2001). *Writ Petition in Delhi High Court.*

Menon, N. (1999). Introduction. In N. Menon (Ed.) *Gender and politics in India.* New Delhi: Oxford University Press.

Nanda, S. (1990). *Neither man norwoman: The hijras of India.* Belmont: Wadsworth Publishing Co.

Nanda, S. (1994). Hijras: An alternative sex and gender role in India. In G. Herdt (Ed.) *Third sex, third gender: Beyond sexual dimorphism in culture and history.* New York: Zone Books.

Narrain, A., & Khaitan, T. (2002). Medicalisation of homosexuality. In B. Fernandez (Ed.) *Humjinsi: A resource book on lesbian, gay and bisexual rights in India.* Mumbai: India Center for Human Rights and Law.

Narrain, A. (2004). The articulation of rights around sexuality and health: Subaltern queer cultures in India in the era of Hindutva. *Health and Human Rights,* 7(2).

Narrain, A., & Gautam, B. (Eds.) (2005). *Because I have a voice: Queer politics in India.* New Delhi: Yoda Press.

People's Union of Civil Liberties-Karnataka. (2003, September). Human rights violations against the transgender community: A study of *kothi* and *hijra* sex workers in Bangalore, India. Bangalore.

Ramasubban, R. (1995). Patriarchy and the risks of STD and HIV transmission to women. In M. Das Gupta, L. C. Chen & T. N. Krishnan (Eds.) *Women's health in India: Risk and vulnerability.* Bombay: Oxford University Press.

Ramasubban, R., & Rishyasringa, B. (2002). *Sexuality and reproductive health and rights: Fifty years of the Ford Foundation's population and health programme in India.* New York: Ford Foundation.

Rege, A. (2002). A decade of lesbian hulla gulla. In B. Fernandez (Ed.) *Humjinsi: A resource book on lesbian, gay and bisexual rights in India.* Mumbai: India Center for Human Rights and Law.

Roy, K. (1995). "Where women are worshipped, there the gods rejoice. In U. Butalia & T. Sarkar (Eds.) *Women and the Hindu right.* New Delhi: Kali For Women.

Sarkar, T. (1996). Colonial lawmaking and lives/deaths of Indian women. In R. Kapur (Ed.) *Feminist terrains in legal domains: Interdisciplinary essays on women and law in India.* New Delhi: Kali For Women.

Seshu, M. (2005). Organising women in prostitution: the case of SANGRAM. In R. Ramasubban & B. Rishyasringa (Eds.) *AIDS and civil society: India's learning curve.* Jaipur and New Delhi: Rawat Publications.

Stree, S. (2002). Women coming together. In B. Fernandez (Ed.) *Humjinsi: A resource book on lesbian, gay and bisexual rights in India.* Mumbai: India Center for Human Rights and Law.

Vanita, R. & Saleem, K. (Eds.) (2000). *Same-sex love in India: Readings from literature and history.* New. Delhi: Macmillan.

Voices Against 377. (2004). Rights for All: Ending Discrimination Against Queer Desire Under Section 377.

7

URBAN POVERTY IN INDIA

Urban poverty is a major challenge before the urban managers and administrators of the present time. Though the anti-poverty strategy comprising a wide range of poverty alleviation and employment generating programmes has been implemented but results show that the situation is grim. More importantly, poverty in urban India gets exacerbated by substantial rate of population growth, high rate of migration from the rural areas and mushrooming of slum pockets. Migration alone accounts for about 40 per cent of the growth in urban population, converting the rural poverty into urban one. Moreover, poverty has become synonymous with slums. The relationship is bilateral, *i.e.* slums also breed poverty. This vicious circle never ends.

Most of the world's poor reside in India and majority of the poor live in rural areas and about one-fourth urban population in India lives below poverty line. If we count those who are deprived of safe drinking water, adequate clothing, or shelter, the number is considerably higher. Moreover, the vulnerable groups such as Scheduled Castes, Scheduled Tribes, minorities, pavement dwellers etc. are living in acute poverty. Housing conditions in large cities and towns are depicting sub human lives of slum dwellers. With the reconstruction of poverty alleviation programmes in urban India, it is expected that social and economic benefits will percolate to the population below the poverty line. However, eradication of poverty and improving the quality of life of the poor remain one of the daunting tasks. Against this view point present study purports to analyse perspective of urban poverty, emerging trends, dimensions, poverty alleviation programmes and to suggest strategies for formulation of micro action plans.

Conceptualisation and Measurement

Poverty generally arises from lack of income or assets. The low income of the poor can be attributed to the following problems facing them: (i) Low access to financial resources and production assets which are necessary to sustain the micro-enterprises beyond day today basis, (ii) Monopolistic control over micro-enterprises by larger entities which, through control over inputs and/or insecurity of wage employment, compel the poor to accept lowest wages and to work overtime without pay. The urban poor have low access to formal education, health services, shelter and safe living environments. Moreover, poverty is also perpetuated by division of labour and time, away from income earning uses and towards daily physical, environmental and energy management tasks, necessary to sustain life itself. This diversion further limits chances of investing household resources in skill attainment and enterprises.

Poverty has been measured on the basis of nutritional requirement, monthly per capita expenditure and housing conditions. Thus, income-based poverty lines set for the whole country do not allow for high costs of living in cities. No single poverty line can take into account the large differences in the availability and cost of food, shelter, water sanitation and health care services. Housing poverty has been defined by UNCHS as lack of safe, secure and healthy shelter with basic infrastructure like piped water and adequate provision for sanitation, drainage and removal of household's wastes. The definition of poverty line in India was set for the first time in 1962 by a working group after taking into account the recommendations of the Nutrition Advisory Committee of the Indian Council of Medical Research regarding balanced diet. The working group proposed the poverty norm in money terms in urban and rural areas. It was based on broad judgment of minimum caloric need. More importantly, the Planning Commission in 1977 constitutes a Task Force on projections of Minimum Needs and Effective Consumption Demand. It defined the poverty line as a per capita consumption expenditure level which meets the average per capita daily caloric requirement of 2400 calories in rural areas and 2100 calories in urban areas long with a minimum of non-food expenditure. The Planning Commission constituted the Expert Group on estimation and number of poor in 1989. It did not redefine the poverty line but estimated separate poverty line for each state by desegregating the national level poverty line. It used the state-wise consumer price index of industrial workers for updating urban poverty line.

The poverty is broadly defined in terms of material deprivation, human deprivation and a range of other deprivations such as lack of voice, vulnerability, violence, destitution, social and political exclusions, and lack of dignity and basic rights. In India, and indeed throughout the world, the conventional approach equates poverty with material deprivation and defines the poor in terms of incomes or levels of consumption. The Planning Commission has defined poverty in terms of the level of per capita consumer expenditure sufficient to provide an average daily intake of 2400 calories per person in rural areas and 2100 calories per person in urban areas, plus a minimal allocation for basic non-food items. There is no doubt that material deprivation is a key factor that underlines many other dimensions of poverty.

Despite uncertain progress at reducing material deprivation, there has been greater progress in human development in the states throughout the 1990's. Human Development Indicators capture important dimensions of well-being and reflect not just the rate of growth in the economy but also levels and quality of public spending. Effective public spending on basic services (education, health, water and sanitation) can compensate for limited capacity of the poor to purchase these services through the market. Education is a key indicator of human development. Many desirable social and economic outcomes are limited to rising levels of education, particularly education of women and of socially vulnerable groups. Health status is another key indicator of human development. Vulnerable, powerlessness, exclusion and social identity crises are some of the issues related with human poverty. Vulnerability is a fact of life for the poor. They are distressed not only by current low levels of resources and incomes, but also by the possibility of falling into deeper poverty and destitution. The poor are at risk because they lack the income, the assets and the social ties that protect the better off from the impact of unexpected setbacks. Illness requires expensive treatment; the temporary or permanent disability of a breadwinner, or a natural or man-made disaster can obliterate a poor household's small savings. Death, disability, disease, etc. are such factors, which are linked with vulnerability. Widowhood or desertion by a spouse, often led to destitution in poor and low caste women. In urban areas, the following types of vulnerability of the poor are reported:

(i) ***Housing Vulnerability*:** Lack of tenure, poor quality shelter without ownership rights, no access to individual water connection/toilets, unhealthy and unsanitary living conditions.

(ii) ***Economic Vulnerability*:** Irregular/casual employment, low paid work, lack of access to credit or reasonable terms, lack of access to formal safety net programmers, low ownership of productive assets, poor net worth and legal constraints to self employment.

(iii) ***Social Vulnerability*:** Low education, lack of skills, low social capital/caste status, and inadequate access to food security programmes, lack of access to health services and exclusion from local institutions.

(iv) ***Personal Vulnerability:*** Proneness to violence or intimidation, women, children and elderly, disabled and destitute, belonging to low castes and minority groups, lack of information, lack of access to justice.

The poor lack the leverage to ensure that state institutions serve them fairly and, thus, often lack access to public facilities or receive goods of inferior quality. More importantly, caste, status and gender is linked to poverty in a number of ways. Deep and continuing social inequalities mark many facets on the society. Individuals with low caste status are for more likely to be employed as low paid; low status labourers live in poorly constructed houses with limited access to water and sanitation. Importantly, poor are the truly destitute. Destitute households have fewer and often very weak ties of mutual assistance and support than their wealthier counterparts. They lack of formal and informal safety nets. Poor women face high risks of destitution. A significant number of women poor belong to female-headed households.

The majority of the urban poor tend to fall within the following generic occupational categories:

(i) Casual workers, unskilled, non-unionised wage workers;
(ii) Unskilled, non-unionised service industry workers;
(iii) Street vendors;
(iv) Construction workers;
(v) Rickshaw pullers;
(vi) Sweepers;
(vii) Domestic workers;
(viii) Rag pickers;
(ix) Sex workers;
(x) Beggars.

In the housing category of poverty, based on physical conditions and environment, urban poor may include:

(i) Pavement dwellers;
(ii) Nomadic pavement dwellers;
(iii) Recognised slum dwellers;
(iv) Unrecognised slum dwellers; and
(v) Squatters.

Three groups tend to be most vulnerable in urban context-women, children and minorities. In general women and children fall at the bottom and of the sub-contracting chain, performing the lowest paid activities such as home based prices and domestic services. In urban settings, the family support chain often breaks down with women facing particular stresses as they attempt to balance their work and domestic tasks. The impact of media, alcohol, drugs etc. on conditions of worsening deprivation of women tend to face harassment and physical abuse form within the households, the community and from employers. The health status of women and children, is also particularly bad in relation to men. Women are forced into becoming sex workers as a result of their economic circumstances, in turn making their health extremely vulnerable.

Social Aspect of Poverty

Poverty has been examined mainly in economic terms, such as per capita income or calorie criterion. The social aspect of poverty, particularly the culture and value aspects, which poverty creates, breeds and transmits and which have larger implications for the overall quality of life have not been seriously examined (Thakur, 1998). Cities and towns generally show the following characteristics (OSD):

1. Very fast rate of population growth due to rural-urban migration for lack of adequate job opportunities in rural areas and small towns;
2. Rapid increase in the scale of urban poverty and deprivation;
3. Increasingly deficient infrastructure and services e.g. housing facility, water supply, sanitation, education, health etc.;
4. Growing shortage of productive jobs;
5. Chronic shortage of financial, managerial and technical resources and
6. Growing gap between the rich and the poor, between the urban elite and poverty stricken rural and urban poor.

There is general consensus that greater part of India's poverty is rural but urban and rural poverty are intimately connected. The problem of rural poverty is flowing into the urban areas. The larger cities are growing in the number of poor people. The urban growth is a result of population shift from poverty stricken hinterland to the cities. Importantly, the vast majority of urban workers come from villages and continue to have their roots there. The poorest among them come from the most helpless strata of rural population.

Thus, the vast majority of the urban poor are migrants, rural poor, landless labourers and petty farmers. Acute impoverishment of these farmers, near hunger situation of rural landless labourers led to their distress and migration to cities. Interestingly, cities provide a market for their cheap labour and they cling to the city, developing a culture of survival. The culture of poverty has the following characteristics:

1. Lack of effective participation and integration of the poor with the major situations of larger society;
2. Low wages, chronic unemployment and under unemployment leading to low income, absence of savings, absence of food reserves and a chronic shortage of cash;
3. Low level of literacy and education, no membership of labour union or any political party, no participation in the national welfare programme;
4. Community spirit in the slums and the slum neighbourhood;
5. The absence of childhood as a specially protected stage in the life cycle, early initiation into sex, a relatively high incidence of abandonment of wives and children;
6. Strong feeling of marginality, helplessness, dependence and inferiority;
7. High incidence of material deprivation, little ability to plan for the future, sense of resignation and fatalism.

Living in a state of perpetual poverty and deprivation, the poor generally develop and acquire habits, which may be characterised as their typical slum habits and which get transmitted to the children as well. These habits generally are:

(i) Idle gossiping;
(ii) Backbiting, leg pulling and slandering;
(iii) Gossiping about the affair of the neighbour;
(iv) Quarrel over small matters;
(v) Bearing tales and spreading rumours;
(vi) Use of abusive language in minor incidents and quarrels among children or women;
(vii) Little regard for public property not much hesitation in breaking street-light, removing lid cover of pit holes etc.;
(viii) Mutual jealousy, suspicion;
(ix) Smoking;
(x) Tobacco, drug abuse, spitting in public places;
(xi) Gambling;
(xii) Playing cards; and

(xiii) Little respect for other's viewpoints, opinion, comforts and time.

Poverty Estimates

Poverty alleviation has been on the national policy agenda for more than 50 years. As early as 1938, the Indian National Congress constituted a National Planning Committee which had declared that social objective should be to ensure an adequate standard of living for the masses. The importance of reduction in poverty and provision of other basic needs has been emphasised in all the five year plans since Independence particularly since the 5th Five Year Plan. The estimates on poverty based on NSS data show that poverty in India in 1997 was around 37 per cent (rural poverty ratio was 38 per cent and urban poverty ratio was 34 per cent).

The concept of poverty is multi-dimensional viz. income poverty and non-income poverty. It covers not only levels of income and consumption but also health and education, vulnerability and risks and marginalisation and exclusion of the poor from the mainstream of society. According to some researchers, reforms would benefit the poor in the medium and long run, although they may have adverse effect in the short-run. Some others argue that reform package has internal contradictions and it might have adverse effect on the poor in both short and long run. The pro-reformers argue that the reforms would increase efficiency and higher growth and in turn reduce poverty. It is also argued that one has to look at counter factional situation while analysing the impact of reforms.

The trends during 24 years of pre-reform period show that the (a) rural poverty varied between 44 per cent and 64 per cent and (b) urban poverty varied between 36 per cent and 53 per cent. Both rural and urban poverty showed a decline in the late 1970's and in the 1980's. The estimates for the period 1973-74 to 1998 are given in Table 1.

The table 1 shows that rural poverty declined in the 1980's but it increased to above 40 per cent in 1992 and 1994-95. On the other hand, urban poverty declined significantly in the 1990's. Gupta's estimates also show similar trends on rural poverty. However, in 1998 the rural poverty increased to around 45 per cent.

Table 1

Trends In Poverty In India (1973-74 to 1998)

Year	*Datta's Estimates*		*S.P. Gupta's Estimates*		
	Rural	*Urban*	*Rural*	*Urban*	*Total*
1	2	3	4	5	6
1973-74	55.72	47.96	—	—	—
1977-78	50.60	40.50	—	—	—
1983	45.31	35.65	45.65	40.79	44.48
1986-87	38.81	34.29	—	—	—
1987-88	39.23	36.20	39.09	38.20	38.86
1988-89	39.06	36.60	—	—	—
1989-90	34.06	33.40	33.70	36.00	34.28
1990-91	36.43	32.76	35.04	35.29	35.11
1991	37.42	32.33	-	-	-
1992	43.47	33.73	41.70	37.80	40.70
1993-94	36.66	30.51	37.27	32.36	35.07
1994-95	41.02	30.51	37.27	32.36	35.07
1995-96	37.15	28.04	38.29	30.05	36.08
1997	35.78	29.99	38.46	33.97	37.23
1998 (Six months)	—	—	45.25	34.58	43.01

Source: Estimates based on NSS data on Consumer Expenditure Quoted from Economic & Political Weekly, March, 2000.

Urban poverty estimates (on 30 day's recall by Planning Commission), shown in Table 2 present the figures of 26.1 per cent of population below the poverty line; 27.09 per cent in rural areas and 23.62 per cent in urban areas.

Table 2

Urban Poverty In India By States During 1999-2000 (30 Day Recall Period)

State	*Rural*		*Urban*		*Combined*	
	No. of Persons Lakh	*% of Persons*	*No. of Persons Lakh*	*% of Persons*	*No. of Persons Lakh*	*% of Persons*
	1	2	3	4	5	6
Andhra Pradesh	58.13	11.05	60.88	26.63	119.01	15.77
Arunachal Pradesh	3.80	40.04	0.18	7.47	3.98	33.47
Assam	92.11	40.04	2.38	7.47	94.55	36.09
Bihar	376.51	44.30	49.13	32.91	425.64	42.60
Goa	0.11	1.35	0.59	7.52	0.70	4.40
Gujarat	39.80	13.17	28.09	15.59	67.89	14.07
Haryana	11.94	8.27	5.39	9.99	17.34	8.74
Himachal Pradesh	4.84	7.94	0.29	4.63	5.12	7.63
Jammu & Kashmir	2.97	3.97	0.49	1.98	3.46	3.48
Karnataka	59.91	17.38	44.49	25.25	104.40	20.04
Kerala	20.97	9.38	20.07	20.27	41.04	12.72
Madhya Pradesh	217.32	37.06	81.22	38.44	298.54	37.43
Maharashtra	125.12	23.72	102.87	26.81	227.99	25.02
Manipur	6.53	40.04	0.66	7.47	7.19	28.54
Meghalaya	7.89	40.04	0.34	7.47	8.23	33.87
Mizoram	1.40	40.04	0.45	7.47	5.49	32.67
Nagaland	5.21	40.04	0.28	7.47	5.49	32.67
Orissa	143.69	48.01	25.40	42.83	169.09	47.15
Punjab	10.20	6.35	4.29	5.75	14.49	6.16
Rajasthan	55.06	13.74	26.78	19.85	81.83	15.28
Sikkim	2.0	40.04	0.04	7.47	2.05	36.55
Tamil Nadu	80.51	20.55	49.97	22.11	130.48	21.12
Uttar Pradesh	412.01	31.22	117.88	30.89	529.89	31.15
West Bengal	180.11	31.85	33.38	14.86	213.49	27.02
Delhi	0.07	0.40	11.42	9.42	11.49	8.23
India	2932.43	27.09	670.07	23.62	2602.50	26.10

Source: Cited from Kuruksheta, April, 2001.

Again, 670.07 lakh persons in urban areas were reported living below poverty line. Importantly, Uttar Pradesh, Maharashtra, Madhya Pradesh, Andhra Pradesh and Bihar account for larger share in urban poor. The percentage of urban poor was recorded highest in Orissa (42.83 per cent), Madhya Pradesh (38.44 per cent), Uttar Pradesh (30.89 per cent), Bihar (32.91 per cent) and Maharashtra (26.81 per cent). Indian poverty is predominant in the rural areas where more than three quarters of all poor people reside, though there is wide variation in poverty across different states. Moreover, progress in reducing poverty is also very uneven across different states of the country (Table 3).

Table 3

Percentage of Population below Poverty Line by States

State	*MISH*			*Planning Commission*		
	1987-88	*1997-98*	*Change*	*1987-88*	*1997-98*	*Change*
	1	2	3	4	5	6
Andhra Pradesh	40.11	15.01	25.1	40.11	38.33	1.78
Assam	9.94	1.71	8.23	9.94	7.73	2.21
Bihar	48.73	24.88	23.85	48.73	34.50	14.2
Gujarat	37.28	7.65	29.63	37.28	27.89	9.39
Haryana	17.98	4.58	13.4	17.64	16.38	1.26
Himachal Pradesh	8.29	1.69	6.6	8.29	9.18	-0.89
Karnataka	48.42	15.45	32.97	48.42	40.14	8.28
Maharashtra	39.78	12.59	27.19	39.78	35.15	4.63
Madhya Pradesh	47.09	15.49	31.60	47.09	48.38	-1.29
Orissa	41.63	20.20	21.43	41.63	41.64	-0.01
Punjab	14.67	2.12	12.55	14.67	11.35	3.32
Rajasthan	41.92	17.41	24.51	41.92	30.49	11.43
Tamil Nadu	38.04	8.00	30.04	38.04	39.77	-1.73
Uttar Pradesh	42.90	15.65	58.55	42.90	35.39	7.51
West Bengal	35.08	8.25	26.83	35.08	22.41	12.67

Note: MIH—Market Information Survey of Households by NCAER, Delhi.
Source: Cited from Economic & Political Weekly, March, 24, 2001.

It showed higher reduction (MISH) in Uttar Pradesh, Kerala, Madhya Pradesh, Tamil Nadu, Karnataka and Gujarat. The poverty reduction as per estimates of Planning Commission during 1987-88 to 1993-94 was recorded highest in Kerala, West Bengal, Rajasthan, Bihar, Gujarat and Uttar Pradesh.

Poverty estimates for urban India are shown in Table 4. The head count ratio in 1993-94 was reported to be 30.03 with poverty gap of 7.62 and square poverty gap of 2.76.

Table 4

Poverty Estimates For Urban India

Period	*Head Count Radio*	*Poverty Gap*	*Square Poverty Gap*	*Gini Coefficient*	
				Urban	*All India*
	1	2	3	4	5
1956-57	51.45	18.16	8.51	0.402	0.3417
1957-58	47.75	15.95	7.00	0.359	0.3536
1958-59	44.76	13.75	5.87	0.348	0.3446
1959-60	49.17	15.83	6.75	0.357	0.3664
1960-61	44.65	13.84	5.83	0.350	0.3259
1961-62	43.55	13.79	6.05	0.357	0.3308
1963-64	44.83	13.29	5.17	0.360	0.3073
1964-65	48.78	15.24	6.38	0.349	0.3105
1965-66	52.90	16.82	6.98	0.339	0.3114
1966-67	52.24	16.81	7.19	0.337	0.3106
1967-68	52.91	16.93	7.22	0.332	0.3055
1968-69	49.29	15.54	6.54	0.329	0.3166
1970-71	44.98	13.35	5.35	0.346	0.3038
1972-73	45.67	13.46	5.26	0.345	0.3185
1973-74	47.96	13.60	5.22	0.317	0.2917
1977-78	40.50	11.69	4.53	0.337	0.3214
1983	35.65	9.52	3.56	0.334	0.3149
1986-87	34.29	9.10	3.4	0.356	0.3222

Table 4 contd...

	1	2	3	4	5
1987-88	35.65	9.31	3.25	0.356	0.3182
1988-89	36.40	9.54	3.29	0.356	0.3182
1989-90	33.40	8.51	3.29	0.356	0.3115
1990-91	32.76	8.51	2.12	0.340	0.2969
1991	33.23	8.24	2.9	0.351	0.3253
1992	33.73	8.82	3.19	0.356	0.3202
1993-94	30.03	7.62	2.76	0.345	—

Source: Cited from Indian Development Report, 1999-2000 IGIDR, Bombay.

Some trends that emerge from assessment of all India poverty situations in pre and post-reform period are (IDR, 2000):

(i) Rural and urban poverty increased during the first two years of the reform period;

(ii) The phenomenon of faster decline of rural poverty in the 1980's has halted in the post 1991 period. The rate of decline in poverty for the period of 1987-88 to 1993-94 has been much slower as compared to that of the 1980's;

(iii) There has been a decline in the absolute number of poor in the 1980's. In contrast, the post 1991 period showed an increase in the absolute number of poor.

(iv) Urban poverty declined much faster than rural poverty in the post-reform period.

Incidence of Poverty

Poverty is a complex, deep-seated pervasive reality. Virtually half of the world lives on less than US $2 a day. More than 1.2 billion people struggle on $1 a day or less. A further 1.6 billion people on $1 to 2 a day and are thus also poor, insecure and at risk of falling to the level of bare subsistence (ILO, 2003). About half of the people living in poverty are of working age (between 15 and 64 years). Although, most family members have to contribute in one way or another to the household's welfare, the earning power of adults is a critical determinant of the well being of the family.

For individuals, poverty is a nightmare. It is vicious circle of poor health, reduced working capacity, low productivity and shortened life expectancy. For families, poverty is a trap. It leads to inadequate schooling, low skills, insecure income, early parenthood, ill health and an early death. For nations, poverty is a curse. It hinders growth, fuels instability and keeps poor countries from advancing on the path to sustainable development (ILO, 2003). There is another face of poverty. People living in conditions of material deprivation draw on enormous reserves of courage, ingenuity, persistence and mutual support to keep on the thread mill of survival. After all, for most people living in poverty, there is no safety net and little state support.

However, poor do not cause poverty. Poverty is the result of structural failures and ineffective economic and social systems. Thus, the poverty may be alleviated only through institutional support, political will and effective administrative machinery for social safety net and creation of employment opportunities.

India has made significant progress in reducing poverty at the national level during the period 1956-2000. Poverty has declined in all states, with substantial differences across states. The absolute number of rural poor, which accounted for about three-fourth of the country's poor rose from 182 million in 1956-67 to 261 million in 1973-74, accounting for nearly half of the additions to the rural population during the period. In the second phase, from the mid 1970s to the close of the year 2000, the country achieved substantial reduction in the incidence of poverty (Table 5).

The proportion of the country's population living in poverty declined from half to one quarter. Due to methodological changes, in the collection of NSS data in the 55th Round comparison of the pre and post-reform period growth rate is problematic. Undoubtedly, India has made substantial progress in the reduction of poverty. Yet, as many as 260 million persons are living below the poverty line. According to UNDP's Human Development Report, 2003, India has the target number of poor among the countries of the world and is home to one fourth of the world's poor. A large number of hardcore poor are located in remote and inaccessible areas.

Table 5
Poverty Estimates For Urban India

Year	*Poverty (Percent)*		*Number of Poor (Million)*		
	Rural	*Urban*	*Rural*	*Urban*	*Total*
1956-57	54.1	—	182	—	—
1957-58	50.2	—	172	—	—
1958-59	46.5	—	162	—	—
1959-60	44.4	—	158	—	—
1960-61	38.9	40.4	141	32	173
1961-62	39.4	39.4	145	32	177
1963-64	44.5	42.5	171	37	208
1964-65	46.8	45.7	184	42	226
1965-66	47.4	46.4	190	44	234
1966-67	56.6	48.4	231	47	278
1967-68	56.5	48.3	236	49	285
1968-69	51.0	45.5	217	47	264
1969-70	49.2	44.4	214	48	262
1970-71	47.5	41.5	210	46	256
1972-73	49.4	44.6	227	53	280
1973-74	56.4	49.6	261	60	321
1977-78	53.1	45.2	264	65	329
1982-83	45.6	40.8	252	71	323
1987-88	39.1	38.2	232	75	307
1993-94	37.3	32.4	244	76	320
1999-2000	27.1	23.6	193	67	260

Source: Tendulkar, S.D. Economic Inequality and Poverty in India IN Uma Kapila (Ed.) Indian Economy Since Independence, Academic Foundation, New Delhi, 2003.

The problem of poverty alleviation is going to be far more difficult than in the past. Since, those who were near the poverty line might have crossed it. The regional differences in poverty reduction are substantial. The decline between 1973-74 and 1999-2000 in state's incidence of poverty in rural areas ranged between

12-50 percentage point during 1973-2000 and 20-40 percentage points in urban areas. The inter-state variations in the rural poverty reduction during 1957-90 has been attributed to the variations in their agricultural productivity improvement. In addition, variations in initial endowments of physical infrastructure and human resources contributed to the inter-state variations in the performance of the states such as Andhra Pradesh, Kerala, and West Bengal, which had a higher rural poverty ratio in the first phase, had lower rural poverty ratios in the second phase (Table 6).

Table 6

Incidence of Urban Poverty Across States

State	*Urban*			*Rural*		
	1973-74	*1993-94*	*1999-2000*	*1973-74*	*1993-94*	*1999-2000*
Andhra Pradesh	50.61	38.33	26.63	48.41	15.92	11.05
Assam	36.92	7.73	7.47	52.67	45.01	40.04
Bihar	52.96	34.50	32.91	62.99	58.21	44.30
Gujarat	52.57	27.89	15.59	46.35	22.18	13.17
Haryana	40.18	16.38	9.99	34.23	28.02	8.27
Karnataka	52.53	40.14	25.25	55.14	29.88	17.38
Kerala	62.74	24.55	20.27	59.19	25.76	9.38
Madhya Pradesh	57.65	48.38	38.44	62.66	40.64	37.06
Maharashtra	43.87	35.15	26.81	57.71	37.93	23.72
Orissa	55.62	41.64	42.83	67.28	49.72	48.01
Punjab	27.96	11.35	5.75	28.21	11.95	6.35
Rajasthan	52.13	30.49	19.85	44.76	26.46	13.74
Tamil Nadu	49.40	39.77	22.11	57.43	32.48	20.55
Uttar Pradesh	60.09	35.39	30.89	56.53	42.28	31.22
West Bengal	34.67	22.41	14.86	73.16	40.80	31.85
India	49.01	32.3 6	23.62	56.44	37.27	27.09

Source: Economic Survey, 2001-02.

The composition of the poor has been changing. The rural poverty is getting concentrated in the agricultural labour and artisan households while urban poverty is concentrated the casual labour households. The share of agricultural labour households, which accounted for 41 per cent of rural poor in 1993-94 increased to 47 per cent in 1999-2000. In contrast, the share of self employed in agriculture in rural poor dropped from 33 to 28 per cent. Casual labour households accounted for 32 per cent of the urban population living in poverty in 1999-2000, increasing from 25 per cent in 1993-94. The increase in its share was due to both the increased dependence of urban households on urban casual labour market as well as higher incidence of poverty among casual labour households. It needs to be recognised that increased dependence of rural and urban households on casual labour market exposes the poor to market risks and tends to increase transient poverty, whereby households move in and out of poverty due to fluctuations in the labour market.

The urban poor have been increasingly concentrated in Uttar Pradesh, Maharashtra, West Bengal, Madhya Pradesh and Andhra Pradesh. Their share in all India urban poverty rose from 56 per cent in 1993-94 to 60 per cent in 1999-2000. Scheduled Castes, Scheduled Tribes and backward castes accounted for 81 per cent of the rural poor in 1999-2000, considerably more than their share in the rural population. The poor among the Scheduled Castes in rural areas were concentrated in Uttar Pradesh, Madhya Pradesh, Bihar and West Bengal. These states accounted for 58 per cent of the Scheduled Castes population living in poverty. In urban areas, Madhya Pradesh and Uttar Pradesh accounted for 41 per cent of the Scheduled Castes population living in poverty. The incidence of poverty among Scheduled Castes was higher in Bihar, Madhya Pradesh, and Uttar Pradesh in both rural and urban areas. The proportion of Scheduled Tribes among the rural population living in poverty has been increasing rapidly from 14.8 per cent in 1993-94 to 17.5 per cent in 1999-2000.

The poverty levels of Scheduled Tribes in rural areas were high in Orissa, Bihar, Madhya Pradesh and West Bengal while in urban areas poverty ratio among Scheduled Tribes was reported high in Orissa, Karnataka, Andhra Pradesh and Bihar. In the terms of human deprivation or poverty, (education, health, etc.) the Scheduled Tribes are at the bottom. The increasing concentration of poverty tribals who suffer from multiple deprivations is a matter of concern. The incidence of poverty among females tended to be marginally higher in both rural and urban areas. The proportion of females living in poor households in rural areas was 37 per cent and 27 per cent in 1993-94 and 1999-2000, respectively with the corresponding percentage for urban areas being 34 and 25 per cent.

In contrast, the percentage of males living in poverty in rural areas was 36 per cent and 26 per cent in 1993-94 and 1999-2000 respectively, while those in urban areas was 32 and 23 per cent, respectively. Females accounted for slightly less than half of the poor, about 49 per cent in both rural and urban areas in both the years. More importantly, child poverty is widespread in India both in rural and urban areas. The percentage of children aged below 15 years living in households below the poverty line in rural areas was 44 per cent and 33 per cent in 1993-94 and 1999-2000, respectively while the corresponding percentages for urban areas stood at 41 and 33 per cent. Among poor people, the share of children in rural areas increased from 44 per cent in 1993-94 to 46 per cent in 1999-2000 and in urban areas from 41 per cent to 42 per cent during corresponding period. The high level of child poverty would result in a high incidence of child malnutrition.

The states with high incidence of human poverty, such as Bihar, Orissa, Madhya Pradesh, Uttar Pradsh and Rajasthan are found at the bottom on the Human Development Index ranking. Kerala was the best performer in both rural and urban areas and Bihar the worst performer in rural areas and Uttar Pradesh in the urban areas. Bihar, Orissa, Madhya Pradesh, and Uttar Pradesh consistently showed poor performance on three indices and Kerala and Punjab showed consistently better performance. Rajasthan performed better on poverty rank than HDI and HPI ranks. Tamil Nadu and Maharashtra performed better on HDI rank than poverty and HPI ranks. The factors contributing to human poverty are not a unique set for the entire country, and vary from state to state and even across regions. The poverty reduction measures are generally focus on livelihood development, employment generation, skill enhancement, rights advocacy, strengthening cooperatives and people's associations and accessibility of micro credit, etc.

Analysis shows that poverty reduction has been uneven between the states. There is no correlation with per capita income or other development indicators like per capita consumption, levels of industrial and infrastructural development etc. in urban areas during the 1990's (Planning Commission, 2001). Again, rapid economic growth has not led to a corresponding decline in poverty. Urban poverty thus, emerges as a more complex phenomenon than rural poverty.

The urban poor faces more problems related with housing amenities, urban infrastructure, size of town or city, and vulnerabilities—housing, economic, social and personal. The urban poor are characterised by deprivation and misery while they are classified as core poor, intermedial poor, and transitional poor. Another study classified them as declining poor, coping poor and improving poor, with different degrees of poverty for three basic needs of survival, security and quality of life.

Government Initiatives

The government policies on urban poverty have followed three paths:

(i) Those that seek to enhance productive employment and income for the poor;

(ii) Those that are directed towards improving the general health and welfare services;

(iii) Those that focus on infrastructure and built environment of poor neighbourhood.

Though several programmes of poverty alleviation have been initiated by government but effective dent on poverty could not be ensured. The schemes had certain limitations, which ultimately resulted in poor results or failure. Environment Improvement of Urban Slums (EIUS) launched in 1972 provided physical infrastructure and could not cover social services like health, education, community development, etc. The scheme could not help in preventing growth of new slums.

Similarly, UBSP was designed to foster Neighbourhood Development Committees in slums for ensuring the effective participation of slum dwellers in developmental activities and for coordinating the convergent provisions of social services, environmental improvement and income generation activities of the specialist departments. The low level of resource allocation for the scheme led to sub critical releases to the state governments, which consequently gave low priority to the scheme. Importantly, NRY scheme was launched in 1989 to provide employment to the unemployed through setting up of micro-enterprises and wage employment through shelter upgradation works and creation of useful pubic assets in low income neighbourhoods. The scheme could not yield good results due to shortfall in employment generation on account of some states not taking up labour intensive schemes. Importantly, progress under Housing and Shelter Upgradation Scheme was recorded slow growth due to non-completion of the necessary documentation and procedural formalities.

Interestingly, PMIUPEP was launched in 1994 and sought to improve the quality of life of the urban poor by creating a facilitating implementation. The scheme provided for the creation of a National Urban Poverty Eradication Fund (NUPEF) with contribution from private sector. The National Slum Development Programme (NSDP) was initiated in 1996 as a centrally sponsored scheme. The scheme highlighted on the creation of community structures as the basis for slum development and gives the maximum possible leeway to the states, ULB's and the community development societies at the slum level to plan and carry out development works as per the local assessed needs. The SJSRY was initiated in 1997 and was designed to replace the UBSP.

Review of Urban Poverty during Plan Period

The review of urban policy framework in historical perspective indicates that until the Sixth Plan (1980-85), the urban policies mainly addressed problems like housing, slum clearance, slum improvement and upgradation, preparation of Master Plans, development of small and medium towns, strengthening of municipal civic administration, etc. The Seventh Plan made a new beginning by recognising the problems of urban poor, which were linked with creation of employment opportunities.

The Integrated Development of Small and Medium Towns (IDSMT) scheme was initiated by government in 1979-80 with a view to reducing the migration of people from rural areas to large cities, generating employment by creating resource generating ventures in the small and medium towns and providing sufficient infrastructure facilities in these towns. Overall, 1058 towns were assisted since inception of the scheme and Rs. 444.94 crores of Central assistance was released. The Urban Basic Services Scheme (UBSS) was initiated on a pilot basis in 1986, with the involvement of UNICEF and the state governments. The programme aimed at child survival and development, provision of learning opportunities for women and children, and community organisation for slum population. The services supposed to be delivered, included environmental sanitation, primary health care, pre-school learning, vocational training and convergence of other social services at slum level. The scheme also included assistance to mentally retarded and handicapped children, rehabilitation of alcoholics and drug addicts, and special programmes for street children. Nehru Rojgar Yojana was launched in 1989, which targeted poor urban households. Within the target group, Scheduled Castes and Scheduled Tribes were to be given special coverage earmarking of funds.

The scheme consists of the following four sub-schemes: (i) the Scheme of Urban Micro Enterprises (SUME) for encouraging self employment ventures, (ii) Scheme of Urban Wage Employment (SUWE) for providing employment to urban poor through creation of socially and economically useful assets in low income neighbourhoods in towns with a population below one lakh, (iii) Scheme of Housing and Shelter Upgradation (SHASHU) for providing employment to persons involved in housing and building activities, (iv) Scheme for Educated Unemployed Employment

Generation in Urban Localities (SEEGUL) for providing self employment opportunities for educated unemployed. Prime Minister's Integrated Urban Poverty Eradication emphasised on poverty alleviation through creation of self-employment opportunities for youth. Swarn Jayanti Swhahari Rojgar Yojana was launched in 1997 and Nehru Rojgar Yojana, PMIUPEP and UBSP were phased out. The pogramme has two sub-schemes namely: (a) urban self-employment programme and (b) urban wage employment programme. The self-employment and wage employment components of NRY and PMIUEP were reorganised under this single programme. The shelter upgradation components of both NRY and PMIUPEP were merged with National Slum Development Programme. The SJSRY sought to provide gainful employment to the urban unemployed or under-employed poor by encouraging setting up of self-employment ventures or provision of wage employment. This progarmme has laid emphasis on creation of suitable community structures on UBSP pattern and delivery of inputs under the programme. The community organisations like Neighbourhood Groups (NHG's), Neighbourhood Committees (NHC's) and Community Development Societies (CDS's) were to be set up in areas based on the USSP pattern. Urban self-employment programme has laid emphasis on setting up gainful self-employment ventures for urban poor, extending assistance to groups of urban poor women for setting up gainful employment ventures, and; training of beneficiaries for upgradation and acquisition of vocational and entrepreneurial skills.

Limitations of UPA Programmes

Viewed from the conceptual framework, one finds that the thrust of the programmes in India has been to reach the urban poor through strategies that are related to employment, urban services and shelter. The impact of these programmes and strategies on the incidence of urban poverty has not been encouraging. The limitations of programmes are:

(i) Inadequate financial resources to ULB's for poverty alleviation in proportion to the magnitude of the problem;

(ii) Lack of guarantee to get institutional finance;

(iii) Lack effective coordination among implementing agencies;

(iv) Lack of a coherent policy framework;

(v) Failure to build partnership with ill-equipped municipal bodies;

(vi) Political interference;

(vii) Poor loan recovery.

Strategies For Poverty Reduction

Global and national structures for poverty reduction should provide a framework for local strategies to escape cycles of low incomes from work and social exclusion International Labour Organisation (2003) has developed policy instruments in the following areas:

(i) Training and skill development;
(ii) Investing in jobs and the community;
(iii) Micro and small enterprises;
(iv) Micro-finance;
(v) Cooperatives;
(vi) Social security;
(vii) Hazards at work;
(viii) Eliminating child labour;
(ix) Overcoming discrimination.

Skills are essential to improve productivity, incomes, and access to employment opportunities. Thus, poverty reduction strategy should focus on vocational education and training since vast majority people living in poverty cannot afford and have access to training opportunities, which are commercially managed. International Labour Organisation has invested in the field of employment intensive infrastructure programmes. It has now widely recognised that these programmes are effective in bringing much needed income to poor families and their communities.

Thus, financial investment in jobs and employment may create addition opportunities to poor youth. The labour intensive projects should respect standards, promote gender equality and encourage enterprise development through contracting systems. The entrepreneurship development may promote income generating enterprises and livelihood development. This will also promote self-employment among educated unemployed youth. Interestingly, it is impossible to build an enterprise without access to credit. Micro-finance activities should be promoted, strengthened and encouraged along with entrepreneurship for enabling poor to borrow for productive purposes.

Moreover, participation and inclusion are central to new approach to poverty reduction. Cooperatives and people's associations including Self Help Groups are an ideal instruments in such a strategy. Cooperatives have proved to be a key organised form in building new models to combat social exclusion and poverty. Similarly, SHG's are proving crucial instrument for availability of micro-finance and social empowerment of poor. Significantly, discrimination is a basis for social exclusion and poverty. Promoting gender equality and eliminating all forms of discrimination at work are essential to defeating poverty. Child labour is both a cause and a system of poverty. The importance of universal access to basic health care and primary and secondary education is well recognised by many countries. For a poor family, securing a basic income, basic health care and school places for the children is a foundation for participating productivity in society and the economy (ILO, 2003). The poor workers need protection from occupational health hazards, accidents, diseases etc. Thus, by focusing directly on creating the conditions for people living in poverty to work for a better future, the decent work approach mobilises the broad spectrum of support across society is needed to maintain progress and harmony and should reach to all poor communities. Eradicating poverty calls for the coordination of policies that focus on different dimensions of the life of people living in poverty.

Policy Recommendations

In the light of the above analysis, the following recommendations are made to make the development programmes for urban poor more effective (Singh, 2001):

1. An attempt is needed to establish an urban information system pertaining to poverty.
2. The programme design requires effective participation by the local NGO's in their formulation, implementation and appraisal.
3. Effective and enhanced participation of urban poor in poverty alleviation programmes is the need of hour.
4. Urban Infrastructure Development Finance Corporation should be established to finance services in the areas where urban poor are concentrated.

5. There is a need to integrate different sectors of infrastructure within an overall plan and bring it under unified public utilities and services distribution agency.
6. Skill upgradation among the urban poor is needed to exploit employment potentials. This can be ensured through local NGO's, academic institutions and private sector partnership.
7. Government intervention is necessary for upgradation of housing conditions and empowerment of poor. The financial assistance should be made according to the paying capacity of the urban poor.
8. Training for urban youths for self-employment is needed to ensure full benefits of employment generation programmes. This may be ensured through strengthening of local NGO's, private institutions and panchayats.
9. Financial assistance provided under UPA Programmes needs to be raised. The banks tend to extend loans only for purchase of fixed assets and do not normally meet the working capital requirements of the beneficiaries.
10. The role of community is crucial for the success of urban poverty alleviation progammes and its sustainability. The local NGO's can perform the function of community mobilisation, organisation and participation in development programmes and should be involved in the task of community organisation, policy formulation, programme implementation, monitoring and appraisal.
11. There is need to take overall requirements into consideration while making allocations so that the problem of urban poverty can be faced in right earnest.
12. The UPA package needs inter-agency linkages at various levels. The grassroot NGO's, academic organisations, resource persons, institutions and government departments—all need effective coordination.
13. The community based approach for planning be used for all UPA schemes. The role of district planning should be ensured in such a manner that UPA programmes are well-designed and effectively implemented.

14. The training for municipal managers, administrators and personnel is required on sustainable basis. Academic institutions, local NGO's, private organisations etc. should be enhanced to cater to the needs of training of municipal personnel.
15. There is an urgent need to develop the urban data base at all levels to conduct action research projects to facilitate grassroot planning and policy formulation.

NOTES AND REFERENCES

Bhaduri, Amit (1996), Employment, Labour Market Flexibility and Economic Liberalisation in India, *Indian Journal of Labour Economics,* Vol. 39 (1).

Bhagawati, J.and Srinivasan, T.N. (1993), India's Economic Reforms, Ministry of Finance, Govt. of India, New Delhi.

Dandekar, N.M. and Rath, N. (1971), *Poverty in India, Indian School of Political Economy,* Bombay.

Datta, G. and M. Rovallion (1997), Micro-Economic Crises and Poverty Monitoring: A Case Study for India, *Review of Development Economics,* Vol. 1 (2), 1997.

Desai, P.B. (1968), Economy of Indian Cities', *Indian Journal of Public Administration*, Vol., XIV (3), July-Sept.

Dev, S.M. (2000), Economic Reforms, Poverty, Income Distribution And Employment, *Economic & Political Weekly,* March.

Dreze, J. (1990), Widows in Rural India, London Schools of Economics, London, STICERD DEP No. 26.

Ghosh, Jayati (1995), Employment and Labour Under Structured Adjustment: India Since 1991, *Indian Journal of Labour Economics*, Vol. 38 (4), 1995.

Gurumukhi, K.T. (2000), Slum Related Policies and Programmes, *Shelter,* Vol. 3 (2), April.

ILO (2003), *Working Out of Poverty, International Labour Organisation,* Geneva.

India Development Report, 1999-2000, IGIDR, Oxford University Press.

Jha, S.S. (1986), *Structure of Urban Poverty*, Popular Prakashan, Bombay.

Joshi, Vijai, and Little (1946), *India's Economic Reforms: 1991:2001,* Oxford University Press, New Delhi.

Kopardekar, H.D. (1986), *Social Aspects of Urban Development,* Popular Prakashan, Bombay.

Nayar, Deepak (1993), *Economic Reforms in India A Critical Assessmen*t, ILO-ARTEP, New Delhi.

ODSG, Overseas Development Paper No. 19, Urban Poverty, Overseas Development Study Group, London.

Radha Krishnan and Rao H. K. (2006), Poverty, Unemployment and Public Intervention, IN India Social Development Report, OUP, Delhi, 2006.

Radha Krishnan and S. Roy (2004), Poverty in India: Dimensions and Character in India Development Report, OUP, Delhi, 2004-05.

Sen, A.K. (2000), Role of Urban Local Bodies in Poverty Alleviation Programmes, Shelter, Vol. 3 (2), April.

Singh Kulwant & Maitra, S. (2000), Urban Poverty in India: Approaches and Initiatives, Shelter Vol. 3 (2), April.

Takru, Rajiv (1997), Issues of Slum Development in India, Paper Presented At National Seminar on Future Cities - Urban Vision 2021, Delhi, Oct.

Tendulkar, S.D. (1998), *Indian Economic Policy Reforms and Poverty: An Assessment* in I.J. Ahluwalia and IMD Little (ed.) 'India's Economic Reforms and Development: Essays for Mohan Singh', Oxford University Press, New Delhi.

Thakur, R.N. and Dhadave, M.S. (1989), *Slum & Social System,* Archives Publishers, New Delhi.

Thakur, R.N. (1988), *Social Aspect by Urban Povertyu*, Nagarlok, Vol. XX (4), Oct.-Dec.

Unni, J. (1998), *Gender Dimensions of Poverty,* SEWA, Gujarat Institute of Development Research, Ahmedabad.

Venkateshwarlu, U. (1998), *Urbanisation in India: Problems and Prospects,* New Age International Publishers, Delhi.

World Bank (2002), *Poverty in India: Challenge of Uttar Pradesh*, World Bank, Delhi.

8

GENDER PERSPECTIVE OF URBANISATION AND POVERTY

Urbanisation and urban growth have accelerated in many developing countries in the past few years. While natural population growth has been the major contributor to urbanisation, rural-urban migration continues to be an important factor. The processes of urbanisation and the nature and scale of rural-urban migration have to some extent been shaped by gender roles and relations. While male migration has been the most predominant form of migration, in parts of Latin America female migration is common and has been influenced by decisions in rural households over who should migrate and for what reason. In other parts of the world, particularly South East Asia, the demand for female labour has meant that more women are migrating in search of employment.

Feminist researchers have pointed out that much of the literature on women, gender and urban poverty issues has fallen outside the mainstream. Urban planning has focused, to a large extent, on physical and spatial aspects of urban development. However, there is increasing recognition of the discrimination women face in relation to access to employment, housing, basic services etc., and the need more effort by some governments and international agencies to reduce this.

A gender equality perspective of urban poverty is important because men and women experience and respond to poverty in different ways. Access to income and assets, housing, transport and basic services is influenced by gender-based constraints and opportunities. Gender-blind urban services provision may not meet the needs of women if their priorities are not taken into consideration.

URBANISATION, URBAN POVERTY AND DEVELOPMENT

Urbanisation

In the past few decades, urbanisation and urban growth have accelerated in many developing countries. In 1970, 37 per cent of the world's population lived in cities. In 1995 this figure was 45 per cent, and the proportion is expected to pass 50 per cent by 2005. Urban populations are growing quickly—2.5 per cent a year in Latin America and the Caribbean, 3.3 per cent in Northern Africa, 4 per cent for Asia and the Pacific and 5 per cent in Africa. But, international comparisons are complicated by differing national definitions of urban areas. In Eastern Europe, Latin America and the Caribbean, the overall ratio of women to men is higher in urban areas than in rural areas, and the inverse is true for Africa and Asia.

Although, in many third world cities natural population growth is the major contributor to urbanisation, rural-urban migration is still an important factor. Internal migration flows are diverse, complex and constantly changing, including rural to urban, urban to rural, urban to urban, and rural to rural. There is much diversity between nations and regions in terms of the age and level of education of migrants, and in the extent to which migration is considered permanent or temporary. A key determinant of migration is the income differential between rural and urban regions. Migration is also affected by crop prices, landowning structures and changes in agricultural technologies and crop mixes in surrounding areas and distant regions. It is also influenced by other factors related to individual or household structures and survival strategies, and wider political, economic and social forces.

Urban Poverty: Definitions, Concepts and Measurement

There is no consensus on a definition of urban poverty but two broad complementary approaches are prevalent: economic and anthropological interpretations. Conventional economic definitions use income or consumption complemented by a range of other social indicators such as life expectancy, infant mortality, nutrition, the proportion of the household budget spent on food, literacy, school enrolment rates, access to health clinics or drinking water, to classify poor groups against a common index of material welfare. Alternative interpretations developed largely by rural anthropologists and social planners working with rural communities in the third world allow for local variation in the meaning of poverty, and expand the definition to encompass perceptions of non-material deprivation and social differentiation.

Anthropological studies of poverty have shown that people's own conceptions of disadvantage often differ from those of professional experts. Great value is attached to qualitative dimensions such as independence, security, self-respect, identity, close and non-exploitative social relationships, decision-making freedom and legal and political rights.

More generally, there has been a widening of the debates on poverty to include more subjective definitions such as vulnerability, entitlement and social exclusion. These concepts have been useful for analysing what increases the risk of poverty and the underlying reasons why people remain in poverty. Vulnerability is not synonymous with poverty, but refers to defencelessness, insecurity and exposure to risk, shocks and stress. Vulnerability is reduced by assets, such as: human investment in health and education; productive assets including houses and domestic equipment; access to community infrastructure; stores of money, jewellery and gold; and claims on other households, patrons, the government and international community for resources at times of need. Entitlement refers to the complex ways in which individuals or households command resources which vary between people over time in response to shocks and long-term trends. Social exclusion is seen as a state of ill-being and disablement or disempowerment, inability which individuals and groups experience. It is manifest in 'patterns of social relationships in which individuals and groups are denied access to goods, services, activities and resources which are associated with citizenship'.

Characteristics of Urban Poverty

Most studies attempting to describe urban poverty have focused on drawing out the characteristics of urban poverty, often by comparing rural with urban poverty. However, there is still much debate as to whether urban poverty differs from rural poverty and whether policies to address the two should focus on different aspects of poverty. In some views, rural and urban poverty are interrelated and there is a need to consider both urban and rural poverty together for they have many structural causes in common, e.g. socially constructed constraints to opportunities (class, gender) and macroeconomic policies (terms of trade). Many point to the important connections between the two, as household livelihood or survival strategies have both rural and urban components. Baker and Wratten illustrate this point in terms of rural-urban migration, seasonal labour, remittances and family support networks. Baker illustrates how urban and rural households adopt a range of diversification strategies, by having one foot in rural activities and another in urban. Conceptualising urban poverty as a separate category from rural poverty is also problematic because of different yardsticks for defining urban in different countries. The urban-rural divide is more a continuum rather than a rigid dichotomy.

Urban Development Policy

It is now widely recognised that the rapid growth of urban populations has led to a worsening in absolute and relative poverty in urban areas. Urban poverty has, until recently, been low on the agenda of development policy because of dominant perceptions of urban bias and the need to counter this with a focus on rural development policy. However, policy interest in urban issues is increasing as a result of two phenomena:

- projections of a large and increasing proportion of poor people living in urban areas, partly as a result of urbanisation;
- and claims that structural adjustment programmes—which have removed some of the urbanbias, by removing price distortions—have lead to a much faster increase in urban poverty than rural poverty.

There have been two broad traditions in policy approaches to urban poverty. The first set of approaches have focused on the physical infrastructure problems of housing, sanitation, water, land use and transportation. Recently there has been more emphasis on private investment and an increased focus on institutional and management aspects of urban development. The second set of broad approaches have focused on economic and social infrastructure issues such as employment, education and community services. Recently, such approaches have put a lot of emphasis on sustainability issues and community involvement/participation in projects and programming.

More recently, concerns with the urban environment and violence and insecurity in urban areas have come to the fore as factors which undermine well-being and quality of life. There is some evidence of a strong relationship between poor health and poor environmental quality. The externalities of urban production are disproportionately borne by the poor because of the spatial juxtaposition of industrial and residential functions, high living densities, overcrowded housing in hazardous and inadequate supply of clean water, sanitation and solid waste disposal services.

Urban violence is estimated to have grown by between three and five per cent a year over the last two decades, although there are large variations between nations and different cities within nations. Violent crimes are more visible in cities and there is growing understanding that violence should be considered a public health problem for which there are prevention strategies. Urban violence is the result of many factors, and there is considerable debate about the relative importance of different factors. Certain specialists stress the significance of inadequate incomes which are usually combined with very poor and overcrowded housing and living conditions, and often insecure tenure, as fertile ground for development violence. Other explanations emphasise more the contemporary urban environment in which attractive goods are continuously on display and create targets for potential criminals. Oppression in all its forms, including the destruction of original cultural identities, together with racism are also cited as causes.

GENDER, URBAN POVERTY AND DEVELOPMENT

Gender issues have been increasingly discussed in the mainstream literature on urbanisation and urban poverty.

Gender and Urbanisation Processes

The urbanisation process is itself shaped by gender roles and relations. For instance the scale and nature of migration into urban areas in Latin America is much influenced by decisions in rural households about who should migrate and for what reason by constraints placed on women's work outside the home by households, and by the demand for female labour in urban areas.

Some studies have highlighted the extent to which migration patterns are differentiated by gender *(ibid.)*. These studies have shown that female migration is of much greater volume and complexity than was previously believed and that migration has gender-differentiated causes and consequences. Female migration is increasing despite the constraints of women's dependent position within the family and society, as households are in need of income, and more employment opportunities are available to women. In some towns and cities in Latin America and the Caribbean, and parts of South East Asia, rural out-migration is female selective, urban sex ratios usually show more women than men and levels of female household headship are higher in urban than rural areas.

Nevertheless, in most of the developing world, single-male migration is more common. The effects of this on family structure, decision-making and women's autonomy and well-being are varied. Where family relations are strained by male absences and remittances are irregular or non-existent, it may lead to increased female poverty. On the other hand, households where women do receive remittances may be among the better off and gain independence and decision-making power through managing household resources.

Gender, Urbanisation and Household Headship

Urbanisation tends to affect gender roles, relations and inequalities (although with great variety in the form and intensity from place to place) since the factors responsible for female-headed household (FHH) formation arise through urbanisation. This is evident in the transformation of household structures, the shifts in household survival strategies and changing patterns of employment.

There is a tendency to equate the growth in FHHs with the growth in poor or disadvantaged households—but female headship may have positive aspects. FHHs are likely to be less constrained by patriarchal authority at the domestic level and female heads may experience greater self-esteem, more personal freedom, more flexibility to take on paid work, enhanced control over finances and a reduction or absence of physical and/or emotional abuse. Female heads may be empowered in that they are more able to further their personal interests and the well-being of their dependants. Studies have shown that the expenditure patterns of female-headed households are more biased towards nutrition and education than those of male-households.

However, while female-headed households may be better off in some ways, they may still face discrimination, may face greater difficulties than men in gaining access to labour markets, credit, housing and basic services, and there are sometimes additional layers of discrimination against female heads. Single parent households, most of which are FHHs also face the difficulties of one adult having to combine income earning with household management and child rearing and this generally means that the parent can only take on part-time, informal jobs with low earnings and few if any fringe benefits.

Gender and Official Assessments of Urban Poverty

There is limited consideration of gender issues with respect to measuring urban poverty, and identifying the urban poor. This has implications for the formation of policy and the design of anti-poverty programmes. A review of current approaches to understanding urban poverty points to the need of broadening the way urban poverty is understood and measured. Official indicators of urban poverty often do not take into account gender-biased aspects of household impoverishment or coping strategies, such as limiting expenditure or resource use in times of economic crisis. Conventional poverty lines give scant attention to health and social indicators, hence failing to demonstrate the social and health dimensions of urban poverty which are heavily borne by women.

Consideration of urban poverty of ten neglects differentials between men and women in terms of their access to income, resources and services. Such differentials may occur within households between men and women or between individuals (i.e. between single men and single women) or between households with women-headed households at a disadvantage to male-headed households. There are also gender-based differentials in vulnerability to illness and violence.

A gender equality perspective draw s attention to the need for gender-sensitive indicators of poverty. A way forward may be to develop indicators that measure gender-biased factors influencing the severity of poverty, such as capacity to achieve success, gender-differentiated needs, social and health dimensions of poverty etc.

Participatory approaches to measuring poverty may have more scope for including a gender analysis. Participatory poverty assessments which are broadly informed by a theory of social capital make visible the social norms and networks of supports of the poor, and highlight their capabilities, assets and resourcefulness. But, they also need to be informed by frameworks which identify processes of social exclusion.

Gender and Urban Development

Feminist researchers have drawn attention to the fact that much of the literature on women, gender and urban development has fallen outside the mainstream. The realm of urban planning has been defined in physical and spatial terms, linked to men's work patterns, dealing with issues such as transport, housing, land and infrastructure whilst issues around health, education and the family, linked to women's work ,have been commonly dealt with as separate national level sectoral concerns.

In general, urban women's priorities have often been ignored in the design of human settlements, the location of housing, and the provision of urban services (Beall 1995a). However, there is increasing recognition of the discrimination faced by women in most aspects of employment, housing and basic services, and greater efforts by some governments and international agencies to reduce or remove this.

BOX 1

Gender-sensitive improvements to official assessments of urban poverty
Need to disaggregate needs since needs are often influenced by gender.

Need to take into account intrahousehold differentials. Households that appear to be above the poverty line may have members who suffer deprivation because they face discrimination in the allocation of resources within the household due to age, gender or social status.

Need to examine social and health dimensions of poverty. The deprivation caused by inadequate income is much reduced if those with low income have access to good quality housing (with adequate provision for water and sanitation) and health care.

Need to take into account non-monetary income sources , e.g. goods and services obtained free, or below their monetary value and differential entitlement to these.

Need to develop more accurate measurements for capacity to achieve access to resources which is influenced by factors such as education, information, legal rights, illness, threatened domestic violence or insecurity.

Greater understanding of men's and women's relative command over assets is required. Low income households may have asset bases that allow them to avoid destitution when faced with shocks, e.g. level of education and training. Women may have limited command over certain assets. On the other hand, women may have greater claims, e.g. on social networks.

Underlying causes of poverty need to be examined. Structural causes of poverty and processes that create or exacerbate poverty (including gender) need to be considered.

Adapted from: Wratten 1995; UNCHS 1995

DIMENSIONS OF URBAN POVERTY

Gender equity considerations are important for any analysis of urban poverty conditions and trends. Men and women experience and respond to urban poverty in different ways as a result of gendered constraints and opportunities (in terms of access to income, resources and services). This section demonstrates why a gender perspective is important to understanding poverty by highlighting gender inequalities in key urban sectors.

Poverty, Employment and Livelihoods

There is gender-differentiated access to employment and income-earning opportunities in urban areas. Unemployment and underemployment have been major concerns for many urban economies. Recent studies suggest the urban poor have suffered significantly from structural adjustment through reduction in employment creation and downward pressure on real wages. New categories of the poor have been identified, for example, former state employees who have been retrenched.

In general terms, there are two broad labour market trends: the feminisation of the labour force; and the deregulation and casualistion of the labour market. The rise in female labour force participation can be attributed in part to a rise in demand for female labour in industries, and in part to household survival strategies during economic restructuring. This has positive benefits for women given that social position within, and access (both social and physical) to, urban labour markets is critical for well-being and survival. However, there is evidence that in many countries gender segmentation in the labour market remains widespread and that women's work remains characterised by insecurity and low returns. Furthermore, many different facets of women's work, both unpaid and paid, are not recognised by urban planners.

Research on two low-income settlements in Madras , India suggests that neither household structure nor the structure of the economy can provide an adequate explanation of either female labour force participation or the type of work women and girls undertake in Madras. Ideological factors and their 'enforcement' at the intermediate social levels of the wider kingroup and community are central to decisions regarding who works in the household and under what conditions. These ideologies are, however, not rigid dictates but guiding principles around which the household respectability is negotiated.

The importance of the informal sector for in come generation and poverty alleviation is well recognised. There is increasing reliance on urban informal employment for both men and women but the ability of the informal sector to absorb the unemployed is limited. There are gender-differentiated patterns of access to informal sector work. Research in Zimbabwe revealed that declines in women's earnings from informal sector activities also meant less control by the women of household budgets, lower self esteem and increased conflict with husbands. Several of those interviewed felt that the men were not fulfilling their obligations as husbands and fathers.

The deregulation and casualisation of the labour market has lead to an increase in homeworking, particularly among women, which sometimes leads to greater exposure to environmental risk, both in terms of human pathogens and industrial toxic compounds at home or in the workplace.

Assets and Consumption Patterns

Evidence from cities as diverse as Guayaquil, Harare, and Guadalajara indicate that with declining incomes and high unemployment, households have modified their consumption and dietary patterns and adjusted household expenditures, in many instances in the direction of cheaper and less nutritious substitutes. In Zimbabwe, there is clear evidence that women have modified their lives to a greater extent than men. Women's responses were mainly individual, taking greater cuts in their own consumption, spending more time shopping for bargains and working longer hours for poorer returns.

The critical importance of assets and debt to the survival strategies of the poor in face of economic shocks has gender dimensions. Moser identifies the major assets of the poor in the face of economic crisis: labour; social and economic infrastructure; housing; household relations; social capital. In many instances, women have less command over assets than men.

Violence in Urban Areas

An emerging area of concern is the increasing levels of crime and violence in urban areas. Important gender differentiation exists in terms of violent response to unemployment. While men turn to crime and violence, women more frequently turn to dependency on men. Research in Jamaica also points to important gender differences in terms of both involvement and impact of violence: economically motivated violence was seen primarily as involving men, while much of interpersonal violence involved women.

There is no conclusive evidence to suggest that gender-based violence is on the increase in urban areas. Some studies suggest that where it does occur, women have cited lack of money and food as the most important cause of marital conflict, and alcohol or drug abuse as the main reason for wife beating. They attributed men's anger to feelings of frustration stemming from insufficient earnings.

Urban Environment, Health and Poverty

The determinants of health in urban areas are complex, but social and cultural factors, including composition of the family and cultural restrictions are important. Poor health can reduce capacity to earn an income, and health treatment can use up scarce savings or lead to debt. Women play a crucial role in informal health care in low-income households and communities in their role as wives and mothers, and continue to be used as conduits to children in promotional and preventative health campaigns, for example around nutrition and immunisation.

For South Asia as a whole, it has been suggested that in the case of the urban poor, ill-health is the most important trigger pushing households into poverty and destitution, particularly when the person sick is the adult wage earner is male. This raises questions as to who in a household gets access to health care when user charges are imposed. This may disadvantage girls and women and privilege boys and men in low-income households.

Indoor air pollution and airborne lead have been identified as among the most serious pollution problems in developing countries. Women and children spend more time at home than men do, are more exposed to indoor pollution, and hardest hit by respiratory disease. Although, women are more exposed to air pollution from household fuels and to contaminated water, there has been little research on the different health consequences of pollution for women and men.

Men and women play different roles in the environmental management in cities. Research in Latin America indicates that poor women are more likely than men to undertake the majority of environmental management tasks such as purification of water and management of domestic waste.

Housing

Lack of access to secure and safe housing is a central feature of urban poverty. At least 600 million urban dwellers in Africa, Asia and Latin America live in housing that is so overcrowded and of such poor quality, with such inadequate provision for water, sanitation, drainage and garbage collection that their lives and their health is continually at risk (UNCHS). Housing is also an important productive asset since access to credit to secure a livelihood may depend on property ownership. The price and availability of land for housing remains an important influence on housing prices and conditions leading to the development of illegal or informal land markets, where the poor have limited capacity to pay. Quantity, quality, accessibility and tenure of housing are all important and have gender-specific dimensions.

There is increased awareness of possible 'gender blindness' in housing and basic service programmes, because they do not recognise and make provision for the particular needs and priorities of women for income-earning, child-rearing and household management, and community-level action and management. Low-cost housing or site and service programmes rarely consider the needs and priorities of women in terms of site design and nature of infrastructure and service provision that meet their needs. The ways and means in which discrimination takes place is well documented, i.e. exclusion of women through eligibility criteria, methods of beneficiary recruitment, cost recovery mechanisms.

There are also gender dimensions to renting and gender-related constraints to owner-occupation. Studies of Latin America and West Africa suggest that female-headed households are more likely to be tenants or sharers than owners, whilst a study in Bangladesh found that female-headed households and supported households were concentrated in the poorest and potentially most vulnerable housing conditions. There are several reasons for this:

- women are often excluded from official housing programmes offering owner occupation;
- female-headed households tend to be poorer and, since poorer households frequently rent, women tend to be tenants;

- female-headed households also frequently lack both time and skills to self-build, but are often required to do so in the absence of funds for professional labour.

However, the tendency to portray women as victims is questionable in light of women's involvement in low-income housing as landlords and illegal developers of urban land. Research on Mexican cities highlights women's direct role in self-help housing construction directly, and their crucial role in underpinning the social relations on which much of the mutually supportive activity of self-help housing construction rests.

Transport, Public Infrastructure and Basic Services

There has been a decline in investment in urban infrastructure such as transport, sanitation, and water provision in many developing country cities. Official statistics suggest that by the early 1990s more than 80 per cent of the urban population in Africa, Asia and Latin America were 'adequately served' with water, at least a third have no proper sanitation, and three-fifths were not connected to a public sewerage system. Governments tend to exaggerate the proportion of people with piped water, and there is much disagreement about the definition of 'adequate'. Inadequate supply of water and sanitation facilities may place time constraints on women, as they are more likely to have the responsibility for tasks that require water.

When planning transport there is no consideration of the fact that women also have to perform reproductive tasks. Women may be severely disadvantaged by the fact that transport often runs infrequently during off-peak periods.

GENDER, URBAN POLICY INTERVENTIONS AND STRATEGIES

There are relatively few examples given of successful anti-poverty policies in urban areas in the development literature. This may be attributed to the fact that most of the work on urban issues has been carried out by geographers, receiving less attention from economists. The increasing sociological and anthropological work on urban issues particularly in Latin America may bring about some change.

One area of urban anti-poverty policy that has witnessed much theoretical and empirical work, and considerable success in benefiting the poor is slum improvement and basic services provision. But, even such initiatives have tended to be biased towards the non-poor.

A significant change during the 1980s and 1990s is the shift from housing needs to housing rights as a result of increasing influence on government actions of international and national law on people's right to housing, largely as a result of much greater use of international and national law by NGOs. Various new approaches to settlements planning and management have been developed over the last 10-15 years in the form of settlement planning, land use control (improved zoning techniques, innovations in land development and management), the management of infrastructure (management of environmental infrastructure, financing investments, paying for water) and transport planning and management.

In recent years, there have been initiatives to reduce discrimination and ensure a greater voice and influence for women's needs and priorities in housing, and more generally human settlements. However, the tendency has been to focus on women's need for income generation rather than their housing needs. It is now more common to find discussions of women's livelihood and housing needs together. Some credit programmes that developed for income generation have also developed credit programmes for housing purchase, construction and improvement, e.g. the Grameen Bank.

Increasing attention is being given to urban employment creation. The new emphasis on self-employment promotion corresponds with changing views on the informal sector. There is also much interest in microenterprise sector development in the context of priorities emerging in liberalising economies such as developing the private sector, creating employment, alleviating poverty and encouraging more equitable income distribution.

The health sector, perhaps more than any other, targets women in urban areas. But, this has not always meant it has addressed women's health needs and rights. Health care remains highly medicalised and professionalised, and poor men and women continue to be excluded from formal or public health care. Cost recovery approaches to financing health services have gendered implications for affordability. A gendered approach which addresses simultaneously and equitably the different preventative and curative health needs of both men and women is required.

The limitations of supply based, top down responses (as epitomised by infrastructure and low-income shelter programmes) has led to various conclusions about what may improve urban conditions. The failure of large scale infrastructure based projects to provide sustainable action has been interpreted in different ways. A range of alternative approaches have been taken particularly by NGOs:

- institutional support; greater use of low cost technology in infrastructure responses (e.g. ITDG smokeless stoves);
- integrated programmes of health, education, shelter and infrastructure support; basic needs support targeted at the poor;
- radical programmes based on community needs and community involvement; involving NGOs more in these community based responses, as an alternative to government/ municipality agencies' support.

The role of women at grassroots or community level is also becoming better appreciated by external agencies. Several case studies suggest that community organisations in which women have a major role are more effective than those controlled by men, e.g. the Integrated Slum Improvement Programme in Visakhpatnam; it is in the few examples of settlements that are led by women that the rhetoric of urban community development has most closely been translated into reality.

There are examples of women's housing projects, or housing projects that address the particular needs of women or women-headed households. Box 2 gives an example of a programme that was developed in Colombia.

Community activism is an important avenue towards participation in city-level planning and policy making processes. But, there is the danger that if women confine themselves to organising self-help and survival strategies they will be left to manage communities on their own, without resources or political and professional support.

Recent concern with urban governance stems from general attention being paid to the issue of 'good governance' in development. It is essentially preoccupied with questions of financial accountability and administrative efficiency, and political concerns related to democracy, human rights, and participation. Urban governance used to be equated solely with urban management but more recently, it has come to be understood both as government responsibility and civic engagement involving a full range of participants, which makes it more possible to integrate a gender perspective. Women need to participate in public office because they have particular experiences of, and relationships to, the urban environment, and they have proved themselves to be effective agents of change at the city or local level on a range of issues (Beall 1995a).

BOX 2

Colombi's programme for the development of families headed by women

In Colombia, in 1990, a local NGO and the Women's World Bank began a credit programme targeted at female heads of household in Cali, the third largest city. Following on from the new constitution passed in 1990 and after the 1991 elections, the Presidential Programme for Women, Youth and the Elderly decided to take up this programme and make it national and permanent, in part to address one of the articles of the new constitution that prescribed special support for women-headed households.

In 1992, the programme was launched in five cities and in 1993 in a further ten, covering 2,750 households. It was supported by many institutions, both governmental and non-governmental. The programme was seen as an effective way of institutionalising gender-aware policy and, in the context of decentralisation, of involving local-level institutions.

The objective of the programme was to improve the quality of life of families headed by women at the lowest socio-economic level in urban areas through the improvement of income generation, household well-being, the condition of children and the promotion of human development of women and their families. The target group is urban women heads of households working in the informal economy in their own small enterprises. The programme includes credit schemes, management training, promotion and support for person development including training in self esteem, health care, legal education and family life.

FUTURE PERSPECTIVES

Poverty analysis must focus on a household's means of survival and its room for manoeuvre in adopting different coping strategies. This necessarily involves a discussion of household composition and gender relations. Such an analysis must go beyond a solely income-based view of poverty and include an understanding of vulnerability, entitlement and social exclusion which emphasises the importance of assets, and processes of exclusion.

The role of governance, institutions and partnerships with individuals, households, communities, voluntary organisation, NGOs, private enterprises, investors and government agencies is continuously emphasised in the urban development literature. There is a need to develop gender-sensitive mechanisms and ways to involve both men and women in the processes of identifying needs and planning. To address the scale and complex nature of urban poverty problems, national and local capacity building institutions will need to be strengthened, ensuring that training is in local languages, gender-sensitive and involves all actors.

New forms of urban partnership are required, to develop participatory processes that include women and men at all stages of urban development. Participation as entitlement refers to how women and men command resources, contribute to, and take responsibility for the well-being of their households, communities and the city. Participation as empowerment relates to processes by which organised groups in cities, and individuals within them, identify and articulate their interests, negotiate change with others, and transform urban organisation life and their role within it. More research is required on women, citizenship, democratisation and decentralisation and its relationship with urban governance. To date the role of women in local municipal government is one of the few areas addressed.

Environmental sustainability issues are very important. More research is required into how gender relations intersect with urban environment and poverty issues in the context of urban development.

Another area requiring some research is social unrest and violence, a continuum that begins within the household and reaches beyond as it becomes a community and city-wide problem.

A review of research agendas relating to gender and urban issues shows that much of it has had little influence on mainstream urban researchers and policy makers. Most of this research remains a specialist concern undertaken by women in separate departments or work areas thus marginalising their work. A major priority is the mainstreaming of this work.

NOTES AND REFERENCES

Amis, P., 1995 'Making sense of poverty', in IIED, 1995, 'Urban poverty: characteristics, causes and consequences', *Environment and Urbanisation,* Vol 7 No 1

Amis, P. and Rakodi, C., 1994, 'Urban poverty: issues for research and policy', *Journal of International Development, Policy, Economics and International Relations.*

Baden, S. and Milward, K., 1995, 'Gender and poverty', *BRIDGE Report No* 30, Brighton: Institute of Development Studies.

Baker, J., 1995, 'Survival and accumulation strategies at the rural-urban interface in north-west Tanzania, in IIED, 1995, 'Urban poverty: Characteristics, causes and consequences', *Environment and Urbanisation,* Vol. 7 No 1.

Beall, J., 1995a, 'Participation in the city: where do women fit in?', *Gender and Development,* Vol.

Beall, J., 1995b, 'In sickness and in health: engendering health policy for development', *Third World Planning Review*, Vol. 17 No 2.

Beall, J, 1997, 'Assessing and responding to urban poverty: lessons from Pakistan', *IDS Bulletin,*Vol. 28 No 2.

Chant, S., (1989), 'Gender and urban planning', in L. Brydon and S. Chant, *Women in the Third World: Gender Issues in Rural and Urban Areas,* London: Earthscan.

Chant, S. (ed), 1992, *Gender and Migration in Developing Countries,* London: Belhaven Press.

—de Haan, 1997, 'Rural-urban migration and poverty: the case of India', *IDS Bulletin,* Vol 28 No 2, Brighton: Institute of Development Studies.

—de Haan, A. with Yaqub, S., 1996, 'Urban poverty and its alleviation', report and conclusions of the Autumn 1995 seminar series at the Institute of Development Studies, *PRUS Working Papers* No. 1, Brighton: Poverty Research Unit at Sussex.

Fustukian, S., 1996, 'Strategies to strengthen urban health and social development', in N. Hall, R. Hart and D. Mitlin, *The Urban Opportunity: The Work of NGOs in Cities of the South,* London: ITDG.

Gilbert, A., 1997, 'Work and poverty during economic restructuring: the experience of Bogota, Colombia', *IDS Bulletin,* Vol 28 No 2, Brighton: Institute of Development Studies.

Gilbert, A. and Gugler, J., 1992, *Cities, Poverty and Development: Urbanisation in the Third World,* Oxford: Oxford University Press.

Hardoy, J., Mitlin, D. and Satterthwaite, D., 1992, *Environmental Problems in Third World Cities,* London: Earthscan.

Hart, R., 1996, 'Introduction and overview', in N. Hall, R. Hart and D. Mitlin, *The Urban Opportunity: The Work of NGOs in Cities of the South,* London: ITDG.

HomeNet, 1996, 'Rights for homeworkers', *HomeNet Newsletter,* No. 5.

ILO, 1996, 'Social exclusion and anti-poverty strategies', research findings on the patterns and causes of social exclusion and the design of policies to promote integration, ILO, Geneva,

Jones, S., 1996, 'Urban development—issues and problems', a background paper prepared for ODA's Economic and Social Committee for Overseas Research for discussion at the ESCOR Workshop on 19th April 1996.

Kanji, N., 1995, 'Gender, poverty and economic adjustment in Harare, Zimbabwe', in IIED, 1995, 'Urban poverty: characteristics, causes and consequences', *Environment and Urbanisation,* Vol. 7 No. 1.

Kruse, 1997, 'Employment generating programmes in the urban context of India, the Nehru Rozgar Yojana', *IDS Bulletin,* Vol. 28 No. 2.

Latapi, A. and de la Rocha, M., 1995, 'Crisis, restructuring and urban poverty in Mexico', in IIED, 1995, 'Urban poverty: characteristics, causes and consequences', *Environment and Urbanisation,* Vol. 7, No. 1.

Lipton, M., 1996, 'Successes in anti-poverty', *Issues in Development Discussion Paper* 8, Development and Technical Co-operation Department, ILO, Geneva.

Masika, R. with Baden, S., 1997, 'Infrastructure and poverty: a gender analysis', *BRIDGE Report* No 51, Brighton: Institute of Development Studies.

Moser, C., 1995, 'Women, gender and urban development policy: challenges for current and future research', *Third World Planning Review,* Vol. 17 No. 2.

Moser, C., 1996, 'Confronting crisis: a comparative study of household responses to poverty and vulnerability in four poor urban communities', *Environmentally Sustainable Development Studies and Monographs Series* No. 8, Washington D.C.: World Bank

Moser, C. and Holland, J., 1995, 'A participatory study of urban poverty and violence in Jamaica: summary finding', Washington D.C.: Urban Development Division, World Bank.

Moser, C. and Peake, L (eds), 1987, *Women, Housing and Human Settlements,* London: Tavistock Publications.

ODA, 1995, 'Urban development review paper', Aid Economics and Small Enterprises Department and Engineering Division, London: ODA.

Paolisso, M. and Gammage, S., 1996, 'Women's response to environmental degradation: poverty and demographic constraints. Case studies from Latin America', Washington: ICRW.

Satterthwaite, D., 1995a, 'The under-estimation and misrepresentation of urban poverty' in IIED, 1995, 'Urban poverty: Characteristics, causes and consequences' *Environment and urbanisation,* Vol. 7 No. 1.

Satterthwaite, D., 1995b, 'Viewpoint—the underestimation of urban poverty and of its health consequences', *Third World Planning Review*, Vol. 17 No. 4.

Sida, 1996, *Promoting Sustainable Livelihoods: A Report from the Task Force on Poverty Reduction,* Stockholm: Sida.

Surjadi, C. and McGranahan, G., 1995, 'Jakarta: environmental problems at the household level', in I. Serageldin, Cohen, A. and Sivaramakrishan, K. (eds), *The Human Face of the Urban Environment,* Proceedings of the Second Annual World Bank Conference on Environmentally Sustainable Development, World Bank, Washington.

United Nations (UN), 1995, *The World's Women: Trends and Statistics,* New York: United Nations.

UNCHS (HABITAT), 1996, *An Urbanising World: Global Report on Human Settlements 1996,* Oxford: Oxford University Press.

Varley, A., 1995, 'Neither victims nor heroines: women, land and housing in Mexican cities', *Third World Planning Review,* Vol 17 No. 2.

Vera-Sanso, P., 'Community, seclusion and female labour force participation in Madras, India', *Third World Planning Review,* Vol 17 No. 2.

Wratten, E., 1995, 'Conceptualising urban poverty', in IIED, 1995, 'Urban poverty: characteristics, causes and consequences', *Environment and Urbanisation,* Vol. 7 No. 1.

9

WOMEN WORKFORCE IN URBAN INDIA

In India, people face a conflict over time spent on housework and childcare versus time spent on paid work. Ironically, if people are paid market rates for childcare and cooking work, rather high valuations are put on these supposedly 'domestic' tasks. Some estimates of the national income have been made which adjust for the unpaid unmarketised domestic work in the USA. These show large increases in the Gross Domestic Product. However, since the work is actually not monetised, people in general don't normatively accord 'domestic work' the values imputed in such studies. Instead, they devalue this work and many people consider it to be women's work.

In India, across a variety of regional and cultural divisions, domestic work and childcare are widely considered to be women's work. It is often implicitly seen as undignified for a man to actually get involved in the dirty work of child cleaning, the messy work of dishwashing, or the time consuming women's jobs of cooking curries or sweeping the floors. Cleaning toilets is universally women's work and the conditions in which some dalit people (i.e., those who were previously called harijans, untouchables or sweepers) work as toilet attenders are unbelievably unsanitary and unpleasant.

The unpleasant aspects of domestic work were analysed by Thorstein Veblen who is better known for his theory of the leisure class. Veblen argued that the dominant people in the leisure class would visibly display time-wasting behaviours (e.g. sports or watching artistic performances) whilst they depend on the devoted or enslaved work of others who would do all the essential services such as cooking, cleaning, and clearing away. Veblen argued that by showing themselves to be cleaner than the working classes, both feudal and capitalist ruling classes displayed their prowess and status. Their physical prowess during military times was augmented by their considerable personal autonomy and control over other people's bodily movements even in peacetime. Veblen is famous for the theory of conspicuous consumption in which even the middle classes were found to emulate the lazy and excessively luxurious behaviours of the rich. Why do middle classes do this? Partly, it is because emulating the behaviours demonstrates one's identification with the higher class. This identification can have subtle cheering effects on someone who is actually oppressed within a hierarchy but prefers to imagine that they are not too far down that hierarchy.

This study examines women's work in India and how huge swathes of women are devoted only to unremunerated work. By contrast, being unemployed is rather rare among men. For women, the orthodox indicators of unemployment do not really apply. Instead it is non-employment time that we need to focus upon. In India, the National Sample Survey Organisation (NSSO) has repeatedly given measures of women's time spent on a variety of activities which broadly one can call the informal sector. These measures are, however, provided *if and only* if the woman first declares that she has no paid work, is not unemployed per se, and is doing domestic work only. She cannot declare herself self-employed either (although many Indian women do) so the category of 'housewives' is an appropriate label for this residual group of non-employed women who were asked the questions about unremunerated work. We provide details of this survey and a summary of the findings in this study. We conclude with a normative discussion of the situation.

The more women's time is allocated to paid employment, the less of their time is available for the unpaid work. Most western feminists would argue that the unpaid work done by women tends to get too little attention, and that its social and economic valuation is unreasonably low. Yet, they do not go so far as to hope for an increase in the time spent on domestic work. The main issue, they would argue, is the rewards and conditions of the work, both domestic and paid work. Women should be autonomous, they should be paid appropriate rates for paid work and they should not be oppressed or coerced in their economic decisions. Ironically, however, most housewives will quickly argue that they 'chose' to be housewives and 'not to work'. This reaction (which we have had in field research in rural Andhra Pradesh in 1985-88 and in 1995-96 as well as in 2005-06) reflects a revaluation in which the woman positively values her role in the family and prefers not to engage in some other set of more public roles.

As indicated by these field data, there is a delicately balanced set of normative principles lying behind all the decisions people make about labouring. Even when we (as researchers) describe labouring, we unintentionally invoke or hint at some of these norms. In this study we tread a fine line between positive and normative description. In a sense we integrate positive description with normative analysis (Olsen, 2005). We take 'labouring' and 'working' to mean the same thing, whilst 'employment' refers to the narrower subset of paid work (including piecework, hourly paid, casual and salaried work).

The International Labour Office (ILO) defines unemployment in a rather open way, requiring that the person be seeking work and also be available for work during the two weeks preceding the interview. For women who are doing child care, it is hard to claim that they are really seeking work even if the woman would, in some hypothetical sense, perhaps be willing to be employed if she could. In the villages, where Olsen did fieldwork in 1995-6, groups of very poor women had created a village level crèche and this had enabled a number of the women to do more paid work. This showed that they had been unemployed previously, due to child care duties. However, in ILO terms, they couldn't have claimed to be unemployed because the child care work kept them from actually seeking work. Andhra Pradesh where the fieldwork occurred has one of the highest female labour force participation rates of all the large Indian states.

The ILO's definition of labour-market inactivity has been changing over time since 1970 and it now tends to include less of the family helpers as 'inactive'. The unpaid family helper nowadays tends to be classified as a contributing family worker. In this way there is a drift toward higher *recorded* labour-force participation of women and children even though this does not necessarily correspond to a real change or increase in their working hours.

Most importantly, the frame of reference of this study considers labour relations—including employment, class and gender relations—to lie behind all outcomes that are measured for groups of individuals in India's large-scale national surveys. We step back from making judgements about which forms of labouring are desirable or otherwise. We describe the tendencies that are currently causing people to do paid work in the Indian economy and, in particular, we examine the tendency to be labour-market 'inactive' in detail.

Both men's and women's labour force involvements are explored here with a view to a balanced, nuanced and in-depth analysis of the differences that emerge between groups of people. These differences have several meanings. Firstly, they imply that causal tendencies are operating concurrently on fairly big homogeneous groups of people. Shared features of the groups include economic poverty, cultural background, health, and demographic conditions. Secondly, homogenous groups may imply that a majority of people of one type make a similar explicit choice, e.g. one group avoids paid work and tends to do domestic work. This interpretation of domestic work sounds rather innocuous and structuralist. But, the career break often has negative effects on a person's lifetime chances in the labour market. Constraints and constraining social norms can lead to such "choices" actually being sub-optimal or disempowering for the individual. Fraser argues that women are exploited through the capitalist system in particular. They do socially necessary labour which was normally not allowed for even in Marxist theorisations of the reserve army of labour. Thirdly, the differences between groups suggest that policy made with one image of 'women's needs' may go wrong if applied to all women. Extending a gender analysis to allow for *men's needs* suggests further nuances: For instance, in India, are employers expecting to pay a breadwinner's wage to each man? Do employed women therefore get a lower wage than men for subjective reasons? One paper cannot answer all these questions but we do succeed in describing the overall situation in terms of employment outcomes in some detail.

Work in India is predominantly conducted outside of paid formal employment contracts. There is a huge formal sector in urban areas, but both rural and urban India also have large numbers of people doing farming, trading and other work in informal enterprises. Instead a range of remuneration arrangements for farmers, traders, other proprietors and their families, non-family helpers, and piece-rate workers cause low employment participation rates. Among women there was a long-term downward trend in the labour-force participation rates 1901-1971. This long-term trend reflected the growth of the distinct role of the housewife over the period 1901-1971 and was unfortunately associated with a rising male sex ratio in the population as a whole. This appearance of lower women's participation was further exaggerated by some changes in the recording of employment in the 1971 Census. The Census of that year was hard to compare with previous years.

Since 1971, there has been a stabilisation of women's employment. The ILO database shows no rise in women's economic activity rates for India 1972-2002. These data show 31 per cent of women working in 1970, 31 per cent in 1980, 27 per cent in 1990, and 30 per cent for India in 2000. In other words there is no substantial change, according to this source.

The measures of work participation obtained by the National Council for Agro-Economic Research (NCAER) in their survey in 1997 showed labour force participation rates of 52 per cent among men and 26 per cent among women. Their calculations used both usual and subsidiary status. The usual status refers to someone having six months per year or more of paid work or self-employment. For those who do not have that regularity of work, the presence of any paid work can then be considered to give a 'subsidiary' status of participating. Mainly women were brought into the records via this subsidiary working status. At the all-India level it raised women's labour force participation from 18 to 26 per cent.

The NCAER figures closely mimic the Indian Census figures for 1991. The Census showed 27 per cent of women and 53 per cent of men were in the labour force using the combination of usual and subsidiary status. (If you leave out subsidiary status, the women's participation rate goes down by about 5 percentage points.) NCAER labels these figures clearly as 'work participation rates' indicating that inactivity, domestic work, and extra domestic work don't count as work. Furthermore state differences in work participation rates are given using NCAER data. The change in female work participation rates due to including subsidiary status has different effects for different states. For those with low participation rates under the heading of 'usual' status (for women), there is a huge difference. Adding subsidiary workers in some cases doubles the work participation rate, e.g. from 9 to 29 per cent in the Punjab, and a similarly large jump occurs in Uttar Pradesh.

The gender differential in participation persists over time, but whether it is narrowing or not is an open question. This study is mainly cross-sectional. There is a strong tendency to be employed among all degree level graduates, including Muslim women. A U-curve of employment probabilities exists over education levels. This U curve is stronger among Muslim women than among other women due to a range of factors. These factors include the expectation (among certain families) that being seen in public could damage a woman's role as protector of the honour of her family; a sense that a woman's education is a way to gain social status and not just future wages; and a sense among household members that they can afford to enable one woman to stay at home most of the time—especially if the household is urban and middle-income.

Among rural households, it is widely believed that it is prestigious for a Hindu woman to cook and serve food to her family and any guests that may come. In rural areas for these women to do domestic work only and nothing else is relatively rare. Instead, doing a range of paid and unpaid work, including some tasks that we call 'extra-domestic work', is more common. The tendency of naming a woman *as being overall a housewife* is very popular. A high status is generally associated with the role of housewife in parts of the country that have implicit cultural values associated with Sanskritisation,

Brahmanical gender norms, and/or the habit of observing *purdah*. Because of the popularity of calling a woman a housewife, we have avoided using the 'principal status' of the person over a whole year and instead have focused upon each person's work during a one-week recall period. We use last week's work status as the main indicator of a person's employment status. Otherwise women's work would be understated as people try to exaggerate the presence of a housewife in each household. We begin with a brief review of literature, then introduce the large-scale data set (NSS 55th round) used in the chapter and finally present the results.

Review of Literature on Women's Labour Force

The relevant literature includes economic theory, institutionalist revisions, gender and development theory, and some additional themes from demography and geography. In the literature on labour-force participation, standard sources begin with the supply of labour and quickly move on to mention human-capital aspects of labour supply. According to this view, 34 per cent of adult Indians participated in the labour market in 1991, and this figure comprised 16 per cent among women and 51 per cent among men. More up-to-date figures show a small decline in both women's and men's labour-force participation between 1993/4 and 1999. 30 per cent of the women in rural areas were working, as recorded in the National Sample Survey of India using a combination of principal and subsidiary employment status, compared with 53 per cent of men. Only 14 per cent of urban women were working, by this measure. Detailed differences in the recall method of record-keeping imply that the two sources are not directly comparable. Mathur used the Indian Census 1991 data. Srivastava used the NSS. *Sarvekshana* (the Bulletin of the National Sample Survey Organisation, 2001: 6; Jacob, 2001) shows a declining female labour force participation rate when comparing 1993/4 and 1999/00 using NSS. Jacob studied four different measures. The weekly and daily status measures of employment status showed the same overall trend. Specifically, over this period using NSS data the rural percentage in the labour force fell by 10 per cent among women and by 4 per cent among men. The urban percentage in the labour force fell 11 per cent among women and there was no change among men.

Basing his statistical analysis upon district-level Census data for 1991, Mathur used averages at the district level to model the 'response' of employment to education levels. A U curve can be seen using Mathur's data, among women since participation first falls between the illiterate group and the next group. Participation rises rapidly after that. Apart from updating the definitive study by Mathur, the present work admits more possibilities into the 'participation' category. Mathur allowed all main farmers, casual labour and employers to be grouped into the active group, following the Indian Census categories, but we add to this various home workers and family labour. In this way we obtain a variant on the labour-force participation rate that is consistent with current ILO definitions.

The human capital theory primarily predicts that wages reflect the rewards earned by human capital in productive enterprises. It has three parts however. First there is the potential worker's subjective reckoning of what they would earn if they worked for pay; secondly there is the act of gaining more education or training (which occurs both at schools and in firms); and third there is the reward firms give to productivity. This complex of factors has been unpicked carefully by other authors, who note that each stage faces certain problems. Basically the theory only relates crudely and roughly to reality. Firstly, it is not a *person* who reckons on earnings that they could make, it is a complex and yet cooperative household which can have one or several bargaining and decision-making processes going on. Secondly, investments in education and training are not merely individual rational choices but are also socially embedded decisions. Fevre has stressed the *habitus* component in which status gains, family enculturation, emulation of role models, and avoidance of stress all play a part. Thirdly, the rewards firms give to education have been shown to differ substantially across countries, regions, sectors, and by sex of worker. Deshpande and Deshpande argue that the gender pay gap observed in urban India occurs because gender-based discrimination is universal and enduring... That women are overcrowded in low-paid, dead-end, insecure and in short, "bad" jobs is easily verified.

Kingdon insists on detailed evidence for such claims since the situation varies from place to place and from job to job. These vagaries of human capital theory leave it wounded but not dead. The theory helps to show that there is an opportunity cost of avoiding labour-force participation. If the individual's returns to working are low, their opportunity cost of not working will be low too. They will then tend toward being labour-market inactive. If they have a degree, the opportunity cost is high since their workplace productivity is likely to be reckoned (by employers) to be high. From human capital theory, one would expect an upward tendency in the labour force participation rate as we move across education levels.

Human capital theory is part of a wide-ranging neoclassical theory of labour supply and demand. Neoclassical theorists argue that supply and demand cause the wage to reward workers according to marginal productivity. Huge gender pay gaps exist. These ranged in 1994 from 43 per cent among illiterate and lower primary workers to 23 per cent among graduates, averaging at 20 per cent overall (all figures are for urban India; the source cited is an NSS report dated 1997.) A neoclassical economist would tend to argue that only market imperfections such as stereotypes, rigid segmentation by gender, and cultural taboos on one sex doing certain operations can be introduced as explanatory factors. To a neoclassical economist, these factors are givens; they act as preferences of individuals; they are not part of the scope of economic science; and they cannot be treated in economic models.

The approach taken here is that the human capital claims can be augmented with a rich array of other claims arising in disciplines close to economics. The neoclassical approach is not necessarily the one that must lead the analysis. Statistical analysis was followed by retroduction—asking why these results came out—and then has been iterated with further statistical and qualitative analysis. The qualitative analysis uses both secondary reports and primary research.

The reason for jettisoning the neoclassical framework as a whole, whilst retaining some of its human capital claims, is that in rural and less-developed country contexts it has become abundantly clear that an individualistic framework is inadequate. Among economists, the "new home economics" evolved to handle this problem. It was applied to Indian labour markets by Skoufias.

According to NHE, the result of the utility-maximising decision at household level is thought to be an optimal distribution of the workers' efforts toward paid and unpaid work, and leisure. Detailed research by Skoufias has uncovered patterns in India which are consistent with this theory. Skoufias' detailed study of seasonal movements in wages and work-time (spent working on farms, either paid or unpaid) concluded that women's labour time is seasonally spread quite differently from men's in India. This generalisation is also supported by older data, but in recent years women have taken on much more of the agricultural work than in the past. Certain tasks are taboo for women in most of rural India, notably plowing the land, but in general a feminisation of agricultural labour has occurred whilst men have tended to take most of the new non-agricultural jobs in rural areas.

Avoiding the whole neoclassical theoretical edifice, we can use political-economy institutionalism as hinted at by Ott and as spelt out in detail by Toye, Hodgson, and Harriss-White. Veblen is one of the famous originators of today's institutionalism, and several associations promote this as a new way to do pluralist economics. Institutionalism refers to an assumption that social norms are in a state of flux as they interact with rules and with personal interpretations that either reproduce those rules or change them. Institutions are never simply given. In the case of India's labour markets, for instance, there are institutionalised norms about the terms of employment. These help to define what people expect from "piecework" "group contracts" "daily casual labour" "exchange labour" and salaried work. Since norms are ever-changing, they are always potentially renegotiable and institutions are also differentiated even within one community (e.g. as we see with marriage and cohabitation occurring side by side in the West).

Institutionalists empirically studying the Indian labour market fall into three main types. First there are the women-in-development specialists, who focus on gender differentiation. Second there are studies of discrimination against women and its causes. Thirdly there are those who have examined the formation of labour gangs, neighbourhood work groups, trade unions, bonded labour relationships, migrant labour and different types of work contracts.

All these three groups are pluralist; it is primarily economists who isolate their arguments away from the details of competing theories.

Specific authors working in the above areas include the following. Firstly, those who describe women's movement into active and visible self-employment indicate that it is perceived as highly desirable among these women for them to validate their work by calling it micro-enterprise or a business. The economic activity of women as a special group is the focus of Gautum and Tripathi in their description of women managing goats. Gulati notes that women's economic and commercial activity in India is restricted by ongoing expectations that they will still also meet a wide range of family expectations. These difficulties, which women face in different ways, vary depending on whether they live as a daughter in the natal home, or as a wife in the marital home, or (rarely) independently. Whilst there is some state variation, notably in the far north and east of India where non-Hindu tribes are more predominant, there is considerable bias against women which links up labour-force inactivity with poor health and low education. Narasimhan goes onward to argue in favour of women organising themselves separately from men in order to resist patriarchy.

Deshpande and Deshpande argue that human capital theory explains why the gender pay gap observed in urban India is a vicious circle:

> 'Asked why women invest less in their education and training, [economists] turn to the sexual division of labour which ascribes to women the role of housekeeper and to men that of the breadwinner. The sexual division of labour weakens women's commitment to the labour market but it maximises the welfare of the household. With their weak commitment, they choose, quite rationally, not to accumulate as much human capital as men do.'

However, Deshpande and Deshpande's own data show that urban women working in the service industries earn as much or more than men of the same educational level if that level is secondary school, and that the gender pay gap falls as education rises. Therefore the bald statements that are sometimes made, as illustrated above, need perhaps to be carefully reconsidered in the light of detailed evidence. Our further research will take up the wage-rate question in detail but so far we are just looking at work participation rates.

Kapadia looked closely at rural labouring and finds that women as well as men often form labour gangs in order to increase their bargaining power *vis a vis* the employers of casual labour. Interviews in 1995 by Davuluri Venkateswarlu also show that women join contracting groups to do casual labour, preferring that to domestic labour and unpaid labour. DaCorta and Venkateswarlu argue that the feminisation of the rural agricultural labour force is not necessarily good for women but it is a strong trend. The variety of labouring contracts has been described in detail by Breman with respect to migrant labour and by Rogaly with respect to field labouring in north India. The bargaining power of the worker is influenced by a whole range of factors which critically affect the wage struck each day. Rogaly is one of the few researchers to have explored this phenomenon although Agarwal has theorised it with regard to women's work choices. A bargaining approach to the evolution of the gender pay gap might be a rich way of challenging neoclassical theory with a substantive alternative.

Thus a rich arena of social relations linked with power-rich hierarchies has been explored by these pluralist, multi-disciplinary authors studying the work economy. All of these institutionalists have paid due attention to unpaid work. Few of them have offered any large-scale statistical evidence. Many insitutionalist studies rest upon a locally based case-study dataset because that is how the terms and conditions of specific labouring contracts are best examined. This study tries to fill the gap whilst being sensitive to the claims made by the women-in-development school in particular.

Authors from another theoretical orientation, the "gender and development" school have argued that households have cultures, households engage in social class relations and households experience both bargaining and cooperation among their members. The gender and development school differs from the women-in-development school in that class and gender are seen as interacting. Women are not simply seen as a homogenous group. GAD and WID are sometimes posed as opposites, but GAD builds upon the insights of WID. See Olsen and Mehta for a GAD analysis of the right to work in India. The use of statistical evidence to back up these theories has been prominent in the work of Dreze and Sen, Swaminathan, Agarwal and Srivastava. These authors attribute the terrible overall outcomes experienced by Indian women due to patriarchal and exploitative capitalist culture. Other than those mentioned here, however, most feminists in India have tended to avoid statistics. In the interests of bridging the chasm between neoclassical economists and some feminists, our methodological pluralist research aims to mediate between schools of thought such as NHE vs. GAD.

When labour-force involvement is classified into employment, self-employment, unpaid family labour, inactivity, and other, we effectively study the labour-force involvement in a reductionist way at the 'individual' unit of analysis. A Marxist view on this augments both GAD and NHE by studying inter-household farm exploitation. Byres and other Marxists have argued that resources owned at household level under the current legal system must be taken into account. In this study we have allowed for the social class system which is an open system of inter-household employment relationships. In regressions we use land owned (and its square), indicators based on employment, and indicators of tenancy and poverty. Self-employment itself is a class outcome (at person-level) which acts as a dependent variable.

Our pluralist approach also included three further hypotheses arising from demographers, the anthropological study of dowry, in which boys' families receive and girls' families give large amounts in cash and in kind and studies of girls' lower education rates. A separate study uses regression to draw out the U curve of housewifisation while controlling for all these important factors. Variables which were controlled for included the number of children in the household, the age of the respondent, allowing curvature and dummies for India's states to have state-wise differentiation in labour markets for a variety of agro-climatic and historical/institutional reasons. The cross-tabulations and Figures in this study arise from gross averages but they are consistent with the regression equations.

It would be ideal to allow for minor work-relevant health differences among the population too. In the UK where 20 per cent of the adult population has a disability of some kind affecting their ability to work, labour-force participation studies routinely control for ill health. However in India's National Sample Survey 55th round there is no indicator of temporary or mild disability. Instead there is a mutually exclusive status known as 'unable to work due to disability'. Such people are simply grouped here into the inactive category. There was no question on 'long-term limiting illness' as found in Western surveys.

Caste differences and the various religious groupings were found to have significant association with work outcomes in India. Important aspects of caste are experienced at the 'upper' end of the spectrum in the differences between Brahman and other 'forward' castes such as the Merchants and the Reddy farming castes. The upper castes are highly differentiated over space, and no records are kept of the specific castes in NSS of the detailed caste name of households.

Analysis of caste in the detailed sense in which it is lived therefore, has to occur within a more detailed, triangulated study. The evidence for main caste groups that is available from NSS 55th round. For details of one fieldwork site in Andhra Pradesh in 1986-7 and 1995 see Olsen and the ESRC Data Set Study Number 3927 respectively. There it was found that the labour relations of merchant castes were particularly strongly gendered, since their womenfolk rarely if ever worked for anyone else. Brahmin women, too, rarely worked for pay at all and were rarely seen in the fields. However among the middle and lower castes, and among Muslim people who were 15 per cent of the local population, work for pay was common for both men and women. The detailed study of caste allows occupational patterns to emerge as linked to small scale caste groups, such as Kshatriya (often landlords) and Chetties (merchants) as well as Kummaaris (potters, who are often small farmers as well as potters), Aacharyas (goldsmiths, who again are often doing farming with the menfolk also doing paid employment in banks as valuers), and so on. For a brief review of gendered aspects of caste and labouring see Raghuram.

Data and Methodology

In our analysis, labour-force involvements are classified as follows: Employed; self-employed, which includes own-account workers and unpaid family labour; unemployed; and inactive. The last category covers 'attending to domestic duties' as well as student, retired, ill and other. Table 1 shows the percentages of the Indian working-age population falling into these categories in 1994. We used ages 16-65 although, in addition, many Indian children also work. For those adults who do domestic work, two collapsed categories are shown here ('inactive' and 'doing extra-domestic work').

Details of the recording of extra-domestic work are in Appendix 1, and the results are summarised in Tables 3 and 4. In the NSS in 1994, a few men aged 16-65 were doing domestic work (about 1 per cent—but many more if the over-65s were included). However in 1999 no men were recorded as such. This step backward in the social construction of housewifery (as female-only) and is unnecessary since many men are labour-market inactive and some of them do informal-sector work. It would be ideal to return to a more sex-blind recording of the employment statuses.

Traditionally, gender theorists have stressed that work in the informal sector should probably appear as 'self-employed', which is possible if the household's respondent argues that that is the best way of categorising a person. For many women, and a few men, 'attending to domestic duties' was the main employment status, but there was nevertheless performance of a wide range of up to 12 activities which would, by many people, be considered to be productive and 'in' the labour market. These are not remunerated activities, but they contribute to the household's livelihood. In the questionnaire, the wording specifies that the person 'attended domestic duties and also engaged in free collection of goods, sewing, tailoring, weaving, etc. for household use.' The activities that are considered here as 'extra-domestic' are:

> These activities were grouped under the headings 'food preparation work', 'fuel and fire work', and 'informal sector unpaid work', respectively that 26 per cent of the urban female domestic workers did 'sewing, tailoring, etc.'. 13 per cent of urban female domestic workers did 'tutoring of own children' and 9 per cent of the urban and 36 per cent of the rural female domestic workers worked in a kitchen garden, did poultry work, or similar. Overall, urban women were more likely to be working purely as housewives than were rural women. This pattern may support Mies's claim that modernisation would imply a growing housewifisation

The National Sample Survey is an integrated survey on household consumer expenditure, employment, unemployment and informal non-agricultural work. It covers both individuals' work (including both paid and unpaid work) and household principal occupation. Detailed indicators of people's personal principal and subsidiary occupation, hours worked, and earnings are provided. At the household level, income estimates are not provided. Instead, the wealth/poverty spectrum is measured using household-level per-capita expenditure. This indicator is not very sophisticated but it does allow the relative spending of households (adjusted for their gross size) to be taken into consideration.

Sampling

The NSS has used a sampling scheme that rotates on the calendar months for its Central samples. Thus all quarters of one calendar year are represented in all regions. The survey period of the 55th Round is 1st July, 1999 to 30th June, 2000. A sample of 10,400 first-stage units (fsu's) (rural and urban combined) were surveyed at all-India level.

In addition to these main 10,400 *fsus,* which are known as the Central sample, there are state samples with additional *fsu's*. All the States/ Union Territories except for Andaman & Nicobar Islands, Dadra & Nagar Haveli and Lakhshadweep participated in the 55th round at least on an equal matching basis compared to the size of the central sample. The state samples did not have the rotating timing found in the central sample. The rotation is useful because it means that when a one-week recall period is used, at least half the overall sample are spread out over the entire year. In this study, both the central sample and state samples have been used together to maximise the sample size.

360,000 people aged 16-65, and 592,000 aged 0 to 99 years were in the survey. The average household size was 5.8 and there were on average 2 children under the age of 16.

Participation of Women Labour Force

The overall level of labour-force participation is seen to be 85 per cent among men and 35 per cent among women using the one-week recall method. In the *National Human Development Report 2001,* published by the Planning Commission in 2002, the same NSS data are used to report the labour-force participation rates as they were recorded at three time-points: 1989, 1994, and 1999/2000. The rates shown there for 1999/2000 are very similar to our estimates: 84 per cent among men and 39 per cent among women. Here the combination "usual principal and subsidiary status or seeking or available for work" was used. Thus, whether one uses one-week recall or the usual-and-subsidiary combination, the results are nearly the same.

Going back in time, this *Report* shows both participation rates declining with men's rates falling from 87 per cent in 1983 to 84 per cent in 1999/2000. Women's rates fell from 44 per cent in 1983 to 39 per cent in 1999/2000—a larger decline on a smaller base. The meanings of this decline are multiple depending on one's policy perspective. Some of the important meanings of withdrawing women from employment are positively valued by many Indian residents quite apart from the commercial effects.

Self-employment is a more important category of work among men than among women. However, as stressed in the *National Human Development Report,* the rates of participation differ depending on which social category the person is in. In the rest of our discussion we will focus on some of the diversity within India's overall averages.

Women's employment rates fall as caste status rises. It is also notable that rural and urban employment rates are very different. In both places however women do plenty of self-employment. In rural areas this is mostly agricultural whereas in urban areas it is mainly informal-sector and small-scale manufacturing.

A logistic regression of employment *per se* also showed that the tendency to have a job first falls with education moving from illiteracy toward middle levels, and then rises. In other words both net and gross patterns showed a U curve. The rapid decline in rates of inactivity among both Hindu and Muslim women as they reach graduate status can be seen. Both Hindu and Muslim women tend to have a typical inverted U of labour-force participation over age-groups. Hindu and Muslim women's rates of labour-force participation are different across a wide spectrum of education levels excepting among graduates. We can test for the differences for other major religions, as done also in the *National Human Development Report,* but we would do this only in the context of detailed evidence about each religious grouping.

The education effects found in the regression indicated only weak support for the human capital theory of labour supply. The rise in labour supply only applied when we compared highly educated women to those in the middle levels of education. Below that there is an apparent perversity. Women of low education levels are more likely to work than those of middle levels. The causal mechanism behind this is a nexus of household-level poverty. We allowed for this in the regression by using a dummy variable for being in a poor household. Poor women are most likely to take casual paid work. Many Indians perceive poor women's employment as being a response to their household income crisis. It is seen as necessary drudgery for them from which housewives have been relieved.

The regression equation allowed for much more than education. Institutional factors were present and statistically significant. The different states' cultural, regulatory and historical backgrounds were allowed for by using state dummies, many of which were highly significant.

Poverty and Labour Market Outcomes

Household level economic poverty was measured by the NSS by getting item-wise recall of monthly expenditure and then adjusting this for the household size, giving a per capita indicator. Those people living in households with less than half of the median monthly expenditure were deemed to be poor for the purposes of the simple regressions here. Such an analysis omits intra-household differentials in the control over expenditure, non-economic aspects of poverty, and differentials in the cost of different types of people (children, adults, elderly). Because they use a recall method, the accuracy of the figures for household economic poverty are further cast into doubt. This study uses the indicator of household economic poverty in a rough and ready fashion because of these caveats.

Poverty is far more prevalent among the rural scheduled castes and scheduled tribes than in other parts of the population. In this way and others, these regression results suffer from endogeneity. The same causal mechanisms that are represented by one variable are also to some extent embedded in other variables. Economic poverty, for instance, is measured directly but then is also proxied by some other variables. Landholding is represented both by the owned holding and the operational landholding (proxied through a dummy for being a tenant). These endogeneities are not too problematic if we take the regression for what it is: a description of the outcomes of a complex array of causal mechanisms which work both actually and counterfactually. They operate not only in their own right, but also only in contexts in which they are able to have effects. We cannot expect regression to simply separate all the causal mechanisms since the operationalisation of social causes is fraught with overlaps between context and specific causes.

We find that people whose work as tenant farmers are less likely to be employed and more likely to be self-employed themselves. We also find that poor households have a reduced tendency to have a woman working purely within the home (as a domestic worker or housewife), because the women in these households tend to go out for employment. Many of these poor women have a double burden of domestic and paid work or even a triple burden of domestic, farming and paid work.

A third warranted argument is much more controversial. Those households which pull themselves out of poverty are more likely to withdraw the woman (or to have her choose to withdraw herself) from the labour market. Women's withdrawal from employment can be an elegant yet silent testimony to the couple's economic success.

Village level fieldwork in Andhra Pradesh helped Olsen to learn that having a woman kept in private is a prestigious and high-status form of invisibility. Many housewives are discouraged from riding bikes even though most learn to ride during their childhood. In a sense most Indian women observe a form of purdah. These patterns cut across castes and religious groupings. The irony of the high-status women often being made invisible via social norms only increases the social distance between them and the poor or low-status women. The norms for different groups of women are quite different and so what a woman 'chooses' is couched in her specific context, her economic / political / caste / religion / lineage and locality as well as her marital status and whether she has borne children. Because of this differentiation it is dangerous to generalise.

Interpretation of Cultural Factors

Qualitative research helps in exploring the meanings people attach to women doing domestic work. Across India, there is a broad cultural tendency to 'Hinduisation', such that even among India's muslims and other minorities some cultural patterns mimic those of the dominant Hindu groups. These include dowry, patrilocality, and arranged marriages for instance. Agarwal's review of inheritance by widows goes so far as to ignore all minority ST and Muslim groups, using only Hinduism-based examples and sources, which is perhaps unfortunate, but does reflect the widespread understanding that the gender order is of a nearly nation-wide nature and is not simply or solely embedded in religious groupings and civil law.

Agarwal's work crosses over between WID, GAD, institutionalism and cultural studies, because she has studied both the dynamics of household bargaining and the roles of religious difference and state-wise policy differentiation across the four countries of South Asia.

The delicate interplay of culture and local social norms leads to about five aspects of housewifery roles which are often perceived (not by all, but predominantly in most places) to be positively valued. These include (1) 'Sanskritisation' a process of displaying upward mobility by invoking and demonstrating honourable roles for women , e.g. as the provider of refreshments at functions, the calm manager of the household, and the beautiful object of admiration. (2) Even women who have professional occupations can successfully continue with their housewifery roles by employing other women to do much of the nitty gritty daily work so there is no problem with the double burden. (3) Women can take care of these matters without involving their employed menfolk. Men's long working hours support the full domestic responsibilities falling upon mothers' and wives' shoulders at home. The exclusion of men from the role of housewife, and from all records of extra-domestic work in NSS 55th round, demonstrates a growing patriarchal role demarcation in India. It is widely seen as more dignified for men to be uninvolved with domestic matters. (4) Women who do farming work can be seen as the helpmeet and unpaid worker of the male household head. This sexist and androcentric approach to farming households is a patriarchal value implicitly held very widely in society (for comparative evidence in which French farm accountants are considered as 'just wives', see Delphy and Leonard, 1992). Finally, (5) many people prefer women to act submissive and deferential toward elders and toward men. Acting deferential is considered to be appropriate and to keep the women in safe relationship networks which protect the women in a patronising way. These women insist that they have a large and valued 'private life' (e.g. women observing purdah who sit with other such women in a household courtyard chatting). However they are effectively then barred from engaging in public life.

To the extent that people hold these values they will intersubjectively create spaces in which middle-income women act as housewives.

The opponents of patriarchy are many and diverse, and their voice has been loudest among the academic authors already cited. They argue that deferential and excessively private roles are bad for women. By listing them, we enable readers to consider the pros and cons of the U curve situation rather systematically. (1) Dependency of most wives on a male breadwinner and his family's property. (2) Low bargaining power of women so that they cannot easily exit, or threaten to exit, a marital home even if there is alcoholism, an affair, or domestic violence. (3) The woman who has neither job nor self-employment can, at times, be isolated and lose confidence. (4) Poor educational outcomes of girls. (5) Women fall behind in their knowledge of their own profession or occupation. (6) Ultimately in this context women are often seen in a diminutive, degraded, and denigrated light. Their work is seen as 'helping' work even if it would be classified as 'employment' or 'self-employment' if done by a man. (7) Women who are not in relationships are seen as exceptional, threatening, odd and often mentally unstable. (8) Sexual harassment of working women goes hand in hand with the patronisation of non-working women. (9) The earnings of girls and women may be seen as 'pin money', as temporary, as nonessential.

Conclusion

The study has described a complex situation in which a U curve of women's employment by education levels is caused by a mixture of economic and cultural factors. The whole study is suffused with interdisciplinary pluralism so that these factors can be taken into account in a balanced way. So-called 'inactive' people can be divided into the inactive *per se* versus those who were recorded as doing some extradomestic work. The ILO definition of unemployment is not sufficiently detailed to help us clarify the nature of the borderline between employment and non-employment. This borderline seems to be permeable and socially constructed.

The U curve was explored in some detail using statistical evidence. The study ended with a list of the felt advantages and disadvantages of women working as housewives—the typical scenario at the bottom of the U among middle-educated women. The standard norms for housewives are adapted for poor women, who often have a double or triple burden of work, and for rich women who can employ others to assist them whilst still being the manager of a household. Great heterogeneity among women is therefore noted. One hopes that a diversification of values (especially about men and women doing domestic work) and a serious ethical discussion of the morality of patriarchy can be based on this kind of overview study. We cited many authors who have engaged in this serious discussion but we also note that the situation appears to be getting worse instead of better in India since its economic liberalisation around 1991.

NOTES AND REFERENCES

Afshar, H. and S. Barrientos (1998). *Women, globalisation and fragmentation in the developing world.* New York, St. Martin's Press.

Agarwal, B. (1994). A *Field of One's Own: Gender and Land Rights in South Asia.* Cambridge: Cambridge University Press.

Agarwal, B. (1997). "Bargaining and Gender Relations: Within and Beyond the Household." *Feminist Economics* 3(1): 1-50.

Agarwal, B. (1998) "Widows versus Daughters or Widows as Daughters? Property, Land, and Economic Security in Rural India", *Modern Asian Studies*, 32:1, 1-48.

Agarwal, B. (2003). "Women's Land Rights and the Trap of Neo-Conservatism: A Response to Jackson." *Journal of Agrarian Change* 3(4): 571-585.

Bhowmik, S. and R. Jhabvala (1996). Rural Women Manage their Own Producer Cooperatives: Self-Employed Women's Association (SEWA) / Banaskantha Women's Association in Western India. Speaking Out: Women's Economic Empowerment in South Asia. M. Carr, M. Chen and R. Jhabvala. London, IT Publications, Aga Khan Foundation and UNIFEM: 105-125.

Chakravarti, U. (1993). "Conceptualising Brahmanical Patriarchy in Early India—Gender, Caste, Class and State." *Economic and Political Weekly* 28(14): 579-585.

Chatterjee, M. (1993). Struggle and Development: Changing the Reality of Self-Employed Workers. Women at the Center: Development Issues and Practices for the 1990s. Eds. G. Young, V. Samarasinghe and K. Kusterer. Connecticut, Kumarian Press: 81-93.

Custers, P. (2000) *Capital Accumulation and Women's Labour in Asian Economies*, London: Sed Press.

DaCorta, L., and Davuluri Venkateswarlu (1999). "Unfree Relations and the Feminisation of Agricultural Labour in Andhra Pradesh, 1970-95." *Journal of Peasant Studies* 26(2-3): 73-139.

Delphy, C. and D. Leonard (1992). Familiar exploitation: a new analysis of marriage in contemporary western societies. Cambridge, Polity 1992.

Deshpande, S. and L. K. Deshpande, (1993), "Gender-Based Discrimination in the Urban Labour Market", ch. 10 in (Papola and Sharma, 1993).

Dijkstra, A. G. and J. Plantenga (1997). Gender and Economics: A European Perspective. London, Routledge.

Dreze, J., and Amartya Sen (1995). India: Economic Development and Social Opportunity. Oxford, Clarendon Press.

Dube, L. (1988). "On the Construction of Gender—Hindu Girls in Patrilineal India." Economic and Political Weekly 23(18): WS11-WS19.

Dunn, D. (1993). "Gender Inequality in Education and Employment in the Scheduled Castes and Tribes of India." Population Research and Policy Review 12(1): 53-70.

Folbre, N. (1986). "Cleaning House: New Perspectives on Households and Economic Development." Journal of Development Economics 22: | 5-40.

Fraser, N. (1994). "After the Family Wage: Gender Equity and the Welfare State." Political Theory 22(4): 591-618.

Gautum, M. and H. Tripathi (2001). "Women in Goat Husbandry." Man in India 81(3&4): 313-320.

Gibbons-Trikha, J. (2003) "Sanctuary: A Women's Refuge in India", Journal of Developing Societies, 19:1, 47-89.

Gulati, L. (1995). "Women and Family in India—Continuity and Change." Indian Journal of Social Work 56(2): 133-154.

Harriss-White, B. (2003). India Working: Essays on Society and Economy. Cambridge, Cambridge University Press.

Hart, G. (1992). "Household Production Reconsidered: Gender, Labour Conflict, and Technological Change in Malaysia's Muda Region." *World Development* 20(6): 809-823.

Heyer, J. (1992) "The Role of Dowry and Daughters' Marriages in the Accumulation and Distribution of Capital in a South Indian Community", *Journal of International Development*, 4:4, August, 419-436.

Hodgson, G. M. (2004). The Evolution of Institutional Economics: Agency, Structure and Darwinism in American Institutionalism. London, Routledge.

Jackson, C. and R. Pearson (1998*). Feminist visions of development: gender, analysis and policy.* London, Routledge.

Jacob, P. (2001). "Magnitude of the Women Work Force in India: An Appraisal of the NSS Estimates and Methods." Sarvekshana XXIV, No. 4

Jejeebhoy, S. J. and Z. A. Sathar (2001). "Women's autonomy in India and Pakistan: The influence of religion and region." Population and Development Review 27(4): 687-.

Kabeer, N. (1994). Reversed realities: gender hierarchies in development thought. London; New York, Verso.

Kalpagam, U. (1994). Labour and Gender: Survival in Urban India. London, New Delhi and Thousand Oaks, Sage.

Kapadia, K. (1995). Siva and Her Sisters: Gender, Caste and Class in Rural South India. Boulder and Oxford, Westview Press.

Kapadia, K. (1999). "Gender ideologies and the formation of rural industrial classes in South India today." *Contributions to Indian Sociology* 33(1-2): 329-352.

Kingdon, G. G. "Labour force participation, returns to education and sex-discrimination." *Gender and Employment in India:* 249-277.

Mathur, A. (1994). "Work Participation, Gender and Economic Development: A Quantitative Anatomy of the Indian Scenario." *The Journal of Development Studies* 30(2): 466-504.

Mies, M. (1980) "Capitalist Development and Subsistence Reproduction: Rural Women in India", Bulletin of Concerned Asian Scholars, XII, 1, pp. 2-14.

Mies, M. (1982). The Lace Makers of Narsapur: Indian Housewives Produce for the World Market. London, Sed Books.

Mies, M. (1998, orig. 1989). *Patriarchy and accumulation on a world scale: women in the international division of labour.* London, Sed.

Mohanty, M., Ed. (2004). Class, Caste, Gender. Readings in Indian Government and Politics. New Delhi, London, Sage Publications.

Narasimhan, S. (1999). Empowering Women: An Alternative Strategy from Rural India. New Delhi, Thousand Oaks and London, Sage.

Narasimhan, S. (2002). "Gender, class, and caste schisms in affirmative action policies: The curious case of India's women's reservation bill." Feminist Economics 8(2): 183-190.

Olsen, W. K. (1996). *Rural Indian Social Relations.* Delhi, Oxford University Press.

Olsen, W. K. (2001). "Social Statistics and the Indian Labour Market." *Journal of Critical Realism* 4: 11-16.

Olsen, W.K. and S. Mehta (2005) The Right to Work and Differentiation in India, conference paper, the Indian Society for Labour Economics, Delhi. Available from the authors.

Olsen, W. K. (2006). "Pluralism, Poverty, and Sharecropping: Cultivating Open-Mindedness in Poverty Studies." *Journal of Development Studies*, forthcoming.

Papola, T. S., A.N. Sharma, et al. (1999). Gender and employment in India. New Delhi, Indian Society of Labour Economics and Institute of Economic Growth Delhi in association with Vikas Pub. House.

Planning Commission, 2002. National Human Development Report 2001. Delhi: Government of India, March.

Poitevin, G. and H. Rairkar (1993 (orig. French 1985)). *Indian Peasant Women Speak Up*. London, Orient Longman.

Raghuram, P. (2001). "Caste and gender in the organisation of paid domestic work in India." *Work Employment and Society* 15(3): 607-617.

Ramachandran, V. K. (1990). *Wage Labour and Unfreedom in Agriculture: An Indian Case Study*. Oxford, Clarendon Press.

Rogaly, B. (1997). "Embedded Markets: Hired Labour Arrangements in West Bengal Agriculture." Oxford Development Studies 25(1): 209-223.

Shariff, Abusaleh (1999) India Human Development Report: A Profile of the Indian States in the 1990s, Delhi: National Council for Applied Economic Research.

Sharma, M. (1985). "Caste, Class, and Gender Production and Reproduction in North India." *Journal of Peasant Studies* 12(4): 57-88.

Skoufias, E. (1992). "Labour market opportunities and intrafamily time allocation in rural households in South Asia." *Journal of Development Economics* 40: 277-310.

Skoufias, E. (1993). "Seasonal Labour Utilisation in Agriculture: Theory and Evidence from Agrarian Households in India." *American Journal of Agricultural Economics* 75: 20-32.

Skoufias, E. (1995). "Household Resources, Transaction Costs, and Adjustment through Land Tenancy." *Land Economics* 71(1): 42-56.

Srivastava, N. (2003). "And Promises to Keep: The Challenge of Gender Disparities in India's Economic Development." *Indian Journal of Economics* LXXXIV(332): 123-146.

Swaminathan, P. (2002). The Violence of Gender-Biased Development: Going Beyond Social and Demographic Indicators. The Violence of Development: The Politics of Identity, Gender and Social Inequalities in India. K. Kapadia. London, Delhi and NY, Kali Books and Sed Press: 69-141.

Toye, J. (2003). Changing Perspectives in Development Economics. Rethinking Development Economics. H.-J. Chang. London, Anthem Press.

Venkateswarlu, D. and L. Dacorta (2001). "Transformations in the Age and Gender of Unfree Workers on Hybrid Cotton Seed Farms in Andhra Pradesh." *Journal of Peasant Studies* 28(3): 1-36.

10

POVERTY, MIGRATION AND URBANISATION IN INDIA

Migration and urbanisation are direct manifestations of the process of economic development in space, particularly in the contemporary phase of globalisation. Understanding the causes and consequences of the former in terms of the changes in the distribution of population and economic activities, along with the success and failures of the interventions by state and other organisations would be extremely important for evaluating the available policy options and exploring areas of possible strategic intervention.

A large part of migration and urbanisation in the less developed countries have historically been linked to stagnation and volatility of agriculture and lack of sectoral diversification within agrarian economy, India being no exception to this. The growth rates in agricultural production and income has been noted to be low, unstable and disparate across regions over the past several decades, resulting in lack of livelihood opportunities in rural areas. A low rate of infrastructural investment in public sector in the period of structural adjustment—necessary for keeping budgetary deficits low—also have affected agriculture adversely. This has led to out-migration from several backward rural areas, most of the migrants being absorbed within urban informal economy. The primary concern of migration related policies must therefore be addressing the problems reflecting ecological footprints of large cities in regions that have become chronically out-migrating and stabilising their agrarian economy through creation of livelihood opportunities. Although, the poor have a right to the city, they should not be forced to shift as "forced migration and transferring encompass more poignant vulnerabilities". Enabling rural people avail urban amenities without having to shift to a town and strengthening rural urban linkages and commutation would also be important maneuver in addressing the problem of rapid urbanisation in a few regions.

Withdrawal or displacement of labour force from rural economy and their absorption in urban sectors have created serious stress in receiving regions as well. The capacity of the cities and towns to assimilate the migrants by providing employment, access to land, basic amenities etc. are limited. The problem have acquired severity as migrants have shown high selectivity in choosing their destinations (understandably linked with availability of employment and other opportunities), leading to regionally unbalanced urbanisation as also distortions in urban hierarchy.

The UNFPA (2007) regards concentration of poverty, growth of slums and social deprivation in cities as the major challenge of development in less developed countries2. It is in this context that the MDG target 11 which stipulates significant improvement in the conditions of 100 million slum dwellers assumes importance. The Report of UN Secretary General of 2000 entitled We the Peoples makes it explicit that there should be no attempt to prevent formation of new slums in order to make the cities more attractive for globalisation through "sanitisation" by pushing out the slum population. The Taskforce for Improving the Lives of Slum Dwellers therefore reformulates the target 11 to suggest improving "substantially the lives of at least 100 million slum dwellers while providing adequate alternatives to new slum formation by 2020". The Taskforce further specifies that the challenge of target 11 will be two-fold. It would be (a) to improve the lives of existing slum dwellers and simultaneously (b) to plan for adequate alternatives for future urban growth. The message comes loud and clear that the national and urban governments, civil society organisations must come forward with policies to mitigate the problems of these large cities, not only through micro level initiatives of improving slum conditions and access to basic amenities but also by adopting macro strategy of balanced regional development.

Growth of Slums

Rural urban migration has often been considered the major factor for growth of slums in urban areas. United Nations has warned that rapid urbanisation and migration would lead to tripling of slum population by 2050, hindering the attainment of the MDG target, noted above. One must however point out that the technological shift from cheap labour based modes of mass production to knowledge based system is likely to bring down the demand for migrant workers, particularly of unskilled labour force and decelerate urbanisation. Given this emerging scenario, one would ask "Is indeed the scale of migration and urbanisation very high and alarming?"

The rates of urbanisation have already declined in many parts of the world, much more than what can be attributed to decline in natural growth in populations. While it is true that the share of natural growth in incremental urban population would decline even the rate of RU migration is likely to decelerate in future years. Most of the mega cities have grown at a rate much below what was projected by UN organisations6. Migrants are often noted to be better off and relatively skilled than those left behind implying that the unskilled peasantry is finding it increasingly difficult to put a foothold in the urban centres in the present globalising environment. Migration to the large cities that have global linkages has become relatively more difficult as persons need access to information, market friendly skills and "some sort of bank roll". The implications of the deceleration in the rates of migration and urbanisation need to be analysed in the context of both sending and receiving regions.

It would be important to look at migration not always as a negative phenomenon -reflecting misery and lack of livelihood opportunities in the outmigrating regions and absence of basic amenities and health hazards in inmigrating regions. It needs to be seen also as an opportunity being taken up by people to improve their socio-economic conditions. There are evidences that this is currently being taken up by skilled and better off sections. A large number of science and technology personnel in backward regions are locating themselves in a handful of cities and developed regions, analogous to the trends and pattern in international migration. While a section of the elite and highly skilled persons are "increasingly enjoying "benefits of migration, barriers to poorer migrants are increasing." It may be possible to "use urban dynamics to help reduce poverty" and make migration an instrument in the strategy of poverty alleviation and hence be incorporated into a programme for meeting the first and the most important target under MDG. It is important to harness the potential of migration in the context of development and poverty alleviation. It would, therefore, make sense to discuss measures to promote orderly migration instead of considering proposals to discourage mobility of population.

The argument that poor constitute a large majority of rural urban migrants and consequently account for much of the incremental urban population is not borne out with the recent data in the Indian context as most of the million plus cities report significant decline in the level of poverty, much more than in small towns. However, with appropriate changes in the nature and form of urban expansion, as envisaged under inclusive growth strategy in the Eleventh Plan, the present exclusionary urban growth based on restrictions to migration and slum evictions can be reversed. Under a more proactive vision of inclusive development, provision of land for the poor can be made within the cities, as envisaged under the above mentioned document. Indeed, all concerned international agencies should examine the possibilities of supporting economic opportunities by providing the migrants access to also infrastructure and basic services, besides removing discriminatory regulations that deny migrants equal access to employment and basic services.

Migration and urbanisation must also be looked in the context of emergence of global cities, many of which have acquired vibrancy in recent years by establishing linkages with national and international market. It is argued that the process of urbanisation in India, as in other developing countries, is being determined by macro economic factors at national and global levels and is not strongly linked to the developments in rural economy. The strategy of economic reform and globalisation has given a boost to growth of industries and business in these global cities, resulting in inflow of capital from outside the region or country as also investment by local entrepreneurs. Given this perspective, it would be important to consider policies to harness the potential of migration in these and other urban centres for promoting a balanced settlement structure, ensuring equity and sustainability in development process.

It would be erroneous to restrict the analysis of urbanisation and migration to a few mega cities and ignore the smaller towns in India as the data suggest that the latter report higher levels of poverty and greater deprivation in terms of quality of life. Furthermore, globalisation strategies have opened up possibilities of resource mobilisation for large cities by strengthening their internal resource base and enabling them to attract funds from global capital market and institutional sources. Unfortunately, most of these avenues have not opened up for smaller towns as their economic base is very low, offering little possibility to local government for internal resource mobilisation with no business opportunity for the actors in capital market. Given this somewhat disturbing scenario, it would be a challenge, as stipulated by UNFPA (2007), to divert and promote "bulk of population growth in smaller cities and towns" that are seriously "underserved in housing, transportation, piped water, waste disposal and other services". These have "fewer human, financial and technical resources at their disposal" and their "capabilities for planning and implementation can be exceedingly weak". This, indeed, is an area of policy intervention in case the government is serious about its commitment to alleviate poverty and usher in a process of sustainable urban development.

Given the above perspective and concerns, the present study begins by overviewing the trends and processes of urbanisation and migration in India at the macro and state levels over the last five decades in the section which follows the present introductory section. An attempt is made here to explain the temporal and regional variation in levels of migration and urbanisation and link it with the growth dynamics in the country. The third section probes further into the factors behind migration in different size class of settlements and its impact on the household and individual characteristics, based on unit level data from National Sample Survey, focusing on women and children. The programmes and schemes for urban development in operation during the last two and a half decades, particularly those launched in the wake of the 74th Constitutional Amendment Act have been reviewed in the fourth section. It also analyses how the emerging institutional structure and new initiatives in urban governance and planning, stipulating a shift away from Master Plan approach to preparation of vision documents, engagement of stakeholders in urban planning, tapping of capital market, judicial interventions etc. are impacting or could impact on the migration, urbanisation and morphology of the cities. The fifth section attempts an assessment of the impact of the programme and policies of the government and rapidly changing institutional system on urban structure and morphology of cities. The final section summarises the major findings, identifies major areas of concern and puts forward a policy perspective for dealing with the problems.

MIGRATION, URBANISATION AND ECONOMIC DEVELOPMENT

Macro Trends in Internal Migration and Urbanisation

It may be pointed out that migration in the Indian sub-continent has historically been low. Researchers like Kingsley Davis have attributed this to prevalence of caste system, joint families, traditional values, diversity of language and culture, lack of education and predominance of agriculture and semi-feudal land relations. By the Davisian logic, too, improvement in the levels of education and that of transport and communication facilities, shift of workforce from agriculture to industry and tertiary activities etc. would increase mobility.

The pattern of internal migration (excluding the international migrants) has been presented in Table 3 using the data from Population Census. It may be seen here that mobility of population measured through percentage of lifetime migrants has declined systematically during 1961-91. This is so both in rural as well as urban areas. An analysis of intercensal migrants (those shifting place of residence during the past decade) reveals a sharper decline. The decline in the mobility of women, wherein socio-cultural factors are likely to be relatively more important, has been less than for men.

The sharp decline in case of male migrants, both in case of rural as well as urban areas, has been attributed, besides the rigidities of the agrarian system, growing regionalism etc., to inhospitable environment they are confronting in the developed regions receiving the migrants as also urban centres.

Focusing on the urban segment, one observes that the sluggish growth of migrants compared to resident population in urban areas has brought down the percentage of lifetime (male) migrants from 37.5 to 26.0 during 1961-91 and that of intercensal migrants from 23.8 to 11.7, although the three decades—particularly seventies—have seen relatively high growth of urban population. Correspondingly, the share of intercensal interstate migrants has declined from 7.9 per cent to 3.3 per cent.

Do the data from Population Census 2001 mark a departure from the past trends? This indeed seems to be the case since, excepting the intercensal migrants, the percentage for all other migration categories have reported a rise during nineties, both for men as well as women. There are nonetheless serious problems of data comparability particularly relating to the duration of stay at the place of enumeration, as discussed above. Consequently, the significant fall in the percentage of intercensal migrants can not be used for temporal comparison, without an adjustment.

The more important questions would be, whether the data on total migrants too have been vitiated as a result of this factor? Are there reasons to believe that given the motivation among migrants to report longer duration of stay than the actual, particularly in the cities, they would be prompted to identify themselves as non migrants? And, has it been possible for them to do that at a much larger scale compared to earlier Censuses? To check this hypothesis, an attempt has been made to estimate the number of rural to urban (RU) migrants coming during a decade through an indirect method, using the population from Census. Using a simple identity, the incremental urban population during a decade can be decomposed into four categories. These are: (a) natural increase, (b) new towns less declassified towns (outside the agglomerations), (c) merging of towns and jurisdictional changes in agglomerations and (d) RU migration.

Based on this, RU migration has been estimated as a residual factor, which should be free from the bias of under-reporting as discussed in the preceding section. This as a percentage of incremental urban population (men and women combined) has been obtained as 21 per cent in the nineties, marginally less than noted in the previous decade. This would be in line with the proposition that the share of intercensal migrants has fallen continuously over the past few decades, including the nineties. One may add that even the percentage of lifetime migrants, which in 2001 is slightly above that of 1991, is significantly below those of 1961 and 1971. There are thus reasons to believe that Indian population has not become more mobile, if their mobility has not actually declined over the years.

The data from NSS for the past two decades too confirm the declining trend of migration for males, both in rural and urban areas, although the fall is less than that reported in the Census. Importantly, the migration rates had declined to all time low levels in 1993 but after that, there has been slight recovery. The fact that percentages of migrants in 1993-94 are marginally above the 1999-00, similar to what was noted using the data from Population Census, may be attributed to more liberal definition of migrants adopted in the 55th round of NSS, as discussed above. However, considering the period from 1983 to 1999-00, one would reconfirm that mobility has declined over the period. In case of women, the percentage of migrants has gone up marginally as this is determined by socio-cultural factors that respond slowly with time. The general conclusion thus emerges unmistakably is that mobility of men, which is often linked to the strategy of seeking livelihood, has gone down systematically over the past few decades.

The increasing immobility in the country has been attributed to growing assertion of regional and language identity, adoption of Master Plans and land use restrictions at the city level etc., that have been considered fallouts of the process of globalisation. All these would discount the proposition that the mobility of labour, operationalised through market, would ensure optimal distribution of economic activities in space. It is important to note that it is no longer the avowed reactionary policies of the state that are restricting migration. It is the functioning of the market for land and basic services combined with a sense of 'otherness' that is the major barrier.

Given the sluggish growth in migration, both in rural and urban areas, one would not expect rapid growth of urban population in the country since the natural growth in urban areas has been less than that in rural areas. There have been, however, significant fluctuations in urban growth rates owing to factors that are not linked with urban dynamics. The growth rate (annual exponential) during 1941-51 was extremely high, 3.5 per cent per annum but that has been attributed to migration from East and West Pakistan at the time of partition of the country which brought in massive inflow from across the border, largely into urban settlements in India. The growth rate declined significantly during fifties to 2.3 per cent but that has been attributed to definitional factors as the Census of 1961 brought in rigorous application of demographic criteria in identifying urban centres. The growth rate would therefore been considered to be an underestimate. The definitional or other exogenous factors affected the growth rates the least in the sixties and consequently the growth rate of 3.2 per cent during 1961-71 can be taken to reflect the real urban tempo in the country.

All time high growth of 3.8 per cent was noted during 1971-81. Partly, this growth can be explained in terms of less rigourous application of criterion relating to non agricultural workforce in identifying urban centres and a more liberal definition of urban agglomeration. The annual growth rate (exponential) of urban population in India has gone from that point onwards. It came down to 3.1 per cent during 1981-91 and further to 2.7 per cent during 1991-2001. This declining trend of urbanisation in the country is in conformity with growing immobility of Indian population, despite growing information flows, accentuation of regional inequality etc. The trend also goes against the popular theories of "urban explosion", "over urbanisation" and "rural exodus".

Regional Pattern and Growth Dynamics

Neo-classical models of growth and labour mobility stipulate that spatial disparity in development, ceteris paribus, would result in migration from backward to developed regions which would help in bringing about optimality in the spatial distribution of labour and economic activities. The mobility pattern observed in India fits well in these models. The analysis of interstate migrants, attempted on the basis of Census at the time of Independence reveals that the less developed states had a high percentage of net out-migrants. The developed states, on the other hand, were in-migrating in character.

In the post Independence period until 1990, however, migration pattern turned out to be different (Table 6). There was a decline in the rates of net outmigration from the backward states like Bihar, Rajasthan, Uttar Pradesh etc. Importantly, Madhya Pradesh and Orissa stood out as exceptions as these reported significant inflow of population. This could be explained in terms of massive public sector investment, resulting in creation of job opportunities in industry and business in the two states. Local population, unfortunately, were not able to take advantage of these developments due to their low level of literacy and skill. Correspondingly, the developed states like Karnataka, Maharashtra, Tamil Nadu and West Bengal that had attracted large scale inmigration during the colonial period, reported decline in inmigration rates. Only the state of Gujarat did not show this decline due to its growing dominance in the industrial map of India. Haryana reporting high inmigration rates may be explained in terms of migration from Punjab due to political instability and communal tensions. The data for the nineties, however, suggest some sort of stepping up of outmigration from poor states and of immigration in to developed states, leading to possibly a marginal increase in the rate of overall migration in the country.

A few scholars have explained the decline in interstate migration (except nineties) in terms of developmental programmes, launched by central and state governments in the post Independence period promoting a spatially balanced development. Furthermore, better transport, communication and commutation facilities are supposed to alleviate the need to shift residence for employment or education, since people can now commute to neighbouring cities and towns. Undoubtedly, there is some truth in these arguments but are not adequate to explain the growing immobility. An analysis of regional structure of development reveals that inter-state inequality in several dimensions of economic and social development has not declined and in certain dimensions, this has gone up.

It would be interesting to look at the migration pattern in relation to that of urbanisation. The pattern of urban growth (or urban rural growth differential) across states during the first four decades since Independence exhibit negative relationship with their level of economic development articulated through income or consumption expenditure in per capita terms, share of industries in state income, agricultural productivity etc. The poor states like Orissa, Bihar, Rajasthan and Madhya Pradesh that experienced rapid demographic growth in urban areas were also those that reported low productivity and high unemployment in agrarian sectors and heavy pressure on urban infrastructural facilities, suggesting presence of push factors behind RU migration. The slowing down of out migration from these to developed states until early nineties, as noted above, meant that the displaced persons from agrarian system sought absorption in the urban centres within the state.

In contrast, urban growth exhibits positive correlation with indicators of infrastructural and economic development both in rural and urban areas, and negative relation with poverty in the nineties. The states that are experiencing low or no growth in farm and non-farm productivity, high unemployment, severe malnutrition etc. are reporting sluggish urbanisation. Most of the cities and towns in developed states have, on the other hand, experienced rapid demographic growth. The data suggest that the RU migrants belong to relatively higher economic and social strata compared to the non-migrants in different size class or urban settlements. Understandably, the cities in developed states are not getting their migrants driven by natural, social or economic calamities but those who have higher levels of skill or economic assets. It is this group who find it easier to establish linkages with the economy of the large cities through socio-cultural channels and avail the "opportunity" offered through migration. Many of them are traveling beyond their states. The negative perspective which characterises and dictates large part of the contemporary literature on migration, therefore, needs to be urgently revisited.

Social Implications of Migration

An analysis of the process of urbanisation since Independence reveals that it has been large city oriented during colonial as also post colonial period. This is manifested in a high percentage of urban population being concentrated in class I cities that offer better employment and earning opportunities. This has gone up systematically over the past few decades. Partly this is due to graduation of lower order towns into class I category. There is nonetheless adequate empirical evidence that these cities have grown at a distinctly higher rate than the lower order towns. The pattern of growth has remained similar over the past few decades although there is a general deceleration in urban growth in all size categories during eighties and nineties. Importantly, the edge that the class I cities have over class II, III, IV and class V towns in terms of the growth rate has gone up during nineties. The gaps in the growth rates have widened. Urban growth has become more unbalanced as developed states and class I cities, with strong economic base, raising resources through institutional borrowing and innovative credit instruments, have successfully attracted population as also economic activities. There, however, has been a modest decline in their population growth but that can be attributed largely to fertility decline.

The small and medium towns with population below 50,000 have on an average grown at a relatively slower pace during the seventies and eighties. In the backward states, however, these had exhibited rapid growth, similar or even higher than that of the class I cities during sixties, seventies and eighties. Detailed empirical analysis reveals that the demographic growth in these towns was not backed up by manufacturing\ commercial activities or infrastructural facilities in these states. Rural poverty, stagnant agriculture, absence of sectoral diversification etc., therefore, were the factors in explaining their demographic growth. Importantly, during nineties, these (Census) towns, have experienced significant deceleration in their demographic growth. Even their number has gone down during 1991-01 which signifies some sort or urban crisis in the context of development dynamics in the country.

Slowing down of the rates of RU migration and urbanisation and concentration of demographic and economic growth in relatively developed states as well as around a few global centres, thus, seems to be a logical outcome of the new economic policy. There has been a paradigm shift in the process of urbanisation, accompanying the programmes of structural reform. Many among the larger cities have been able to corner much of the resources, available for infrastructural and industrial development both from private and public sector, as noted above. The small and medium towns located away from these "global centres of growth", particularly those in backward regions, have failed in this which explains their low demographic growth.

Poverty and Vulnerability as Correlates of Migration and Urbanisation

A cross classification of migration data across consumption expenditure categories reveals that at the macro level, economic deprivation is less of a factor in migration, both in rural and urban areas. There is a sharp decline in the percentage of persons reporting economic factors as the reason for mobility in recent years. As many as 36 per cent of the migrants of less than one year duration, among rural men have reported new/better employment or transfer as the reason for their migration decision in 1983, as per the NSS data. This has come down to 25 per cent only in 1999-00. For women, the percentage has declined from 5 to 3 only. The economic factors have become less important in migration decisions among migrants in urban areas as well. For men, the percentage has gone down from 46 to 34 while in case of women, the corresponding are 8 to 3. The increase in the share of women among migrants under all categories and durations is yet another indication of growing importance of non-economic factors since marriage and joining the family are the major factors responsible for their mobility.

The migration rate for males is as high as 23.3 per cent in the category with the highest monthly per capita expenditure (MPCE) in rural areas in 1999-00. The figure goes down systematically in lower expenditure categories, the rate being as low as 4.3 at the bottom. The same is valid in case of women migrants, the percentage varying from 31.6 to 57.0. An identical pattern is observed in urban areas as well. The above, however, is not a clinching evidence that economically better off people are more likely to migrate to avail new economic opportunities elsewhere, since the reported expenditure levels reflect the post migration situation. One can stipulate that the migrants have moved to higher consumption expenditure category after or because of their mobility. However, such post migration upward movement may not be high so as to render the hypothesis that the people in high expenditure categories are more likely to migrate, invalid.

The persons who have gone to any other place for 60 days or more during the last six months from the date of survey and returned back may be termed as seasonal or short duration migrants. A large segment of them in urban areas could be those who are adopting coping strategies or making temporary shifts in lean seasons for livelihood and survival. One would then stipulate a positive association of seasonal migrants with poverty. Alternately, seasonal migration can be attributed not to push factors but to short duration transfer of regular workers, temporary posting of marketing and extension workers etc. Interestingly, migration pattern reveals that poverty is not the key factor behind seasonal migration in urban areas. Indeed, this mobility is not very high among the poor when compared to middle class households. The bottom 40 per cent of the population account for only 29 per cent of the total seasonal migrants. The share of the third quintile is, however, 29 per cent, much above its population share. These suggest that even such short term opportunities are taken more by the well off sections in urban areas.

Migration rates for Scheduled Castes (SC) and Scheduled Tribes (ST) are around 20.4 per cent in rural areas in 1999-00. The rate for the remaining segment of the population is about 25 per cent. Among women, too, the migration rate for the non-backward classes is marginally above that of the others. One would infer that poverty and immiserisation, often linked with SC, ST and other backward castes, have not led to massive push factor migration.

A unit level analysis of the 55th Round data has been attempted focusing on the urban areas. It is noted that urban households/ population are equally distributed into the three categories based on mobility—rural to urban (RU) migrant, urban to urban (UU) migrant and non migrant. A large section of UU migrants may be reporting mobility due to transfer of jobs, business trips and availing better employment opportunities and hence has the least poverty, less than even the non-migrants. RU migrant category which has a substantial proportion of socially and economically displaced persons understandably reports a high incidence of poverty.

Poverty among urban households classified by the number of members reporting migration brings out yet another dimension of social dynamics. It is evident that the poorest households are those that send one or a few of their members to other destinations. However, the entire household shifts to a new place when the in-migrant belongs to economically better-off strata. These households are in fact more affluent than the non-migrant households as the incidence of poverty here is the lowest.

Percentage of immigrants in different employment categories reveals an interestimg pattern. Poverty among the salaried persons and those in regular employment is the lowest which is understandable. The next lowest is reported, not very surprisingly, by the unemployed persons. This is a reflection of the capability of these persons to stay out of the labour market (linked to their assets, savings etc.) as they can afford to wait for appropriate jobs. Casual workers report the highest level of poverty which should be a matter of concern for the architects of National Employment Guarantee Scheme which excludes the urban areas. The next highest poverty is recorded by the persons classified as others, comprising largely those outside labour force. This is because large sections of these people are children and aged dependents. Indeed, the households that report a large number of dependents have greater risk of falling below the poverty line. Importantly, this category claims more than 64 per cent of the total urban population in the country implying that in absolute terms this would be the single largest component, requiring urgent attention under any anti poverty programme.

Poverty declines smoothly as one moves from illiteracy to graduation level of education and above. This could be a manifestation of the economic pay-off of education but could also be due to the capability of richer sections of population to send their children to schools and higher/better institutions of learning.

Probabilities for the individuals to fall below poverty line have been calculated from the logit regression model (excluding the seasonal migrants). The plotting of the probability values for the RU migrants, UU migrants and the non-migrants across different size class of urban centres. Noticeably, the probability of falling below poverty line is the highest for non-migrants, followed by RU migrants.

The lowest probability is noted in case of UU migrants. Further, the vividly shows that the probability of being poor declines as one moves from small to medium and large cities, for all the migration categories.

The relationship between incidence of poverty and levels of education for RU and UU migrants and non-migrants. Probability of falling below poverty line declines monotonically with increase in level of education, for all the three categories. However, the curve for the non-migrants is above that of the other two categories. One would note a higher incidence of poverty among the locals than the RU migrants which again is higher than UU migrants, for all levels education. Impact of education is seen as positive in all city sizes.

The data from the 55th and 61st round of NSS suggest that the country is coming out of the jobless growth syndrome. The employment rates by usual (principal) status in 15-59 age-group have gone up both for men and more for women during 1999-04. New employment opportunities are coming up within affluent domestic sector as also select industries and regions/urban centres that are linked to global market. While poor constitute a segment among the migrants, a substantial number of them belong to the middle and high income categories who are able to grab the new opportunities. This improved employment opportunities, nonetheless, has not restored the workforce participation rates (WPR) to the level of 1993-94 for men. In case of women, however, the WPR in 2004-05 are higher not only than those of 1999-00 but also than that of 1993-94. One gets a relatively less alarming picture by weekly and daily status as the growth rates by these are higher than by usual status during the entire decade ending in 2004-05. Increase in current status employment has generally been considered to be a positive factor for generation of income at the lowest economic stratum.

The overview suggests that the employment trend during last five years (1999-04) is disconcerting, particularly in case of urban India. This can be linked with the fact that the annual rate of decline in urban poverty has been significantly below that in rural poverty. The rate of decline has been estimated to be lower in case of urban areas during the entire decade 1993-2004 than rural areas but the gap between the two rates is very high during the later half.

One must look at urban employment scenario by considering the small medium and large cities separately. It is indeed true that large cities have successfully attracted infrastructural and industrial investment during the past decades of structural adjustment and thereby recorded reasonably high growth in employment. Poverty levels in large cities, however work out to be very low—about half compared to smaller towns. Anti-poverty strategy therefore must have a thrust on the livelihood related activities in small and medium towns. It may also be noted that the share of casual employment, which has a high incidence of poverty, has gone down in urban areas, being replaced by increase in self employment for men and women and regular employment for women. The new employment opportunities are however being taken by skilled and semi skilled persons. Employment for persons up to secondary as also higher levels of education has gone up significantly with a corresponding decline in their unemployment rates. The benefits have, however, not gone to the weaker segment within the workforce like the illiterates and women.

Understandably, a large segment of migrants in urban centres comprises not of destitutes or economically and socially displaced persons, moving from place to place as a part of their survival strategy. In fact, the percentage of migrants declining over time and their economic and social status being better than that of non-migrants and even improving over time, reflect barriers to mobility for the poor. With growing regionalism, service provision being based on market affordability, changes in skill requirements in urban labour market etc., the emerging productive and institutional structure have become hostile to poor newcomers. The migration process has become selective wherein unskilled labourers are finding it difficult to access the livelihood opportunities coming up in developed regions and large cities.

Changing Policy Framework, Programmes and Institutional Structure for Urban Governance

The policy and strategy of urban development have undergone major changes during the past two and a half decades. This has resulted in transformation of the organisational structure for managing urban sector schemes and the supporting financing system that need to be analsed in some detail.

A review of the evolution of policy perspective on urban development indicates that until the Sixth Plan (1980-85), the policies addressed largely the problems of housing, slums and provision of civic amenities. It did sometimes put forward vision of Master Plans for large cities and development of small and medium towns in the context of regional development but did not propose specific programmes or projects to move towards the vision at national level. The Seventh Plan explicitly recognised the problems of urban poor but the issues of employment generation, pro-poor growth strategy, infrastructural requirement etc. did not strategy for this sector.

The Eighth Plan (1992-97) for the first time talked of urban policies that could directly contribute to the goals of employment generation and poverty reduction by directing growth in certain directions. It envisaged a role for the local bodies in city development and stipulated cost recovery to be built into the municipal finance system. This perspective has further been reinforced in the Ninth Plan period (1997-2002) which talks of cities as engines of growth. It also puts forward a vision of market oriented growth with substantial reduction in budgetary allocations for development of urban infrastructure.

Overview of Central and State Government Schemes and Projects

The basic concern of public agencies in urban sector during the past couple of decades has been infrastructural deficiency in water supply, sanitation, solid waste management, and urban transport, particularly in large cities. This led to launching of Mega City scheme in 1993-94 but that covered only five mega cities. Delhi which was not a part of the above was covered under National Capital Region Plan with much larger dose of central assistance. Ahmedabad and Hyderabad had the advantage of mobilising resources through tax-free bonds. Accelerated Urban Water Supply Programme, another scheme launched in the same year 1993-94, had a wider spatial coverage although a large part of the benefits went to the large cities. The infrastructural problems in smaller towns have been addressed through the centrally assisted Integrated Development of Small and Medium Towns programme launched in 1979-80. Projects have been undertaken under the programme in 1854 towns and cities up to March 2007 with central subsidy of Rs. 10696.5 million. There has been serious inequality in disbursement of funds since eight states namely Andhra Pradesh, Gujarat, Karnataka, Madhya Pradesh, Maharashtra, Tamil Nadu, Uttar Pradesh and West Bengal have received 70 per cent of the total. Unfortunately, the total disbursement under this scheme in per capita terms was low which went down further in the nineties. It is also important to point out that external assistance came in a big way in the urban sector during nineties. By the tenth Plan, multilateral lending agencies like the Asian Development Bank (ADB), World Bank and several bilateral agencies had become key players. Unfortunately, here again the thrust was in favour of metropolitan and other class I cities.

The Tenth Plan document expressed concern regarding decline in the rate of growth of urban population during nineties but failed to mention that this was primarily due to decline in the absolute number of Census towns and significantly higher decline in demographic growth of small and medium town compared to average urban growth in the country. It recognised the need to address the disparity in the availability of infrastructure and services across different size class of urban centres underlining the fact that "very small towns with extremely limited resources rarely see any improvement". It noted that larger cities generally have the capacity to raise resources from domestic as well as international sources. Unfortunately, the Plan proposed very little to address the problems of serious deficiency in infrastructure and basic amenities in small towns.

The Eleventh Plan (The Approach Paper) too expresses concern, like its predecessor, regarding deteriorating infrastructural situation in cities that "provide large economies of agglomeration" and are absorbing large proportions of the incremental urban population. It lays major emphasis on Jawaharlal Nehru National Urban Renewal Mission launched in the fourth year of the last plan "in a mission mode". Never before have the select large cities received per capita allocation on such a large scale for infrastructural investment with

Additional Central Assistance coming as grants. The other special feature is that the Mission has succeeded to a large extent in getting the state and city governments to commit themselves to structural reforms which the Central government had failed to achieve despite adopting several measures and incentive schemes since early nineties. "It would be particularly necessary to ensure that there is no dilution in these reform requirements", the approach paper has stipulated. Also, sanctioning of the funds under the Mission is contingent on the City Development Projects (CDP) and detailed project reports being approved by the government, for which the bulk of the resources would have to be mobilised from non-governmental channels.

Like the predecessor, the Eleventh Plan talks of bringing about spatially balanced urbanisation through development of new townships and growth centres. The Task

Force for Slum Development for the Plan proposes improving the level of basic services for non-Mission cites through Integrated Housing and Slum Development Programme (IHSDP) which would replace National Slum Development Programme and Valmiki Ambedkar Awas Yojna. The IHSDP has been placed within JNNURM, which otherwise was for promoting infrastructural development only in sixty three large cities. Consequently, it is possible to project that the Mission is not for large cities alone but for promoting balanced urbanisation in the country. However, the resources available for other than 63 cities are too meager to stall the alarming trend of urban deceleration, particularly in less developed regions.

The Mission, besides attempting infrastructural development with market reforms, is to provide the poor access to basic services and land with tenurial security. Unfortunately, the component of infrastructure and reform in governance is being looked after by the Ministry of Urban Development while provision of shelter, basic services and slum development are the responsibilities of a separate sub-mission administered by the Ministry of Housing and Urban Development. It may further be noted that the milestones for implementation of reform agenda are unambiguous and easy to monitor as these can be ascertained based on an overview of the legislative changes, administrative orders etc. The indicators for ensuring access to basic amenities and land to the poor, on the other hand, are far too complicated and difficult to construct based on official information. Unfortunately, the CDP have not even tried to provide a framework or an institutional structure for fulfillment of these goals and the sanctioning authorities have failed to take note of this lacuna.

In the recently launched programme of UIDSSMT under JNNURM, projects have been launched only in 321 towns. The spatial disparity under the Programme can be inferred from the fact that 65 per cent of the resources has been utilised by four states namely Andhra Pradesh, Maharashtra, Tamil Nadu and Uttar Pradesh. This analysis clearly reveals that funds are utilised by a few states and concentration is in large towns and cities.

In the context of promoting livelihood for the poor, the Tenth Plan had launched Swarna Jayanti Shahari Rozgar Yojna (SJSRY) which basically subsumed Nehru Rozhar Yojna, Prime Minister's Integrated Urban Poverty Eradication Programme and Urban Basic Services for Poor, following the recommendations of Hashim Committee. The shelter and housing upgradation component was taken out and combined with National Slum Development Programme and Urban Basic Services for Poor under the new scheme IHSDP, mentioned above. The recent Evaluation Reports for SJSRY, however, reveals serious problems in its designing and implementation. As the cost ceiling for individual projects, skill upgradation etc. are low, economic viability of the self help enterprises set up under the scheme has become a casualty. The problems in identification of poor beneficiaries and implementation of the scheme without any dedicated cadre have resulted in significant leakages. Bankability of the projects also has emerged as an area of concern due to lack of marketing support to the enterprises as also difficulties in passing on the risk of running the enterprises from an individual to a group of asset less persons.

An analysis of ILCS programme indicates that only one-sixth of the towns and cities located in only 23 states of the country have opted for this sanitation programme designed for provision of clean environment especially for the poor. This reflects a basic flaw in designing of the programme as it is being taken up in only 864 places though the programme despite its substantial subsidy component and all the cities and towns in the country reporting deficiency in terms of coverage of sanitation facility. The funds under ILCS have been distributed in a highly skewed manner as four states namely Andhra Pradesh, Rajasthan, Uttar Pradesh and West Bengal have cornered over three quarters of the allocated funds.

Empowerment of Local Bodies

With the passing of the 74th Amendment Act to Indian Constitution and corresponding legislations, amendments, ordinances etc. at the state level, decentralisation has been hailed as a panacea for the problems of urban management in the country. All these basically attempt to achieve two objectives: one, enabling\facilitating the local bodies to undertake management, planning and development responsibility; and two, transferring powers to these bodies for generating adequate tax and non-tax revenue for this purpose.

Constitutional assignment of the responsibility of planning to city level agencies, however, has not automatically enabled them to prepare the Master Plans based on a development perspective for the city or region. A large majority of the agencies are simply not equipped to take up the responsibility of planning, especially of launching capital projects. Considerable expertise is required to identify the infrastructural and industrial projects appropriate for the growth of the city or town, assess their environmental implications and mobilise resources for these. This assistance is unlikely to come from the state government departments since they too have serious financial problems and may not be able to augment their professional staff. The only choice for the local bodies has, therefore, been to resort to financial intermediaries, credit rating agencies and private consultants. A large number of such agencies have come up in recent years in the private sector with assistance from international organisations. Projects have been prepared or identified in formal or informal consultation with interested companies or the "stake-holders" through the intermediation of the financial institutions. Understandably, identifying projects with high credit rating that would attract corporate investment is a different exercise from that of preparing a Master plan to answer the needs and aspirations of local people and then breaking it down to meaningful projects.

The second objective of the Amendment Act—increasing the resource availability at the local level—is an extremely doubtful proposition. Understandably, the outcome in different states has been different, contingent on materialisation of a number of conditions. Wllingness of the state government to devolve the powers of generating tax and non tax revenues, that of local bodies to actually utilise these opportunities, that of the people to make the tax and non-tax payments etc. are the determining factors. The data available at the micro level from various sources do not lend support to the stipulation that the Amendment has indeed enhanced the resources of the local bodies, except a few large cities.

Financial Institutions Supporting Urban Sector

The major players in urban sector currently are financial institutions including the public sector agencies that have been given the mandate and autonomy to leverage larger part of their funds from the market. Housing and Urban Development Corporation (HUDCO), the major player in public sector, established in 1970 basically to provide loans for urban development projects and associated institutional support had opened a new window in 1989 to provide funds for infrastructure projects. Availability of loans from this window, generally at less than the market rate, had made the state and city level agencies including the municipalities depend increasingly on it. This is more so in case of cities and towns with less than a million population since their capacity to mobilise internal resources were limited. HUDCO also became the premiere financial institution for disbursing loans under the Integrated Low Cost Sanitation Scheme which had a major subsidy component for different beneficiary categories. Also, the Corporation charged lower interest rates from local bodies in smaller cities. Its loans for upgrading and improving the basic services in slums were available at a rate much lower than the normal schemes until early nineties, below that under similar schemes of the World Bank.

The provision of such loans from HUDCO has either been totally withdrawn or the volume sanctioned has been drastically reduced. Furthermore, the small bias in favour of smaller cities that had enabled a few of them to borrow funds has also been given up. Further, it was financing up to 90 per cent of the project cost in case of infrastructural schemes for "economically weaker sections" which has declined over the years. In fact, the cost of borrowing for all social sector projects has increased, resulting in reduction in the interest rate differentiation. It is important to note that HUDCO has been upgraded as 'miniratna company' in August 2004 and consequently it is not entitled to any equity support from the government which has further reduced its capacity to direct funds to social sectors at low interest rates. It has been pointed out that the cities with strong economic base, that are attracting private sector investment both from within as well as outside the country, are able to get also a disproportionate share of the subsidised HUDCO funds.

The Infrastructure Leasing and Financial Services (ILFS), established in 1989, have emerged as an important financial institution in recent years. Its activities have more or less remained confined to development of industrial townships and roads and highways where risks are comparatively less. It basically undertakes project feasibility studies and provides a variety of financial as well as engineering services. With the increasing dependence on funds from private sector and capital market, the need to study the projects' financial viability, to safeguard the interests of the investors, has come to the forefront, which explains the growing importance of ILFS. Its contribution to the total infrastructural finance in the country however is very low and its role is being recognised more as a merchant banker rather than of a mere loan provider.

ILFS has helped local bodies, para-statal agencies and private organisations in preparing feasibility reports for infrastructure projects, detailing out the pricing and cost recovery mechanisms and establishing joint venture companies called Special Purpose Vehicles (SPV). Further, it has become equity holders in these companies along with other public and private agencies, including the operator of the BOT project. The role of ILFS may, thus, be seen as a promoter of a new perspective of development. Understandably, the projects for the provision of basic amenities in slums or low income areas, not having clear stipulations for total cost recovery within a reasonable period and therefore not fancied by private or joint sector companies are unlikely to find favour of this organisation.

Life Insurance Corporation (LIC) of India provides loans directly to municipalities and other local and state level agencies and indirectly through financial organisations like HUDCO, for infrastructure development. Unfortunately, the LIC format of funding the local bodies has not been very popular since it entails substantial contribution from the borrowing organisations that often have proved to be a bottleneck. Besides there have been problems with regard to recovery of dues.

Setting up of Infrastructure Development Finance Corporations at the state level has been hailed as a landmark in this field. These are expected to play an important role in channeling the central government and HUDCO funds to local bodies and augmenting their infrastructural investment. Their role in strengthening urban infrastructural base of urban centres, particularly those located in backward regions, however, is yet to be assessed.

New System of Urban Governance

Reduction of public sector intervention, ensuring appropriate prices for infrastructural services and urban amenities through elimination or reduction of subsidies, development of capital market for resource mobilisation, facilitating private and joint sector projects, simplification of legislative system to bring about appropriate land use changes and location of economic activities etc. are being advocated as a package, heralding a new system of urban governance. Some kind of "financial discipline" has been imposed by the Central government and Reserve Bank of India on the concerned state government departments and urban local bodies to ensure that their programmes and projects rely increasingly on internal resource mobilisation, loans from development cum banking institutions and capital market at non-subsidised interest rates.

The para statal agencies created in the post-Independence period like Housing Boards, Water Supply and Sewerage Boards, Development Authorities etc., that had taken over many of the functions of local bodies, have particularly come in for sharp criticism on grounds of inefficiency, lack of cost effectiveness and continued dependence on grants for sustenance. The allocations for these agencies have been cut down drastically along with that for the government departments, allowing them only limited possibility to undertake capital projects. A strong case has been made for making all organisations in urban sector financially viable and accountable to the users. Projects for the provision of sanitation facilities, improving slum colonies etc., that had a substantial component of subsidy, too have received less funds in this changed policy perspective.

Urban infrastructure projects have generally been considered commercially non-viable in India and consequently direct private investment in these from within or outside the country has been limited. Consequently, funds are being made available under Employees State Insurance Scheme and Employer's Provident Fund that have a longer maturity period and thus are more suited for infrastructure financing. The stipulations and requirements for channeling investment into government securities are being relaxed so that larger funds can be made available as per the principle of commercial profitability.

The local and regional bodies and para-statal agencies have floated bonds carrying varying interest rates for financing their infrastructure projects. Unfortunately, the weak financial position and revenue sources of the urban local bodies often make it difficult to issue general obligation bonds as investors are reluctant to depend solely on the general revenue of the local bodies as their security. As a consequence, a new type of credit instruments has been designed to enable the local bodies tap the capital market. "Structured debt obligations" (SDOs) are arrangements through which bonds are issued on the condition that the borrowing agency would pledge or escrow certain buoyant sources of revenue for debt servicing. This is a mechanism by which the debt repayment obligations are given utmost priority and kept independent of the overall financial position of the borrowing agency. It ensures that a trustee would monitor the debt servicing and that the borrowing agency would not have access to the pledged resources until the loan is repaid. Understandably, this constraints "the local fiscal flexibility" for carrying out its normal functions as also meeting some exigencies.

It may, however, be noted that only a handful of large cities with reasonably strong economic base have benefited from the "opportunity", opening up owing to the Constitutional Amendment. These cities have been able to introduce new taxes, increase the rates of the old ones and at the same time liberate themselves from the legislative and administrative controls of the state government in their day to day functioning. A few of these cities have also been able to raise resources by issuing bonds or SDOs or borrowings from international organisations. It may be mentioned that the issuance of such credit instruments as also securing institutional loans have been contingent on the local bodies accepting stringent conditionalities, as discussed above. Unfortunately, the small and medium towns with weak and unstable economic base, have not been able to benefit in a similar fashion. Tamil Nadu raising Rs 304 million (unsecured and privately placed) infrastructure bonds for 15 year period in 2001 was the first case of water and sanitation pooled fund in the country. The fund thus raised were passed on to several local bodies for part financing of their sanitation project. This obligated the local bodies to route their revenue earnings through an escrow account in a bank. The state of Karnataka has also tried a similar mode of resource mobilisation for small towns. The Ministry of Urban Development has proposed guidelines on the pattern of Tamil Nadu and Karnataka for resource mobilisation for smaller towns through reform agenda under JNNURM. Unfortunately, mobilisation of resources for pooled funds for capitalminvestment in small towns has been difficult. Consequently, the disparity in per capita expenditure and consequently the level of amenities, across the size class of urban centres has accentuated in recent years.

The central government and the Reserve Bank of India have proposed restrictions on many of the states for giving guarantees to local bodies and para-statal agencies, in an attempt to ensure some fiscal discipline. As a consequence, in most of the states, only the para-statal agencies and municipal corporations have been able to get the state guarantee, with the total exclusion of smaller municipal bodies. Needless to mention that getting bank guarantee is even more difficult for the latter.

AN ASSESSMENT OF THE IMPACT OF THE NEW SYSTEM OF GOVERNANCE ON URBAN STRUCTURE

The Problem of Regional and Size Class Disparity

Taking a holistic view, one is not very certain that the recent programmes of liberalisation, new system of urban governance and tapping of capital market for infrastructure investment has helped mitigate problems of urbanisation and migration in the country, as discussed in the preceding sections. The level of inequity in the provision of basic services across the states and size categories of urban centres have been extremely high in early eighties due to higher capacity of the people and the government in developed states to make investment in the services. The transfers of resources from the central to states had not favoured the backward states. More importantly, the state governments and para-statal institutions had not exhibited sensitivity in favour of small and medium towns.

A process of shifting the tasks and responsibilities to the local bodies has manifested clearly since mid eighties but unfortunately this has been done without examining the economic base and resource raising capacity of these bodies on the one hand and their requirements on the other. Increasing dependency of para statal agencies as also the local governments on their internal resources and institutional finance have further accentuated the disparity in the levels of amenities across the states and size class of urban settlements.

Recent studies on the disparity in the income of local bodies and its various components across size class of urban centres at all India level suggest that the larger cities are financially in a stronger position and can take up public works and social infrastructure projects on their own which is not so for smaller towns. The Constitutional Amendment, making the civic bodies increasingly dependent on their own tax and non-tax resources, has further increased the disparity in the level of services and economic infrastructure across size class of urban centres. This has adversely affected the level of basic services in small and medium towns and their capacity to absorb future growth of population or attract new economic activities, particularly in less developed states. With the decline in central or state assistance in the era of decentralised governance, it is not surprising that most of these towns do not make any investment for improving infrastructure and basic services. This has compounded their problems of inadequacy of basic amenities. Institutional borrowings of the para-statal agencies, involved in the provision of the amenities, at high rates of interest, reduction in their grants from government etc. are likely to further erode their capacity to invest in backward states, smaller order towns, slums and low income areas. Unfortunately, much of the subsidised amenities, provided through the governmental programmes during the seventies and eighties, had gone to a few large cities and benefited mostly the high and middle income colonies. These could not have continued in a more liberalised regime of the nineties. However, withdrawing government support and relegating the provision of the services to the market are creating serious problems of regional inequality.

Intra Urban Disparity

The impact of the Constitutional Amendment on intra-urban disparity is likely to be adverse, leading to socio-economic segmentation of large cities. The Amendment, stipulates that the ward level committees are to be constituted in all cities having more than 0.3 million people and that these will have the powers take decisions regarding the level and nature of amenities, based on the capability and willingness of the residents to pay. The slum populations in the heart of the large cities or their peripheries, with low affordability or willingness to pay, would understandably accept a low level of civic amenities. The elite colonies, on the other hand, would be able attract private entrepreneurs and even the subsidised government programmes for improving the quality of services, based on their capacity to pay higher user charges and political connections. This would accentuate the disparity in the availability of basic amenities across the wards and between the city and the periphery.

The decade of the nineties has witnessed a sea change in urban governance, the most significant aspect being participation or engagement of civil society organisations in urban governance and planning. The institutional vacuum created by the withdrawal of the state and hesitation in the entry of private sector agencies has been sought to be filled up by non-governmental organisations and community based organisations. The limited success of the wards committees to usher in decentralised governance has led to the mushrooming of civil societies that have strived to become partners in urban management of the different localities within the cities with diverse agenda. The functioning of these societies, that have come up mainly in the planned colonies has serious implications in accentuating intra-city inequalities in the level of amenities and infrastructural facilities and slowing down migration into big cities.

The major concern of the RWAs in metropolitan cities has been able to increase safety for their residents, strive for better delivery of public amenities and more efficient management of development projects. In the process they have tried to sanitize their neighbourhood by removing encroachments, slums, squatter and petty commercial establishments that pose a threat to local security and hygiene. Undoubtedly, better policing of urban land and prevention of squatting by the migrants are important fall outs of decentralised governance through citizen welfare associations in the major metropolises in the country. Many of these associations have filed petitions against vendors, encroachment by squatters etc. Courts have taken a serious view of the PILs filed by them and often directed the local authorities to remove the squatters.

Given the resource crunch in the government agencies in the era of globalisation, privatisation, partnership arrangements and promotion of community-based projects have become the only options for undertaking such investments. The projects that are now being sub contracted to private agencies or being launched with public private partnership have been responsible for exclusion of the poor due to various stipulation of cost recovery. The same is the case with public sector projects as well since these have increasingly been made to depend on institutional borrowings and capital market. All these have accentuated the gaps between rich and poor localities within the cities, particularly in the context of water and sanitation facilities, resulting in serious problems of health and hygiene. Growing disparity in the quality of micro environment has also been responsible for law and order problem resulting in individual and group violence.

The arrangements worked out by the local bodies with financial intermediaries including the credit rating institutions for tapping the capital market have often forced the former to pledge their regular earnings from octroi, grants from the state etc. as a guarantee for debt servicing. Importantly, the projects that are likely to be financed through such arrangements are commercially viable so as to ensure profitability to the investors and other stakeholders. The arrangements, thus, lead to a situation wherein the finances generated from the common people get escrowed as a security for projects that are likely to benefit better off sections of population or elite colonies. Similarly, the assignment of certain revenue channels to a separate fund, whose management is controlled by an outside financial institution or trustee can become a serious infringement on the rights of the local bodies. It, thus, appears that the policy of liberating the local governments from the regulatory and legislative controls of the state has brought the former under the direct control of financial institutions. This would be all very desirable from the development of capital market but may not answer the needs of basic amenities for the majority of urban poor and migrant workers.

The funds being made available to local bodies through Infrastructure Lease and Financial Services (ILFS) and Financial Institutions Reform and Expansion (FIRE) Programme and even HUDCO are expected to be matched by an equal amount raised from the domestic debt market. Further, a mandatory agenda for policy reform pertaining to urban governance, land management, pricing of services etc. have also been proposed for the participating institutions. Similarly, for obtaining World Bank loan under the IDA (International Development Assistance) the Corporations are required to maintain a separate account for the facilities created under the credit scheme, outside the overall municipal budget, as a pre-condition for getting the loan. Proposals have been put forward for revising the user charges for these facilities and making a group of sectors independent of the general municipal budget. All these are likely to place obligations constraining the local bodies in undertaking capital and even current expenditure out of their own revenues in slums and other low income colonies.

Conclusions

A macro overview of migration pattern reveals that economic deprivation is not the most critical factor for migration decisions in contemporary times. This factor does not emerge as important even in case of seasonal migrants which discounts the proposition that short duration mobility is restricted to the poor. Indeed, both poor and rich households report out-migration although the reasons for sending out their family members and the nature of jobs sought by them are different.

An analysis of unit level data in urban areas suggests that poor households are likely to send out one or more of their adult members to other locations, possibly for creating an outside support system for livelihood. In case of economically better-off strata, however, migration often means shifting of the entire family. The motivations for migration are, thus, diverse and varied depending on the socio-economic characteristics of the household. All these question the proposition that push factors have been the major determinants of mobility or that poverty holds the key to migration in the nineties.

Migration to urban centres emerges as a definite instrument of improving economic wellbeing and escaping poverty, irrespective of the size of the towns. The probability of being poor is less among the migrants compared to local population, in all size class of urban centres. What must however be pointed out is that large cities report low levels of poverty, irrespective of the migration status and nature of employment. However, the proposition that large cities have greater capacity of poverty alleviation for the residents or in-migrants needs to be postulated with caution. It can be argued that these cities have become less hospitable and less accommodating for the poor, reducing the absorption of economically dispossessed migrants and consequently reports lower poverty risk when compared to smaller towns.

Educational attainment emerges as the single most significant factor impacting on poverty. The poverty mitigating role of education is noted as significant for RU and UU migrants as also the non-migrant population. It suggests that there is a definite economic payoff to education in present urban context of the country but this is being enjoyed by those who are able to get regular jobs.

Despite the evidence of poverty mitigating impact of migration, the basic stipulation of the globalisation model that mobility of labour, operationalised through the market, would automatically ensure optimal distribution of economic activities and population needs to be examined with rigour. The growth of manufacturing and modern service activities in India during nineties has been concentrated in a few developed states and regions as the locational controls and programmes to promote industries in backward regions have been withdrawn gradually. This understandably has accentuated interstate disparity in development. Many of the backward states, particularly their backward districts, are facing serious problems of unemployment and under employment. Unfortunately, certain specificities and fragmentations in labour market as also policies of development are hindering mobility of workers, particularly those belonging to low economic strata. Programmes of structural reform, leading to relaxation and even removal of the restrictions on movement of commodities, have unfortunately failed to make a dent on socio-economic factors constraining movement of labourforce or people.

The process of globalisation has led to weakening of institutions like family, community, common property resources etc. This has increased vulnerability of poor both in rural and urban areas, despite reported decline in poverty. Migration which brought about redistribution of population from poorer to developed regions and helped them in finding a survival strategy is yet another institution which has come under strain. Despite increase in regional imbalances, Indian population has become somewhat immobile due to emerging socio-political factors. This poses a major challenge for the development strategy, currently being pursued in the country. The policy of unbalanced development, if continued despite this ominous trend, can have serious negative implications.

The decline in population mobility would undermine the proposition that the peasantry, eking out their distressed livelihood within an overstretched agrarian economy, would be able to find their escape route and grab the growing employment opportunities in industries and business coming up in and around a few large cities. Unless the reasons for increasing immobility are properly understood and the factors responsible for it are appropriately tackled, it would be dangerous to follow the strategy of unbalanced development or leave the spatial structure of development to be determined by forces of global and national market and hope that labour market would ensure equity in the accrual of benefits. The analysis of the urban dynamics in the past few decades, as attempted above, questions these solutions, emerging from the neo liberal paradigm.

In view of this macro scenario, a case can be made for providing special assistance to the less developed states that are not in a position to allocate requisite funds to their urban centres for this purpose. Particularly, small and medium towns in these states need to be supported in financing capital projects as their economic bases are not strong to generate adequate revenues for the purpose. This would imply increasing the resources allocated for urban development. There must, however, be explicit stipulations in the urban sector schemes to ensure that most of this fund goes to small and medium towns and for the provision of basic services for the urban poor.

The seriousness of the problem of intra urban inequality demands that the concerned public agencies take the overall responsibility of ensuring the basic amenities to all sections of population in different size class of urban centres, irrespective of their income or affordability. For this purpose, it would be important to set up the "minimum standards" for the amenities in realistic terms. The public agencies may, however, fulfil this responsibility by engaging/ supporting private organisations, NGOs and CBOs or strengthening the local bodies. It is unfortunate that all urban centres have been excluded from the purview of the wage employment scheme under National Employment Guarantee Act, although the small and medium towns in most states report poverty level equal to or higher than that in rural areas. The capacity of the local governments to create livelihood opportunities on a long term basis through self-employment programmes through skill formation and asset creation is limited. The past experiences suggest that there has been considerable leakage in these programmes. Banks and other financial institutions have been unwilling to give loans to the poor as the risk of non-recovery is very high. Also, the assets created through wage employment programmes have not contributed significantly to the development potential or long-term income generating capacity of the poor. It is, therefore, recommended that the anti-poverty programmes in small urban areas should primarily be focussed on provision of basic amenities.

The new programmes must be designed to cover all vulnerable sections of population in the entire hierarchy of settlements. Importantly, the capacity of the small and medium towns in less developed states as also the urban poor to pay for basic services would remain low during the next few years of structural adjustment as the prospect of an increase in their real income does not seem very bright. The programmes must, therefore, be specifically targetted and the subsidies should become explicit. The justification for all these must be sought in the context of a regional development plan.

It is important that regional and city development plans are formulated and implemented through a process relatively independent of the financing system, so that all the "stakeholders", including those financing component of the projects, are obliged to function within the framework of a development plan. Also, there should be proper monitoring of the scheme so that the vested interests at the local level do not corner a large part of the benefits on the basis of their financial contribution in the project.

Constitutional amendment for decentralisation of financial powers is not sufficient for augmenting resources of the local bodies. This must be backed up by actual devolution of powers and responsibilities and their use by the municipal bodies. The management capacities of these bodies need to be strengthened by giving more technical personnel and training the existing staff. They should be able to organise their affairs better, including mobilisation of tax and non-tax resources for infrastructure development. Manufacturing activities at the town level are noted to exhibit a strong relationship with the availability of infrastructure and amenities. One may, therefore, argue that the provision of these services in small urban settlements, besides being a goal in itself, would help in generating non-agricultural employment and diversifying their economic base. This in turn would decelerate migration from backward to developed states and large cities. Further, it would enable the small towns develop better linkages with their hinterland through provision of infrastructural support and greater capacity to absorb large sections of migrants in productive activities.

NOTES AND REFERENCES

American India Foundation (2006): Locked Homes, Empty Schools, A Zubaan Original, New Delhi.

Central Council of Local Governments (Zakaria Committee): A Report on Augmentation of Financial Resources of Urban Local Bodies, Government of India, New Delhi.

Credit Rating Information Services of India Limited (1996): Credit Rating of Municipal Bonds: Rating Report on Ahmedabad Municipal Corporation, New Delhi.

Davis, Kingsley (1951): The Population of India and Pakistan, Princeton University Press, New Jersey.

Dutta, A. (1999): "Institutional Aspects of Urban Governance", in Mathur, O. P. (ed.) jndia: the Challenge of Urban Governance, National Institute of Public Finance and Policy, New Delhi.

Dubey, A., S. Gangopadhyay and W. Wadhwa (2001), "Occupational Structure and Incidence of Poverty in Indian Towns of Different Sizes", Review of Development Economics, 5(1), pp.49-59.

Expert Group of Commercialisation of Infrastructure (1996); The India Infrastructure Report: Policy Imperatives for Growth and Welfare, Ministry of Finance, Government of India, New Delhi.

Kundu, A, (2003): Urbanisation and Urban Governance: Search for a Perspective beyond Neo-Liberalism, Economic and Political Weekly, vol. 38, no 29.

—(2006): "Globalisation and the Emerging Urban Structure: Regional Inequality and Population Mobility", India: Social Development Report, Oxford, New Delhi Kundu, A., Bagchi, S. and Kundu, D. (1999): "Regional Distribution of Infrastructure and Basic Amenities in Urban India", Economic and Political Weekly, 34(28).

Maitra, S. (1999): "Access of Urban Poor to Basic services: An Analysis in the Changing Perspective of Urban Governance in India" in Mathur, O. P. (ed.) India: the Challenge of Urban Governance,.National Institute of Public Finance and Policy, New Delhi and N. Sarangi (2005), "Employment Guarantee: Issue of Urban Exclusion", Economic and Political Weekly, August 13, pp.3242-46.

—, and N. Sarangi (2007), "Migration, Employment Status and Poverty: An Analysis across Urban Centres", Economic and Political Weekly, Jan 27, 2007.

Mathur, O. P. (1999): "Fiscal Innovations and Urban Governance" in Mathur, O. P. (ed.)India: the Challenge of Urban Governance, National Institute of Public Finance and Policy, New Delhi.

Ministry of Social Justice and Empowerment (1999): First Report of the Expert Committee for Devising a Pension System for India, Government of India, New Delhi.

Ministry of Urban Development (1992): The Constitution Seventy-fourth Amendment Act 1992 on Municipalities, Government of India, New Delhi.

National Institute of Public Finance and Policy (1995): Redefining State-Municipal Fiscal Relations, vol. I (mimeo), NIPFP, New Delhi.

National Institute of Urban Affairs (1983): A study of Resources of Urban Local Bodies in India and the Level of Services Provided, National Institute of Urban Affairs, New Delhi.

— (1998): Compendium of Major Legislation in Conformity with Constitution Seventy-fourth Amendment Act, Study Series no. 70, NIUA, New Delhi.

National Sample Survey Organisation (2001): Employment and Unemployment Situation in India 1999-2000, Fiftieth Fifth Round, Department of Statistics, New Delhi.

—(2002): Migration in India: 1999-2000, Report No. 470, Fiftieth Fifth Round, Department of Statistics, New Delhi

(2006): Employment and Unemployment Situation in India 2004-05 (Part I & II), Sixty-first Round, Department of Statistics, New Delhi.

Palnitkar, S and Kundu, D. (2005): Achieving the Millennium Development Goals, Financing Housing, Water and Sanitation in the Cities of Middle-Income Countries: The Case of Delhi, (mimeo) UNDP

Planning Commission (1983): Task Forces on Housing and Urban Developments, Government of India, New Delhi.

—(1993): Report of the Expert Group on Estimation of Proportion and Number of Poor Government of India, New Delhi.

—(1997): Ninth Five Year Plan 1997-2002, Government of India, New Delhi.

Racine, Jean Luc (ed.) (1997): Peasant Moorings: Village Ties and Mobility Rationales in South India, Sage, New Delhi.

Rao, P. S. N. (1999): "Financing Urban Infrastructure—The Emerging Trends", Papers of the International Seminar on Financing and Pricing of Urban Infrastructure, Human Settlement Management Institute, New Delhi.

Sivaramakrishna, and Singh, B. N. and Kundu, A. (2005): Handbook of Urbanisation, Oxford University Press, New Delhi.

Srivastava, Ravi S. (2003): "India's Uneven Development: An Analysis of Some Recent Trends and their Implications" The Indian Journal of Economics, July 2003.

Tendulkar, Suresh D., Sundaram, K. and Jain L. R. (1993): Poverty in India, 1970-71 to 1988-89, ILO-ARTEP Working Paper, New Delhi.

UNFPA (2007): State of World Population 2007: Unleashing the Potential of Urban Growth, UNFPA, New York, 2007.

UNFPA (2006): State of World Population 2006: A Passage to hope, Women and International Migration, UNFPA, New York, 2007.

United Nations (1995): Population and Development, United Nations, New York United Nations (2005): World Urbanisation Prospects, New York.

World Bank (1995b): Better Urban Services: Finding the Right Incentives, World Bank, Washington DC.

—(1998): Reducing Poverty in India: Options for More Effective Public Services, World Bank, Washington, D.C.

11

URBAN SOCIOLOGY IN THE NEW MILLENNIUM

The city has long been a strategic site for the exploration of many major subjects confronting society and sociology. It would be impossible for an article to summarise the enormous scholarship urban sociology produced in the century coming to a close. But, behind this sustained work lie marked shifts. In the first half of this century, the study of cities was at the heart of sociology. Since then urban sociology has gradually lost this privileged role as a lens for the discipline, as producer of key analytic categories. But, now, at the end of this century, it is argued that the city is, once again, emerging as a strategic site for understanding major new trends that are reconfiguring the social order. Can urban sociology seize the moment and once again produce path-breaking scholarship that will give us some of the analytic tools for understanding the broader social transformation under way?

It is perhaps one of the ironies at this century's end that some of the old questions of the early Chicago School of Urban Sociology should re-emerge as promising and strategic to understand certain critical issues today, notably the importance of recovering place and undertaking ethnographies at a time when dominant forces such as globalisation and tele-communications seem to signal that place and the details of the local no longer matter. Yet, the old categories of analysis are not enough.

The invitation to write a think piece about urban sociology at the millennium frees the author to look forward, at what are some of the major challenges facing urban sociology, given its traditions and lineages rather than summarising past accomplishments. The study aims to examine some of the major conditions in cities today that are such challenges for theorisation and empirical analysis. This is then a partial account, beyond the fact that questions of positionality are inevitable. It seeks to locate the new frontiers that demand new forms of theorisation and research.

The challenges arise out of the intersection of major macro-social trends and their particular spatial patterns. The city and the metropolitan region emerge as strategic sites where these macro-social trends materialise and hence can be constituted as an object of study. Among these trends are globalisation and the rise of the new information technologies, the intensifying of transnational and translocal dynamics, and the strengthening presence and voice of socio-cultural diversity. Each one of these trends has its own specific conditionalities, contents and consequences for cities, and for theory and research. Cities are also sites where each of these trends interacts with the others in distinct, often complex manners, in a way they do not in just about any other setting.

All three trends are at a cutting edge of actual change that sociological theory and urban sociology in particular need to factor in to a far greater extent than they have. By far the best developed and most studied is socio-cultural diversity as it lends itself to the micro-sociological treatments that prevail in much urban sociology.

These trends do not encompass the majority of social conditions; on the contrary, most social reality probably corresponds to older continuing and familiar trends. That is why much of urban sociology's traditions and well-established sub-fields will remain important and constitute the heart of the discipline. Further, there are good reasons why most of urban sociology has not quite engaged the characteristics and the consequences of these three trends: current data sets are quite inadequate for addressing these issues at the level of the city. Yet, although these three trends may involve only parts of the urban condition and cannot themselves be confined to the urban, they are strategic in that they mark the urban condition in novel ways and the latter is, in turn, a key research site for their examination. In thinking about the challenges facing urban sociology at the millennium, it is necessary to confront these strategic developments.

Conceptual Framework

Among the dominant forces reconfiguring the social, the economic, the political, and the subjective at century's end are globalisation and the new information technologies. The implications for the urban of these three trends are pronounced: globalisation and telecommunications are about dispersal, transnational and translocal networks cut across the boundaries of cities, and much of the new cultural diversity is embedded in new subjectivities and narratives, not common foci for urban sociology. If one were to take the traditional tools of urban sociology and social science one could factor in some aspects of these trends. But, theorisation is lagging, even though there are important exceptions. Economic geography and cultural studies have contributed rather more.

'Embedded statism', which has marked the social sciences generally is one obstacle to a full theorisation of some of these issues. We can characterise this in terms of the explicit or implicit assumption about the nation-state as the container of social processes and the national as the appropriate scale for studying major social, economic and political processes. These assumptions work well for many of the subjects studied in the social sciences.

But, they are not helpful in elucidating a growing number of situations when it comes to globalisation and to a whole variety of transnational processes now being studied by social scientists. Nor are those assumptions helpful for developing the requisite research techniques. Further, while they describe conditions that have held for a good part of this century in much of the world, we are now seeing their partial unbundling. Their unbundling demands the introduction of additional qualifications to the major assumptions described above. Of particular interest here is the implied correspondence of national territory with the national, and the associated implication that the national and the non-national are two mutually exclusive conditions. We are now seeing their partial unbundling.

For instance, it has been argued that one of the features of the current phase of globalisation is that the fact a process happens within the territory of a sovereign state does not necessarily mean that it is a national process. Conversely, the national (such as firms, capital, culture) may increasingly be located outside the national territory, for instance, in a foreign country or in digital spaces. This localisation of the global, or of the non-national, in national territories, and of the national outside national territories, undermines a key duality running through many of the methods and conceptual frameworks prevalent in the social sciences, that the national and the non-national are mutually exclusive.

This partial unbundling of the national has significant implications for our analysis and theorisation of cities, especially major cities where the forces of globalisation and telecommunications come together. The city as an object of study has long been a debatable construct, whether in early writings or in very recent ones. But, the unbundling of urban space and of the traditional hierarchies of scale we are seeing today further raises the ante in terms of prior conceptualisations. Major cities can be thought of as nodes where a variety of processes intersect in particularly pronounced concentrations. In the context of globalisation, many of these processes are operating at a global scale. Cities emerge as one territorial or scalar moment in a trans-urban dynamic. This is, however, not the city as a bounded unit, but the city as a node in a grid of cross-boundary processes. Further, this type of city cannot be located simply in a scalar hierarchy that places it beneath the national, regional and global. It is one of the spaces of the global, and it engages the global directly, often by-passing the national. Some cities may have had this capacity long before the current era; but today these conditions have been multiplied and amplified to the point that they can be read as a qualitatively different phase. Pivoting theorisation and research on the city might be a fruitful way of cutting across embedded statism and capturing the rescaling of some major social, economic and political processes at the level of the city.

Besides the challenge of overcoming embedded statism, there is the challenge of recovering place in the context of globalisation, telecommunications, and the intensifying of transnational and translocal dynamics. One obvious tradition of scholarship that comes to mind in this regard is the old school of ecological analysis developed by Ernest Burgess and Robert Red-field as well as the work by Park and by Wirth. One might ask if their methods might be of particular use in recovering the category place. Robert Park believed the geography of the city was determined by the political economy and immigration. Louis Wirth stressed the ethnicity of geography at the expense of class analysis. Their students, such as Harvey Zorbaugh turned to fieldwork in an effort to understand the clashing interpretations of urban geography made by their teachers. They contributed many detailed studies mapping distributions and assuming functional complementarity among the diverse 'natural areas' they identified in Chicago.

As a matter of fact, detailed fieldwork is a necessary step in capturing many of the new aspects in the urban condition, including those having to do with the major trends focused on in this article. But, assuming functional complementarity brings us back to the notion of the city as a bounded space rather than one site or scale, albeit a strategic one, where multiple trans-boundary processes intersect and produce distinct socio—spatial formations. Recovering place can only partly be met through the techniques of research of the old Chicago School of Urban Sociology. I do think we need to go back to some of the depth of engagement with urban areas that the School represented and the effort towards detailed mappings. The type of ethnographies done by Duneier the scholars in Burawoy et al., are excellent examples, using many of the techniques yet working within a different set of assumptions.

But, that is only part of the challenge of recovering place. Large cities around the world are the terrain where a multiplicity of globalisation processes assume concrete, localised forms. These localised forms are, in good part, what globalisation is about. Recovering place means recovering the multiplicity of presences in this landscape. The large city of today has emerged as a strategic site for a whole range of new types of operations—political, economic, 'cultural,' subjective. It is one of the nexi where the formation of new claims materialises and assumes concrete forms.

The loss of power at the national level produces the possibility for new forms of power and politics at the sub-national level. Further, in so far as the national as container of social process and power is cracked it opens up possibilities for a geography of politics that links sub-national spaces across borders. Cities are foremost in this new geography. One question this engenders is how and whether we are seeing the formation of a new type of transnational politics that localises in these cities.

Immigration, for instance, is one major process through which a new transnational political economy and translocal household strategies are being constituted. It is one largely embedded in major cities in so far as most immigrants, certainly in the developed world, whether in the USA, Japan or Western Europe, are concentrated in such major cities. It is, in my reading, one of the constitutive processes of globalisation today, even though not recognised or represented as such in mainstream accounts of the global economy.

This configuration contains unifying capacities across national boundaries and sharpening conflicts within cities. Global capital and the new immigrant workforce are two major instances of transnationalised actors that have unifying properties internally and find themselves in contestation with each other inside cities. Researching and theorising these issues will require approaches that diverge from the more traditional studies of political elites, local party politics, neighbourhood associations, immigrant communities, and so on, through which the political landscape of cities and metropolitan regions has conventionally been conceptualised in urban sociology.

IMPACT OF GLOBALISATION ON URBANISATION

The concept of the city is complex, imprecise, and charged with specific historical meanings. A more abstract category might be 'centrality', one of the properties cities have historically provided and produced. Such a focus would not concern matters such as the boundaries of cities or what cities actually are. These are partly empirical questions: each city is going to have a different configuration of boundaries and contents. The question is, rather, what are the conditions for the continuity of centrality in advanced economic systems in the face of major new organisational forms and technologies that maximise the possibility for geographic dispersal, at the regional, national and indeed, global scale, as well as simultaneous system integration? Historically, centrality has largely been embedded in the central city. One of the changes brought about by the new conditions is the reconfiguring of centrality: the central city is today but one form of centrality. Important emerging spaces for the constitution of centrality range from the new transnational networks of cities to electronic space.

A second major issue essential for thinking about the future of the city concerns the narratives that we have constructed about the city and their relation to the global economy and to new technologies. The understandings and the categories that dominate mainstream discussions about the future of the advanced urban economy signal that the city has become obsolete for leading economic sectors. We need to subject these notions to critical examination. There are instantiations of the global economy and of the new technologies that have not been recognised as such or are contested representations.

Finally, and on a somewhat more theorised level, there are certain properties of power that make cities strategic. Power needs to be historicised to overcome the abstractions of the concept, it is actively produced and reproduced. Many of the studies in urban sociology focused on the local dimensions of power have made important contributions in this regard. Beyond this type of approach, one of the aspects today in the production of power structures has to do with new forms of economic power and the re-location of certain forms of power from the public political realm to the private economic realm. This brings with it questions about the built environment and the architectures of centrality that represent different types of power. Does power have spatial correlates, does it have a spatial moment? In terms of the economy this question could be operationalised more concretely: Can the current economic system, with its strong tendencies towards concentration in ownership and control, have a space economy that lacks points of physical concentration?

To some extent, it is the major cities in the highly developed world which most clearly display the processes. However, increasingly these processes are emerging in cities in developing countries as well. But, they are often submerged under the megacity syndrome: sheer population size and urban sprawl create their own orders of magnitude. While size and sprawl may not much alter the power equation, they do change the weight, and the legibility, of some of these properties.

One way of framing the issue of centrality is by focusing upon larger dynamics rather than beginning with the city as such. For instance, we could note that the geography of globalisation contains both a dynamic of dispersal and one of centralisation, the latter a condition that has only recently begun to receive recognition. Most of the scholarship on these issues, and it is vast, has focused on dispersal patterns. The massive trends towards the spatial dispersal of economic activities at the metropolitan, national and global levels that we associate with globalisation have contributed to a demand for new forms of territorial centralisation of top-level management and control operations.

The fact, for instance, that firms world-wide had half a million affiliates outside their home countries by 1997 signals that the sheer number of dispersed factories and service outlets that are part of a firm's integrated operation creates massive new needs for central co-ordination and servicing. In brief, the spatial dispersal of economic activity made possible by globalisation and telecommunications contributes to an expansion of central functions *if this* dispersal is to take place under the continuing concentration in control, ownership and profit appropriation that characterises the current economic system.

It is at this point that the city enters the discourse. Cities regain strategic importance because they are favoured sites for the production of these functions. National and global markets as well as globally integrated organisations require central places where the work of globalisation gets done. Finance and advanced corporate services are industries producing the organisational commodities necessary for the implementation and management of global economic systems. Cities are preferred sites for the production of these services, particularly the most innovative, speculative, internationalised service sectors. Further, leading firms in information industries require a vast physical infrastructure containing strategic nodes with hyperconcentration of facilities; we need to distinguish between the capacity for global transmission/communication and the material conditions that make this possible. Finally, even the most advanced information industries have a production process that is at least partly place-bound because of the combination of resources it requires even when the outputs are hypermobile. The tendency in the specialised literature has been to study these advanced information industries in terms of their hypermobile outputs rather than the actual work processes which include top level professionals as well as clerical and manual service workers.

Further, when we start by examining the broader dynamics in order to detect their localisation patterns, we can begin to observe and conceptualise the formation, at least incipient, of transnational urban systems. The growth of global markets for finance and specialised services, the need for transnational servicing networks due to sharp increases in international investment, the reduced role of the government in the regulation of international economic activity and the corresponding ascendance of other institutional arenas with a strong urban connection—all these point to the existence of a series of transnational networks of cities. The data are still inadequate; one of the most promising data sets at this time is that organised by Taylor and his colleagues. But, much remains to be done in this field. To a large extent it seems that the major business centres in the world today draw their importance from these transnational networks. I have long argued that there is no such thing as a single global city, and in this sense there is a sharp contrast with the erstwhile capitals of former empires.

These networks of major international business centres constitute new geographies of centrality. The most powerful of these new geographies of centrality at the global level binds the major international financial and business centres: New York, London, Tokyo, Paris, Frankfurt, Zurich, Amsterdam, Los Angeles, Sydney, Hong Kong, among others. But, this geography now also includes cities such as Bangkok, Seoul, Taipei, Sao Paulo, Mexico City. The intensity of transactions among these cities, particularly through the financial markets, trade in services, and investment has increased sharply, and so have the orders of magnitude involved. There has been a sharpening inequality in the concentration of strategic resources and activities between each of these cities and others in the same country. This has consequences for the role of urban systems in national territorial integration. Although, the latter has never quite been what its model signals, the last decade has seen a further acceleration in the fragmentation of national territory. National urban systems are being partly unbundled as their major cities become part of a new or strengthened transnational urban system.

But, we can no longer think of centres for international business and finance simply in terms of the corporate towers and corporate culture at their centre. The international character of major cities lies not only in their telecommunication infrastructure and foreign firms: it lies also in the many different cultural environments in which these workers and others exist. This is one arena where we have seen the growth of an enormously rich scholarship. Today's major cities are in part the spaces of post-colonialism and indeed contain conditions for the formation of a post-colonialist discourse. It seems to me that this is an integral part of the future of such cities.

A NEW TRANSNATIONAL POLITICAL GEOGRAPHY

The incorporation of cities into a new cross-border geography of centrality also signals the emergence of a parallel political geography. Major cities have emerged as a strategic site not only for global capital, but also for the transnationalisation of labour and the formation of translocal communities and identities. In this regard, cities are a site for new types of political operations. The centrality of place in a context of global processes makes possible a transnational economic and political opening for the formation of new claims and hence for the constitution of entitlements, notably rights to place. At the limit, this could be an opening for new forms of 'citizenship'. The emphasis on the transnational and hypermobile character of capital has contributed to a sense of powerlessness among local actors, a sense of the futility of resistance. But, an analysis that emphasises place suggests that the new global grid of strategic sites is a terrain for politics and engagement.

This is a space that is both place-centred in that it is embedded in particular and strategic locations; and it is transterritorial because it connects sites that are not geographically proximate yet are intensely connected to each other. Is there a transnational politics embedded in the centrality of place and in the new geography of strategic places, such as is for instance the new world-wide grid of global cities? This is a geography that cuts across national borders and the old North-South divide. But, it does so along bounded 'filieres'. It is a set of specific and partial rather than all-encompassing dynamics. It is not only the transmigration of capital that takes place in this global grid, but also people — both rich — the new transnational professional workforce, and poor, most migrant workers. And it is a space for the transmigration of cultural forms, the re-territorialisation of 'local' subcultures.

If we consider that large cities concentrate both the leading sectors of global capital and a growing share of disadvantaged populations—immigrants, many of the disadvantaged women, people of colour generally and in the megacities of developing countries, masses of shanty dwellers—then we can see that cities have become a strategic terrain for a whole series of conflicts and contradictions. We can then think of cities also as one of the sites for the contradictions of the globalisation of capital, even though, heeding Katznelson's observation, the city cannot be reduced to this dynamic.

One way of thinking about the political implications of this strategic transnational space anchored in cities is in terms of the formation of new claims on that space. The city has indeed emerged as a site for new claims: by global capital which uses the city as an 'organisational commodity', but also by disadvantaged sectors of the urban population, frequently as internationalised a presence in large cities as that of capital. The 'de-nationalising' of urban space, and the formation of new claims by transnational actors, raise the question *Whose city is it?*

Foreign firms and international business people have increasingly been entitled to do business in whatever country and city they chose—entitled by new legal regimes, by the new economic culture, and through progressive deregulation of national economies. They are among the new city users. The new city users have made an often immense claim on the city and have reconstituted strategic spaces of the city in their image. Their claim to the city is rarely contested, even though the costs and benefits to cities have barely been examined. They have profoundly marked the urban landscape. For Martinotti, they contribute to change the social morphology of the city; the new city of these city users is a fragile one, whose survival and successes are centred on an economy of high productivity, advanced technologies, intensified exchanges. It is a city whose space consists of airports, top level business districts, top of the line hotels and restaurants, in brief, a sort of urban glamour zone.

Perhaps, at the other extreme, are those who use urban political violence to make their claims on the city, claims that lack the *de facto* legitimacy enjoyed by the new 'city users'. These are claims made by actors struggling for recognition, entitlement, claiming their rights to the city. These claims have, of course, a long history; every new epoch brings specific conditions to the manner in which the claims are made. The growing weight of'delinquency' (such as smashing cars and shop-windows; robbing and burning stores) in some of the uprisings over the last decade in major cities of the developed world, is perhaps an indication of sharpened socio-economic inequality — the distance, as seen and as lived, between the urban glamour zone and the urban war zone. The extreme visibility of the difference is likely to contribute to further brutalisation of the conflict: the indifference and greed of the new élites versus the hopelessness and rage of the poor.

There are two aspects in this formation of new claims that have implications for the transnational politics that are increasingly being played out in major cities. One is the sharp and perhaps sharpening differences in the representation of claims by different sectors, notably between international business and the vast population of low income 'others'—immigrants, women, people of colour generally. The second aspect is the increasingly transnational element in both types of claims and claimants. It signals a politics of contestation embedded in specific places but transnational in character. One challenge for urban sociology is how to capture such a cross-border dynamic with existing or new categories and, in doing so, how not to lose the city itself as a site.

GLOBALISATION AND INSCRIPTION IN THE URBAN LANDSCAPE

Although, globalisation as a process involves multiple economies and work cultures, it is in terms of the corporate economy and the new transnational corporate culture that economic globalisation is usually represented in the urban landscape. Yet, the city concentrates diversity. Its spaces are inscribed with the dominant corporate culture but also with a multiplicity of other cultures and identities, notably through immigration. The slippage is evident: the dominant culture can encompass only part of the city. And while corporate power inscribes non-corporate cultures and identities with 'otherness,' thereby devaluing them, they are present everywhere. The immigrant communities and informal economy in cities such as New York and Los Angeles are only two instances.

How can we expand the terrain for this representation so as to incorporate those other conditions? And how can we make a new reading of the locations where corporate power is now installed, a reading that captures the non-corporate presences in those same sites? Once we have recovered the centrality of place and of the multiple work cultures within which economic operations are embedded, we are still left confronting a highly restricted terrain for the inscription of economic globalisation. Sennett observes that 'the space of authority in Western culture has evolved as a space of precision'. And Giddens notes the centrality of 'expertise' in today's society, with the corresponding transfer of authority and trust to expert systems. Corporate culture is one representation of precision and expertise. Its space has become one of the main spaces of authority in today's cities. The dense concentrations of tall buildings in major downtowns or in the new 'edge' cities are the site for corporate culture—though as I will argue later they are also the site for other forms of inhabitation, but these have been made invisible. The vertical grid of the corporate tower is imbued with the same neutrality and rationality attributed to the horizontal grid of American cities.

Through immigration a proliferation of, in their origin, highly localised cultures now have become presences in many large cities, cities whose élites think of themselves as cosmopolitan, that is, as transcending any locality. Cultures from around the world, each rooted in a particular country or village, now are reterritorialised in a few single places, places such as New York, Los Angeles, Paris, London, and most recently Tokyo.

The space of the immigrant community, of the black ghetto, and increasingly of the old decaying manufacturing district emerges as the space of a compound other, constituted as a devalued, downgraded space in the dominant economic narrative about the post-industrial urban economy. Corporate culture collapses differences, some minute, some sharp, among the different socio-cultural contexts into one amorphous otherness, an otherness represented as having no place in the economy, or, supposedly, only marginally attached to the economy. It therewith reproduces the devaluing of those jobs and of those who hold such jobs. By leaving out these articulations, by confining the referent to the centrally placed sectors of the economy, the dominant narrative about the urban economy can present the economy as containing a higher order unity rather than as segmented.

The corporate economy evicts these other economies and its workers from economic representation, and the corporate culture represents them as the other. What is not installed in a corporate centre is devalued or will tend to be devalued. And what occupies the corporate building in noncorporate ways is made invisible. The fact that most of the people working in the corporate city during the day are low paid secretaries, mostly women, many immigrants, is not included in the representation of the corporate economy or corporate culture. And the fact that at night a whole other work force installs itself in these spaces, including the offices of the chief executives, and inscribes the space with a whole different culture (manual labour, often music, lunch breaks at midnight) is an invisible event.

Another dimension along which to explore some of these issues is the question of the body. The body is citified, urbanised as a distinctively metropolitan body. The particular geographical, architectural, municipal arrangements constituting a city are one particular ingredient in the social constitution of the body. For some scholars, they are by no means the most important one. She argues that the structure and particularity of the family and neighbourhoods is more influential, though the structure of the city is also contained therein. 'The city orients perception insofar as it helps to produce specific conceptions of spatiality.' The city contributes to the organisation of family life, of work-life in so far as it contains a distribution in space of the specific locations for each activity; similarly, architectural spatiality can be seen as one particular component in this broader organisation of space.

This citified body is inscribed by the many socio-cultural environments present in the city and it, in turn, inscribes these. There are two forms in which this weaves itself into the space of the economy. One is that these diverse ways in which the body is inscribed by socio-cultural contexts that exist in the city works as a mechanism for segmenting and, in the end, for overvaluing and devaluing, and it does so in very concrete ways.

The other way in which this diversity weaves itself into the space of the economy is that it re-enters the space of the dominant economic sector as merchandise and as marketing. Of interest here is Stuart Hall's observation that contemporary global culture is different from earlier imperial cultures: it is absorptive, a continuously changing terrain that incorporates the new cultural elements whenever it can. In the earlier period, Hall (1991) argues, the culture of the empire, epitomised by Englishness, was exclusionary, seeking always to reproduce its difference. At the same time today's global culture cannot absorb everything, it is always a terrain for contestation, and its edges are certainly always in flux. The process of absorption can never be complete. Today's large cities are a strategic site where these diverse dynamics materialise in concrete patterns.

NOTES AND REFERENCES

Abbott, Andrew, 1999 *Department and Discipline: Chicago Sociology at One Hundred,* Chicago: University of Chicago Press.

Abu-Lughod, J. L. 1994 *From Urban Village to 'East Village': The Battle for New York's Lower East Side,* Cambridge: Blackwell.

— 1999 *New York, Los Angeles, Chicago: America's Global Cities,* University of Minnesota Press.

Allen, J. 1999 'Cities of Power and Influence: settled formations', in Allen, J. et al. (eds) *Unsettling Cities,* New York: Rout-ledge.

Allen, J., Massey, D. and Pryke, M. (eds) 1999 *Unsettling Cities,* New York: Routledge.

Anderson, E. 1990 *Streetwise,* Chicago: University of Chicago Press.

Appadurai, Arjun, 1996 *Modernity at Large,* University of Minnesota Press.

Bhachu, P. 1985 *Twice Immigrants,* London: Tavistock Publications.

Berner, E. and Korff, R. 1995 'Globalisation and Local Resistance: The Creation of Localities in Manila and Bangkok', *International Journal of Urban and Regional Research* 19 (2).

Bobo, L., Schuman, H. and Steeh, C. 1986 'Changing Racial Attitudes toward residential Integration', in John Goering, (ed.). *Housing Desegregation and Federal Policy,* Chapell Hill: University of North Carolina Press.

Body-Gendrot, S. 1993 *Ville et Violence,* Paris: Presses Universitaires de France.

—, 1999 *Economic Globalisation and Urban Unrest,* London: Blackwell.

Bonacich, E., Cheng, L. Chinchilla, N. Hamilton, N. and Ong, P. (eds) 1994 *Global Production: The Apparel Industry in the Pacific Rim,* Philadelphia: Temple University Press.

Bonilla, F., Melendez, E. Morales, R. and de los Angeles Torres, M. (eds) 1998 *Borderless Borders,* Philadelphia: Temple University Press.

Bourgeois, P. 1995 *In Search of Respect: Selling Crack in El Barrio,* New York: Cambridge University Press.

Boyd, M. 1989 'Family and Personal Networks in International Migration: Recent Developments and New Agendas', *International Migration Review* 23(3): 638-70.

Brar, H., P. Martin, J. Wrench (with M. Johnson) 1993 *Invisible Minorities. Racism in New Towns and New Contexts,* Coventry: Warwick University.

Brenner, N. 1998 'Global cities, glocal states: global city formation and state territorial restructuring in contemporary Europe', *Review of International Political Economy* 5(1).

Brewer, J.D. 1998 'Informal social control and crime management in Belfast', *The British Journal of Sociology* 49(4).

Brotchie, J., Blakely, E., Hall, P. and Newton, P. (eds) 1995 *Cities in Competition: Productive and Sustainable Cities for the Twenty-First Century,* Melbourne: Longman Australia.

Burawoy, M. et al. 1991 *Ethnography Unbound: Power and Resistance in the Modern Metropolis,* Berkeley: University of California Press.

Burgel, G. and Burgel, G. 1996 'Global Trends and City Politics: Friends or Foes of Urban Development?' in M. Cohen, B. Ruble, J. Tulchin, A. Garland (eds) *Preparing for the Urban Future. Global Pressures and Local Forces,* Washington D.C.: Woodrow Wilson Center Press (distributed by The Johns Hopkins University Press).

Castells, M. 1989 *The Informational City,* London: Blackwell.

Clark, T. and Hoffman-Martinot, V. (eds) 1998 *The New Public Culture,* Oxford: West-view Press.

Cohen, M., Ruble, B., Tulchin, J. and Garland, A. (eds) 1996 *Preparing for the Urban Future. Global Pressures and Local Forces,* Washington D.C.: Woodrow Wilson Center Press (distributed by The Johns Hopkins University Press).

Comstock, G. 1991 *Violence Against Lesbians and Gay Men,* New York: Columbia University Press.

Copjec, J. and Sorkin, M. (eds) 1999 *Giving Ground,* London: Verso.

Cybriwsky, R. 1991 *Tokyo: The Changing Profile of an Urban Giant,* London: Bel-haven.

Dawson, M. 1999 'Globalisation, the Racial Divide, and a New Citizenship', in R. Torres, L. Miron and J. X. Inda (eds) 1999 *Race, Identity, and Citizenship,* Oxford: Blackwell.

De Sena, J. 1990 *Protecting One's Turf: Social Strategies for Maintaining Urban Neighbourhoods,* Lanham: University Press of America.

Dogan, M. and J. D. Kasarda (eds) 1988 *A World of Giant Cities,* Newbury Park, CA: Sage.

Domhoff, G.W. 1991 *Blacks in White Establishments: A study of Race and Class in America,* New Haven: Yale University Press.

Duncan, O. 1959 'Human Ecology and Population Studies,' in P. Hauser and O. Dudley (eds) *The Study of Population,* Chicago: The University of Chicago Press.

Duneier, M. 1999 *Sidewalk,* New York: Farrar, Strauss & Giroux.

Dunn, S. (ed.) 1994 *Managing Divided Cities,* Staffs, UK: Keele University Press.

Fainstein, S. 1997 'Justice, Politics, and the Creation of Urban Space', in A. Merrifield and E. Swyngedouw (eds) *The Urbanisation of Injustice,* New York: New York University Press.

Fainstein, S.I., Gordon, I. and Harloe, M. 1993 *Divided City: Economic Restructuring and Social Change in London and New York,* New York: Blackwell.

Fainstein, Susan and Judd, Dennis (eds) 1999 *Urban Tourism.* New Haven, Conn: Yale University Press.

Featherstone, M. (ed.) 1990 *Global Culture: Nationalism, Globalisation and Modernity,* Newbury Park, Ca: Sage.

Feagin, J.P. and Vera, H. 1996 *White Racism,* New York: Routledge.

Gans, H. 1995 *The War Against the Poor,* New York: Basic Books.

Georges, E. 1990 *The Making of a Transnational Community: Migration, Development, and Cultural Change in the Dominican Republic,* New York: Columbia University Press.

Giddens, A. 1990 *The Consequences of Modernity,* Oxford, U.K.: Polity Press.

Gottdiener, M. 1985 *The Social Production of Urban Space,* Austin: University of Texas Press.

Graham, S. and Marvin, S. 1996 *Telecommunications and the City: Electronic Spaces, Urban Places,* London: Routledge.

Gravesteijn, S.G.E., Griensven, S. van and de Smidt, M. C. (eds) 1998 *Timing Global Cities, Nederlandse Geografische Studies,* 241, Utrecht.

Green, D., Strolovitch, D. and Wong, J. 1998 'Defended Neighbourhoods, Integration, and Racially Motivated Crime', *American Journal of Sociology* 104(2): 372-404.

Grosz, E. 1992 'Bodies-Cities', in B. Colom-ina (ed.) *Sexuality and Space,* Princeton Papers on Architecture. Princeton: Princeton Architectural Press.

Hall, S. 1991 'The Local and the Global: Globalisation and Ethnicity', in A. King (ed.) *Current Debates in Art History 3. Culture, Globalisation and the World-System: Contemporary Conditions for the Representation of Identity,* Department of Art and Art History, State University of New York at Binghamton.

Hannerz, U. 1992 *Cultural Complexity. Studies in the Social Organisation of Meaning,* New York: Columbia University Press.

Holston, J. (ed.) 1996 'Cities and Citizenship', a Special Issue *of Public Culture8(2).*

Hondagneu-Sotelo, P. 1994 *Gendered Transitions,* Berkeley: University of California Press.

Hutchison, R. (ed.) 1997 *Research in Urban Sociology, Vol. 4: New Directions in Urban Sociology,* Greenwich: JAI Press.

Indiana Journal of Global Legal Studies, 1996. *Special Issue: Feminism and Globalisation: The Impact of the Global Economy on Women and Feminist Theory* 4(1 Fall).

Jacobson, David (ed.) 1998 *The Immigration Reader: America in a Multidisciplinary Perspective,* Oxford: Blackwell.

Jessop, R. 1999 'Reflections on Globalisation and its Illogics', in Olds, K. et al. (eds) *Globalisation and the Asian Pacific: Contested Territories,* London: Routledge.

Katznelson, I. 1992 *Marxism and the City,* Oxford: Clarendon Press.

Kempen, R. van, and Ozuekren, A. Sule 1998 'Ethnic Segregation in Cities: New Forms and Explanations in a Dynamic World', *Urban Studies* 35(10): 1631-57.

King, A.D. 1990 *Urbanism, Colonialism, and the World Economy. Culture and Spatial Foundations of the World Urban System,* The International Library of Sociology. London and New York: Routledge. (ed.) 1996 *Re-presenting the City.* Ethnicity, Capital and Culture in the 21st Century, London: Macmillan.

Klopp, B. 1998 'Integration and Political Representation in a Multicultural City: The Case of Frankfurt am Main', *German Politics and Society* Issue 49, 16(4): 42-68.

Knox, P. and Taylor, P. J. (eds) 1995 *World Cities in a World-System,* Cambridge, UK: Cambridge University Press.

Lash, S. and Urry, J. 1994. *Economies of Signs and Space,* London: Sage publications.

Logan, J. R. and Molotch, H. 1987 *Urban Fortunes: The Political Economy of Place,* Berkeley: University of California Press.

Mahler, S. 1995 *American Dreaming: Immigrant Life on the Margins,* Princeton, NJ: Princeton University Press.

Marcuse, Peter 1987 'The Grid as City Plan: New York City and Laissez-Faire Planning', *Planning Perspectives* 2: 287—310.

Martinotti, G. 1993 *Metropolis,* Bologna: Il Mulino.

Massey, D. and Denton, N. 1993 *American Apartheid,* Cambridge: Harvard University Press.

Mayer, Margit and Ely, John (eds) 1998 *Green Politics.* Philadelphia, PA: Temple University Press.

McDowell, L. 1997 *Capital Culture,* Oxford: Blackwell Publishers.

Meyer, D. 1991 'Change in the World System of Metropolises: The Role of Business Intermediaries', *Urban Geography* 12(5): 393-416.

Nakhaie, M. 1997 'Vertical Mosaic among the Elites: The new Imagery Revisited', *Canadian Review of Sociology and Anthropology* 34(1): 1-24.

Olds, K., Dicken, P., Kelly, P., Kong, L. and Wai-Chung Yeung, H. (eds) 1999 *Globalisation and the Asian Pacific: Contested Territories*, London: Routledge.

Palumbo-Liu, D. 1999 *Asian/American*, Stanford: Stanford University Press.

Park, R.E., Burgess, E. W. and McKenzie R. D. (eds) 1967 *The City*, Chicago: University of Chicago Press.

Portes, A. (ed.) 1995 *The Economic Sociology of Immigration*, New York: The Russell Sage Foundation.

Portes, A., Castells, M. and Benton, L. (eds) 1989 *The Informal Economy: Studies in Advanced and Less Developed Countries*, Baltimore: Johns Hopkins University Press.

Porter, J. 1965 *The Vertical Mosaic*, Toronto: University of Toronto Press.

Rodriguez, N.P. and Feagin, J.R. 1986 'Urban Specialisation in the World System', *Urban Affairs Quarterly* 22(2): 187-220.

Ruggiero, V. and South, N. 1997 'The late-modern city as bazaar: drug markets, illegal enterprise and the barricades', *The British Journal of Sociology* 48(1): 54-71.

Sachar, A. 1990 'The global economy and world cities', in A. Sachar and S. Oberg (eds) *The World Economy and the Spatial Organisation of Power*, Aldershot: Avebury.

Santos, M., De Souze, M.A. and Silveira M. L. (eds) 1994. *Territorio Globalizacao e Frag-mentacao*, Sao Paulo: Editorial Hucitec.

Sassen, S. 1991 *The Global City: New York London and Tokyo*, Princeton: Princeton University. (Updated edition 2000.)

—, 1996 *Losing control? Sovereignty in an Age of Globalisation*, the 1995 Columbia University Leonard Hastings Schoff Memorial Lectures. New York: Columbia University Press.

—, 1998 *Globalisation and Its Discontents*, New York: New Press. *(ed.)* 2000 *Cities and Their Crossborder Networks*, Tokyo: UNU Press.

Sennett, R. 1990 *The Conscience of the Eye*, New York: Knopf.

—, 1994 *Flesh and Stone: The Body and the City in Western Civilisation*, New York: Norton.

Short, John Rennie and Kim, Yeong-Hyun 1999 *Globalisation and the City,* Essex: Longman.

Skeldon, R. 1997 'Hong Kong: Colonial City to Global City to Provincial City?', *Cities 14(5).*

Skillington, T. 1998 'The City as Text: constructing Dublin's identity through discourse on transportation and urban re-development in the press', *The British Journal of Sociology* 49(3): 456—74.

Sklair, L. 1991 *Sociology of the Global System: Social Changes in Global Perspective,* Baltimore: Johns Hopkins University Press.

Smith, David 1995 'The New Urban Sociology Meets the Old: Re-reading Some Classical Human Ecology', *Urban Affairs Review* 30(3): 432-57.

Smith, D.A. and Timberlake, M. 2000 'Cities in global matrices', in S. Sassen (ed.) *Cities and Their Crossborder Networks,* Tokyo: UNU Press.

Snow, David and Anderson, Leon (eds) 1993 *Down on Their Luck: the Lives of Homeless Street People,* Berkeley: University of California Press.

Stren, R. 1996 'The Studies of Cities: Popular Perceptions, Academic Disciplines, and Emerging Agendas', in M. Cohen, B. Ruble, J. Tulchin, A. Garland (eds) 1996 *Preparing for the Urban Future. Global Pressures and Local Forces,* Washington D.C.: Woodrow Wilson Center Press (distributed by The Johns Hopkins University Press).

Suttles, G. D. 1968 *The Social Order of the Slum,* Chicago: University of Chicago Press. Taylor, Peter J. 1995 'World Cities and Territorial States: The Rise and Fall of their Mutuality', in P. J. Taylor and P. L. Knox (eds) *World Cities In a World-System,* Cambridge: Cambridge University Press.

—, 1996 'On the Nation-State, The Global and Social Science', *Environment and Urban Planning* A28:1917-28.

Timberlake, M. (ed.) 1985 *Urbanisation in the World Economy,* Orlando: Academic.

Torres, R., Miron, L. and Inda, J. X. (eds) 1999 *Race, Identity, and Citizenship,* Oxford: Blackwell.

Wacquant, L. 1997 'Inside the Zone', *Theory, Culture, and Society* 15(2): 1—36.

Watson, S. and G. Bridges (eds) 1999 *Spaces of Culture,* London: Sage.

Wilson, W. J. 1987 *The Truly Disadvantaged: The Inner City, the Underclass and Public Policy,* Chicago: University of Chicago Press.

—, 1997 *When Work Disappears,* New York: Alfred A. Knopf.

Wright, T. 1997 *Out of Place,* Albany: State University of New York Press.

Yuval-Davis, N. 1999 'Ethnicity, Gender Relations and Multiculturalism', in R. Torres, L. Miron and J. X. Inda (eds) *Race, Identity, and Citizenship,* Oxford: Blackwell.

Zukin, S. 1991 *Landscapes of Power,* Berkeley: California University Press.

Zweigenhaft, Richard L. and Domhoff, G. W. 1999 *Diversity in the Power Elite: Have Women and Minorities Reached the Top ?* New Haven: Yale University Press.

BIBLIOGRAPHY

Abu-Lughod, J.L. (1994). *From Urban Village to 'East Village': The Battle for New York's Lower East Side,* Cambridge: Blackwell.

Afshar, H. and S. Barrientos (1998). *Women, globalisation and fragmentation in the developing world.* New York, St. Martin's Press.

Agarwal, B. (1994). *A Field of One's Own: Gender and Land Rights in South Asia.* Cambridge: Cambridge University Press.

Agarwal, B. (1997). "Bargaining and Gender Relations: Within and Beyond the Household." *Feminist Economics* 3(1): 1-50.

Agarwal, B. (1998) "Widows versus Daughters or Widows as Daughters? Property, Land, and Economic Security in Rural India", *Modern Asian Studies*, 32:1, 1-48.

Agarwal, B. (2003). "Women's Land Rights and the Trap of Neo-Conservatism: A Response to Jackson." *Journal of Agrarian Change* 3(4): 571-585.

Aggarwal, S. (2002). ABVA writ petition for repeal of Section 377. In B. Fernandez (Ed.) *Humjinsi: A resource book on lesbian, gay and bisexual rights in India.* Mumbai: India Center for Human Rights and Law.

Aguilar, A. G. and Ward, P.W. (2003): "Globalisation, Regional Development, and Mega-city Expansion in Latin America: Analysing Mexico City's Peri-urban Hinterland", *Cities*, 20(1), 3-21.

Allen, J. (1999). 'Cities of Power and Influence: settled formations', in Allen, J. *et al.* (eds) *Unsettling Cities,* New York: Rout-ledge.

Allen, J., Massey, D. and Pryke, M. (eds) 1999 *Unsettling Cities,* New York: Routledge.

Amis, P. and Rakodi, C., (1994). 'Urban poverty: issues for research and policy', *Journal of International Development, Policy, Economics and International Relations.*

Amis, P., 1995 'Making sense of poverty', in IIED, 1995, 'Urban poverty: characteristics, causes and consequences', *Environment and Urbanisation,* Vol 7, No 1.

Anderson, E. 1990 *Streetwise,* Chicago: University of Chicago Press.

Appadurai, Arjun, 1996 *Modernity at Large,* University of Minnesota Press.

Baden, S. and Milward, K., 1995, 'Gender and poverty', *BRIDGE Report No* 30, Brighton: Institute of Development Studies.

Baker, J., 1995, 'Survival and accumulation strategies at the rural-urban interface in north-west Tanzania, in IIED, 1995, 'Urban poverty: Characteristics, causes and consequences', *Environment and Urbanisation,* Vol. 7 No 1.

Bayly, C.A., 1983 *Rulers, Townsmen and Bazaars: North Indian Society in the Age of British Expansion, 1770-1870,* Cambridge.

Beall, J., 1995b, 'In sickness and in health: engendering health policy for development', *Third World Planning Review*, Vol. 17 No 2.

Berner, E. and Korff, R. 1995 'Globalisation and Local Resistance: The Creation of Localities in Manila and Bangkok', *International Journal of Urban and Regional Research* 19 (2).

Bhachu, P. 1985 *Twice Immigrants,* London: Tavistock Publications.

Bhaduri, Amit (1996), Employment, Labour Market Flexibility and Economic Liberalisation in India, *Indian Journal of Labour Economics*, Vol. 39 (1).

Body-Gendrot, S. 1999 *Economic Globalisation and Urban Unrest,* London: Blackwell.

Bonacich, E., Cheng, L. Chinchilla, N. Hamilton, N. and Ong, P. (eds) 1994 *Global Production: The Apparel Industry in the Pacific Rim,* Philadelphia: Temple University Press.

Bonilla, F., Melendez, E. Morales, R. and de los Angeles Torres, M. (eds) 1998 *Borderless Borders,* Philadelphia: Temple University Press.

Boyd, M. 1989 'Family and Personal Networks in International Migration: Recent Developments and New Agendas', *International Migration Review* 23(3): 638-70.

Brar, H., P. Martin, J. Wrench (with M. Johnson) 1993 *Invisible Minorities. Racism in New Towns and New Contexts,* Coventry: Warwick University.

Breman, J. (2003). *The labouring poor in India: patterns of exploitation, subordination, and exclusion*. Delhi; Oxford, Oxford University Press.

Brewer, J.D. 1998 'Informal social control and crime management in Belfast', *The British Journal of Sociology* 49(4).

Brotchie, J., Blakely, E., Hall, P. and Newton, P. (eds) 1995 *Cities in Competition: Productive and Sustainable Cities for the Twenty-First Century,* Melbourne: Longman Australia.

Burawoy, M. et al. 1991 *Ethnography Unbound: Power and Resistance in the Modern Metropolis,* Berkeley: University of California Press.

Burgel, G. and Burgel, G. 1996 'Global Trends and City Politics: Friends or Foes of Urban Development?' in M. Cohen, B. Ruble, J. Tulchin, A. Garland (eds) *Preparing for the Urban Future. Global Pressures and Local Forces,* Washington D.C.: Woodrow Wilson Center Press (distributed by The Johns Hopkins University Press).

Castells, M. 1989 *The Informational City,* London: Blackwell.

Castells, Manuel. 1977. *The urban question: A Marxist approach* (translated by Alan Sheridan). London: Edward Arnold.

Central Council of Local Governments (Zakaria Committee): A Report on Augmentation of Financial Resources of Urban Local Bodies, Government of India, New Delhi.

Chakravarti, U. (1993). "Conceptualising Brahmanical Patriarchy in Early India—Gender, Caste, Class and State." Economic and Political Weekly 28(14): 579-585.

Chakravarty, U. (1993, April 3). Conceptualising Brahmin Patriarchy. *Economic and Political Weekly.*

Chant, S. (ed), 1992, *Gender and Migration in Developing Countries,* London: Belhaven Press.

Chant, S., (1989), 'Gender and urban planning', in L. Brydon and S. Chant, *Women in the Third World: Gender Issues in Rural and Urban Areas,* London: Earthscan.

Chaplin, Susan E. 2007. 'Partnerships of hope: New ways of providing Sanitation services in India', in Annapurna Shaw (ed.): *Indian cities in transition* (83-103). Chennai: Orient Longman.

Chatterjee, M. (1993). *Struggle and Development: Changing the Reality of Self-Employed Workers.* Women at the Center: Development Issues and Practices for the 1990s. Eds. G. Young, V. Samarasinghe and K. Kusterer. Connecticut, Kumarian Press: 81-93.

Childe, V. Gordon. 1957. 'Civilisation, cities, and towns', *Antiquity* (March): 210-13.

Clark, T. and Hoffman-Martinot, V. (eds) 1998 *The New Public Culture*, Oxford: West-view Press.

Cohen, D.J. and Volkmar, F. (1997). *Handbook of Autism and Pervasive Developmental Disorders.* New York: Wiley.

Cohen, M., Ruble, B., Tulchin, J. and Garland, A. (eds) 1996 *Preparing for the Urban Future. Global Pressures and Local Forces,* Washington D.C.: Woodrow Wilson Center Press (distributed by The Johns Hopkins University Press).

Comstock, G. 1991 *Violence Against Lesbians and Gay Men,* New York: Columbia University Press.

Counsel Club. (2002). A self-help story. In B. Fernandez (Ed.) *Humjinsi: A resource book on lesbian, gay and bisexual rights in India.* Mumbai: India Center for Human Rights and Law.

Custers, P. (2000) *Capital Accumulation and Women's Labour in Asian Economies*, London: Sed Press.

Cybriwsky, R. 1991 *Tokyo: The Changing Profile of an Urban Giant,* London: Bel-haven.

DaCorta, L., and Davuluri Venkateswarlu (1999). "Unfree Relations and the Feminisation of Agricultural Labour in Andhra Pradesh, 1970-95." *Journal of Peasant Studies* 26(2-3): 73-139.

Daley, T.C. (2002). The need for cross-cultural research on Pervasive developmental disorder, *Transcultural Psychiatry,* 39(4): 531-551.

Daley, T.C. (2004). "From Symptom Recognition to diagnosis: Children with Autism in urban India," *Social Science and Medicine,* 58:1323-1335.

Dandekar, N.M. and Rath, N. (1971), *Poverty in India,* Indian School of Political Economy, Bombay.

Davis, Kingsley (1951): *The Population of India and Pakistan*, Princeton University Press, New Jersey.

Dawson, M. 1999 'Globalisation, the Racial Divide, and a New Citizenship', in R. Torres, L. Miron and J. X. Inda (eds) 1999 *Race, Identity, and Citizenship,* Oxford: Blackwell.

De Sena, J. 1990 *Protecting One's Turf: Social Strategies for Maintaining Urban Neighbourhoods,* Lanham: University Press of America.

Dear, Michael J. 2000. *The Postmodern Urban Condition.* Oxford: Blackwell.

Delphy, C. and D. Leonard (1992). *Familiar exploitation: a new analysis of marriage in contemporary western societies.* Cambridge, Polity 1992.

Desai, M. (2002). Civil laws affecting gay men and lesbians. In B. Fernandez (Ed.) *Humjinsi: A resource book on lesbian, gay and bisexual rights in India.* Mumbai: India Center for Human Rights and Law.

Desai, P.B. (1968), Economy of Indian Cities', *Indian Journal of Public Administration*, Vol., XIV (3), July-Sept.

Deshpande, S. and L. K. Deshpande, (1993), "Gender-Based Discrimination in the Urban Labour Market", ch. 10 in (Papola and Sharma, 1993).

Dijkstra, A. G. and J. Plantenga (1997). *Gender and Economics: A European Perspective*. London, Routledge.

Dobbin, Christine, 1972 *Urban Leadership in Western India: Politics and Communities in Bombay City, 1840-85,* Oxford.

Dogan, M. and J. D. Kasarda (eds) 1988 *A World of Giant Cities,* Newbury Park, CA: Sage.

Domhoff, G.W. 1991 *Blacks in White Establishments: A study of Race and Class in America,* New Haven: Yale University Press.

Doniger, W. (2000). *Splitting the difference: Gender and myth in ancient Greece and India.* New Delhi: Oxford University Press.

Dreze, J. (1990), *Widows in Rural India*, London Schools of Economics, London, STICERD DEP No. 26.

Dreze, J., and Amartya Sen (1995). *India: Economic Development and Social Opportunity*. Oxford, Clarendon Press.

Dubey, A., S. Gangopadhyay and W. Wadhwa (2001), "Occupational Structure and Incidence of Poverty in Indian Towns of Different Sizes", *Review of Development Economics*, 5(1), pp.49-59.

Dubey, Bharati. 2009. 'Hindu soc [housing society] slams door on actor' and 'No ban on Muslims, says society secy [secretary]', *The times of India,* Mumbai, 31 July 2009: 1 and 9.

Duncan, O. 1959 'Human Ecology and Population Studies,' in P. Hauser and O. Dudley (eds) *The Study of Population,* Chicago: The University of Chicago Press.

Duneier, M. 1999 *Sidewalk,* New York: Farrar, Strauss & Giroux.

Dunn, D. (1993). "Gender Inequality in Education and Employment in the Scheduled Castes and Tribes of India." Population Research and Policy Review 12(1): 53-70.

Dunn, S. (ed.) 1994 *Managing Divided Cities,* Staffs, UK: Keele University Press.

Durkheim, Emile. 1964/1893. *The division of labour in society.* New York: The Free Press. Dürrschmidt, Jörg. 2000. *Everyday lives in the global city: The delinking of locale and milieu.* London: Routledge.

Dutta, A. (1999): "Institutional Aspects of Urban Governance", in Mathur, O. P. (ed.) India: the Challenge of Urban Governance, National Institute of Public Finance and Policy, New Delhi.

Dutta, A. (2004, August 9). Homosexual victim exposes the Delhi press. *Media South Asia.* http://www.thehoot.org.

Eckert, J.M. 2003. *The charisma of direction action: Power, politics, and the Shiv Sena.* New Delhi: Oxford University Press.

Ellin, Nan. 2006. *Integral Urbanism.* New York: Routledge.

Fainstein, S. 1997 'Justice, Politics, and the Creation of Urban Space', in A. Merrifield and E. Swyngedouw (eds) *The Urbanisation of Injustice,* New York: New York University Press.

Fainstein, S.I., Gordon, I. and Harloe, M. 1993 *Divided City:Economic Restructuring and Social Change in London and New York,* New York: Blackwell.

Fainstein, Susan and Judd, Dennis (eds) 1999 *Urban Tourism.* New Haven, Conn: Yale University Press.

Feagin, J.P. and Vera, H. 1996 *White Racism,* New York: Routledge.

Featherstone, M. (ed.) 1990 *Global Culture: Nationalism, Globalisation and Modernity,* Newbury Park, Ca: Sage.

Fernandez, B. (Ed.) (2002). *Humjinsi: A resource book on lesbian, gay and bisexual rights in India.* Mumbai: India Center for Human Rights and Law.

Fishman, Robert. 1992. The Regional Plan and the Transformation of the Industrial Metropolis. in David Ward and Oliver Zunz, eds., *The Landscape of Modernity*. New York: The Russell Sage Foundation.

Flanagan, William G. 1993. *Contemporary urban sociology.* Cambridge: Cambridge University Press.

Folbre, N. (1986). "Cleaning House: New Perspectives on Households and Economic Development." *Journal of Development Economics,* 22: 5-40.

Fustukian, S., 1996, 'Strategies to strengthen urban health and social development', in N. Hall, R. Hart and D. Mitlin, *The Urban Opportunity: The Work of NGOs in Cities of the South,* London: ITDG.

Gans, H. 1995 *The War Against the Poor,* New York: Basic Books.

Gans, Herbert, 1968. *People and Plans: Essays on Urban Problems and Solutions*. New York: Basic Books.

Gautum, M. and H. Tripathi (2001). "Women in Goat Husbandry." Man in India 81(3&4): 313-320.

Georges, E. 1990 *The Making of a Transnational Community: Migration, Development, and Cultural Change in the Dominican Republic,* New York: Columbia University Press.

Ghosh, Jayati (1995), Employment and Labour Under Structured Adjustment: India Since 1991, *Indian Journal of Labour Economics*, Vol. 38 (4), 1995.

Gibbons-Trikha, J. (2003) "Sanctuary: A Women's Refuge in India", *Journal of Developing Societies*, 19:1, 47-89.

Giddens, A. 1990 *The Consequences of Modernity,* Oxford, U.K.: Polity Press.

Gilbert, A. and Gugler, J., 1992, *Cities, Poverty and Development: Urbanisation in the Third World,* Oxford: Oxford University Press.

Goffman, E. (1963). *Stigma: Notes on the management of Spoiled Identity.* Englewood Cliffs, N.J: Prentice Hall. Gray, D.

Gohain, Manash Pratim and Dipak Dash. 2009. 'Muslims in Delhi too find doors slammed on them', *The times of India,* Mumbai, 3 August, 2009: 13.

Gopalan, A. (2005). Client advocacy and service provision: the Naz Foundation's mission. In R. Ramasubban & B. Rishyasringa (Eds.) *AIDS and civil society: India's learning curve.* Jaipur and Delhi: Rawat Publications.

Gottdiener, M. 1985 *The Social Production of Urban Space,* Austin: University of Texas Press.

Graham, S. and Marvin, S. 1996 *Telecommunications and the City: Electronic Spaces, Urban Places,* London: Routledge.

Graham, S. and S. Marvin. *Telecommunications and the city: Electronic spaces, urban places.* London: Routledge.

Gravesteijn, S.G.E., Griensven, S. van and de Smidt, M.C. (eds) 1998 *Timing Global Cities, Nederlandse Geografische Studies,* 241, Utrecht.

Green, D., Strolovitch, D. and Wong, J. 1998 'Defended Neighbourhoods, Integration, and Racially Motivated Crime', *American Journal of Sociology* 104(2): 372-404.

Grosz, E. 1992 'Bodies-Cities', in B. Colom-ina (ed.) *Sexuality and Space*. Princeton Papers on Architecture. Princeton: Princeton Architectural Press.

Gulati, L. (1995). "Women and Family in India—Continuity and Change." *Indian Journal of Social Work* 56(2): 133-154.

Gupta, A. (2002). Trends in the application of Section 377. In B. Fernandez (Ed.) *Humjinsi: A resource book on lesbian, gay and bisexual rights in India.* Mumbai: India Center for Human Rights and Law.

Gupta, Dipankar. 1982. *Nativism in a metropolis: the Shiv Sena in Bombay.* New Delhi: Manohar.

Gupta, Narayani, 1981 'Twelve Years On: Urban History in India', *Urban History Yearbook*, p. 76.

Gurumukhi, K.T. (2000), Slum Related Policies and Programmes, *Shelter*, Vol. 3 (2), April.

Hall, S. 1991 'The Local and the Global: Globalisation and Ethnicity', in A. King (ed.) *Current Debates in Art History 3. Culture, Globalisation and the World-System: Contemporary Conditions for the Representation of Identity,* Department of Art and Art History, State University of New York at Binghamton.

Hannerz, U. 1992 *Cultural Complexity. Studies in the Social Organisation of Meaning,* New York: Columbia University Press.

Hansen, Thomas Blom, 2001 *Violence in Urban India: Identity Politics, 'Mumbai' and the Postcolonial City,* Delhi; Nair, *Promise of the Metropolis,* pp. 271-98.

Hardoy, J., Mitlin, D. and Satterthwaite, D., 1992, *Environmental Problems in Third World Cities,* London: Earthscan.

Harriss-White, B. (2003). India Working: Essays on Society and Economy. Cambridge, Cambridge University Press.

Hart, G. (1992). "Household Production Reconsidered: Gender, Labour Conflict, and Technological Change in Malaysia's Muda Region." World Development 20(6): 809-823.

Hart, R., 1996, 'Introduction and overview', in N. Hall, R. Hart and D. Mitlin, *The Urban Opportunity: The Work of NGOs in Cities of the South,* London: ITDG.

Harvey, David. 1985. *The urbanisation of capital: Studies in the history and theory of capitalist urbanisation.* Baltimore: Johns Hopkins University Press.

Holston, J. (ed.) 1996 'Cities and Citizenship', a Special Issue *of Public Culture8(2).*

Hondagneu-Sotelo, P. 1994 *Gendered Transitions,* Berkeley: University of California Press.

Human Rights Law Network. (2002). Perspectives on gay and lesbian rights. In B. Fernandez (Ed.) *Humjinsi: A resource book on lesbian, gay and bisexual rights in India.* Mumbai: India Center for Human Rights and Law.

Human Rights Watch. (2002). Epidemic of abuse: Police Harassment of HIV/AIDS outreach workers in India, 14(5).

Hutchison, R. (ed.) 1997 *Research in Urban Sociology, Vol. 4: New Directions in Urban Sociology,* Greenwich: JAI Press.

ILO (2003), Working Out of Poverty, International Labour Organisation, Geneva.

India Development Report, 1999-2000, IGIDR, Oxford University Press.

Indiana Journal of Global Legal Studies, 1996. *Special Issue: Feminism and Globalisation: The Impact of the Global Economy on Women and Feminist Theory* 4(1 Fall).

Jackson, C. and R. Pearson (1998). *Feminist visions of development: gender, analysis and policy*. London, Routledge.

Jacob, P. (2001). "Magnitude of the Women Work Force in India: An Appraisal of the NSS Estimates and Methods." *Sarvekshana* XXIV, No. 4

Jacobson, David (ed.) 1998 *The Immigration Reader: America in a Multidisciplinary Perspective,* Oxford: Blackwell.

Jaffrey, Z. (1996). *The invisibles: A tale of the eunuchs of India.* New York: Vintage Books.

Jejeebhoy, S.J. and Z.A. Sathar (2001). "Women's autonomy in India and Pakistan: The influence of religion and region." Population and Development Review 27(4): 687-.

Jessop, R. 1999 'Reflections on Globalisation and its Illogics', in Olds, K. et al. (eds) *Globalisation and the Asian Pacific: Contested Territories,* London: Routledge.

Jha, S.S. (1986), *Structure of Urban Poverty*, Popular Prakashan, Bombay.

Joshi, Vijai, and Little (1946), *India's Economic Reforms: 1991:2001,* Oxford University Press, New Delhi.

Kabeer, N. (1994). Reversed realities: gender hierarchies in development thought. London; New York, Verso.

Kalpagam, U. (1994). Labour and Gender: Survival in Urban India. London, New Delhi and Thousand Oaks, Sage.

Kanji, N., 1995, 'Gender, poverty and economic adjustment in Harare, Zimbabwe', in IIED, 1995, 'Urban poverty: characteristics, causes and consequences', *Environment and Urbanisation,* Vol. 7 No. 1.

Kapadia, K. (1995). *Siva and Her Sisters: Gender, Caste and Class in Rural South India*. Boulder and Oxford, Westview Press.

Kapadia, K. (1999). "Gender ideologies and the formation of rural industrial classes in South India today." *Contributions to Indian Sociology* 33(1-2): 329-352.

Katznelson, I. 1992 *Marxism and the City,* Oxford: Clarendon Press.

Kaur, Ravinder. 2001. 'The eclipse or the renaissance of "community"? The career of the concept', in Surinder S. Jodhka (ed.): *Community and identities: Contemporary discourses on culture and politics in India* (80-94). New Delhi: Sage Publications in association with The Book Review Literary Trust, New Delhi.

Kempen, R. van, and Ozuekren, A. Sule 1998 'Ethnic Segregation in Cities: New Forms and Explanations in a Dynamic World', *Urban Studies* 35(10): 1631-57.

Khilnani, Sunil. 2002. *The Idea of India* , Penguin Books, New Delhi.

King, A.D. 1990 *Urbanism, Colonialism, and the World Economy. Culture and Spatial Foundations of the World Urban System,* The International Library of Sociology. London and New York: Routledge. (ed.) 1996 *Re-presenting the City.* Ethnicity, Capital and Culture in the 21st Century, London: Macmillan.

King, Anthony D., 1976 *Colonial Urban Development: Culture, Social Power, and Environment,* London.

Kingdon, G. G. "Labour force participation, returns to education and sex-discrimination." *Gender and Employment in India*: 249-277.

Klopp, B. 1998 'Integration and Political Representation in a Multicultural City: The Case of Frankfurt am Main', *German Politics and Society* Issue 49, 16(4): 42-68.

Knox, P. and Taylor, P.J. (eds) 1995 *World Cities in a World-System,* Cambridge, UK: Cambridge University Press.

Kofman, Eleonore and Elizabeth Lebas. 1996. 'Lost in transposition: Time, space and the city', Introduction to Henri Lefebvre: *Writings on cities* (translated and edited by Eleonore Kofman and Elizabeth Lebas) (3-60). Oxford: Blackwell Publishers.

Kopardekar, H.D. (1986), *Social Aspects of Urban Development*, Popular Prakashan, Bombay.

Kundu, A. (2006): "Globalisation and the Emerging Urban Structure: Regional Inequality and Population Mobility", India: Social Development Report, Oxford, New Delhi Kundu, A., Bagchi, S. and Kundu, D. (1999): "Regional Distribution of Infrastructure and Basic Amenities in Urban India", Economic and Political Weekly, 34(28).

Kundu, A. and N. Sarangi (2007), "Migration, Employment Status and Poverty: An Analysis across Urban Centres", Economic and Political Weekly, Jan 27, 2007.

Kundu, A., (2003): Urbanisation and Urban Governance: Search for a Perspective beyond Neo-Liberalism, *Economic and Political Weekly*, vol. 38, no 29.

Lash, S. and Urry, J. 199 4 *Economies of Signs and Space*, London: Sage Publications.

Latapi, A. and de la Rocha, M., 1995, 'Crisis, restructuring and urban poverty in Mexico', in IIED, 1995, 'Urban poverty: characteristics, causes and consequences', *Environment and Urbanisation*, Vol. 7, No. 1.

Law Commission of India. (2000). *One hundred and seventy-second report: Review of rape laws.* New Delhi: Government of India.

Lefebvre, Henri. 1996. *Writings on cities* (Selected, translated and introduced by Eleonore Kofman and Elizabeth Lebas). Oxford: Blackwell Publishers.

Lewis, Oscar. 1966. *The Culture of Poverty.* Scientific American.

Lipton, M., 1996, 'Successes in anti-poverty', *Issues in Development Discussion Paper* 8, Development and Technical Co-operation Department, ILO, Geneva.

Logan, J. R. and Molotch, H. 1987 *Urban Fortunes: The Political Economy of Place,* Berkeley: University of California Press.

M.S.A. Rao (ed.), 1974 *Urban Sociology in India: Reader and Sourcebook,* Hyderabad, p. 11.

Macionis, J. J., & Parrillo, V. N. (1998). *Cities and Urban Life*. Upper Saddle River, New Jersey: Prentice Hall.

Maciver, R.M. and Charles H. Page. 1962/1950. *Society: An introductory analysis.* London: Macmillan. Mahadevia, Darshini. 2007. 'A city with many borders: Beyond ghettoisation in Ahmedabad', in Annapurna Shaw (ed.): *Indian cities in transition* (341-389). Chennai: Orient Longman.

Mahler, S. 1995 *American Dreaming: Immigrant Life on the Margins,* Princeton, NJ: Princeton University Press.

Marcuse, Peter 1987 'The Grid as City Plan: New York City and Laissez-Faire Planning', *Planning Perspectives* 2: 287—310.

Massey, D. and Denton, N. 1993 *American Apartheid,* Cambridge: Harvard University Press.

Mathur, A. (1994). "Work Participation, Gender and Economic Development: A Quantitative Anatomy of the Indian Scenario." *The Journal of Development Studies* 30(2): 466-504.

Mayer, Margit and Ely, John (eds) 1998 *Green Politics.* Philadelphia, PA: Temple University Press.

McDowell, L. 1997 *Capital Culture,* Oxford: Blackwell Publishers.

Mehta, Suketu. 2004. *Maximum city: Bombay lost and found.* New Delhi: Penguin Books. Mitchell, William J. 1995. *City of bits: Space, place, and the infobahn.* Cambridge, Mass.: Massachusetts Institute of Technology.

Menon, N. (1999). Introduction. In N. Menon (Ed.) *Gender and politics in India.* New Delhi: Oxford University Press.

Meyer, D. 1991 'Change in the World System of Metropolises: The Role of Business Intermediaries', *Urban Geography* 12(5): 393-416.

Mies, M. (1980) "Capitalist Development and Subsistence Reproduction: Rural Women in India", *Bulletin of Concerned Asian Scholars*, XII, 1, pp. 2-14.

Ministry of Law and Land Reforms (1949), "East Bengal Act XXIII of 1949, The Non-Agricultural Tenancy Act, 1949, Dhaka, Pakistan.

Ministry of Law and Land Reforms (1976), "The Local Government Ordinance, 1976", E. B. Act XIII of 1953, Ministry of Law and Land Reforms, Government of the Peoples' Republic of Bangladesh, Dhaka, Bangladesh.

Ministry of Law and Parliamentary Department (1953), "The Town Improvement Act, 1953", Ministry of Law and Parliamentary Affairs,

Government of the Peoples' Republic of Bangladesh, Dhaka, Bangladesh.

Ministry of Social Justice and Empowerment (1999): First Report of the Expert Committee for Devising a Pension System for India, Government of India, New Delhi.

Ministry of Urban Development (1992): The Constitution Seventy-fourth Amendment Act 1992 on Municipalities, Government of India, New Delhi.

Mohanty, M., Ed. (2004). *Class, Caste, Gender. Readings in Indian Government and Politics*. New Delhi, London, Sage Publications.

Moser, C. and Chant, S., 1985, 'The role of women in the execution of low-income housing projects training module', *DP U Gender and Planning Working Paper* No 6, London: University College London.

Moser, C. and Holland, J., 1995, 'A participatory study of urban poverty and violence in Jamaica: summary finding', Washington D.C.: Urban Development Division, World Bank.

Moser, C. and Peake, L (eds), 1987, *Women, Housing and Human Settlements,* London: Tavistock Publications.

Moser, C., 1995, 'Women, gender and urban development policy: challenges for current and future research', *Third World Planning Review,* Vol. 17 No. 2.

Moser, C., 1996, 'Confronting crisis: a comparative study of household responses to poverty and vulnerability in four poor urban communities', *Environmentally Sustainable Development Studies and Monographs Series* No. 8, Washington D.C.: World Bank

Nakhaie, M. 1997 'Vertical Mosaic among the Elites: The new Imagery Revisited', *Canadian Review of Sociology and Anthropology* 34(1): 1-24.

Nanda, S. (1990). *Neither man norwoman: The hijras of India.* Belmont: Wadsworth Publishing Co.

Nanda, S. (1994). Hijras: An alternative sex and gender role in India. In G. Herdt (Ed.) *Third sex, third gender: Beyond sexual dimorphism in culture and history.* New York: Zone Books.

Narasimhan, S. (2002). "Gender, class, and caste schisms in affirmative action policies: The curious case of India's women's reservation bill." Feminist Economics 8(2): 183-190.

Narasimhan, S. (1999). *Empowering Women: An Alternative Strategy from Rural India.* New Delhi, Thousand Oaks and London, Sage.

Narrain, A. (2004). The articulation of rights around sexuality and health: Subaltern queer cultures in India in the era of Hindutva. *Health and Human Rights,* 7(2).

Narrain, A., & Khaitan, T. (2002). Medicalisation of homosexuality. In B. Fernandez (Ed.) *Humjinsi: A resource book on lesbian, gay and bisexual rights in India.* Mumbai: India Center for Human Rights and Law.

National Institute of Urban Affairs (1983): A study of Resources of Urban Local Bodies in India and the Level of Services Provided, National Institute of Urban Affairs, New Delhi.

Nayar, Deepak (1993), *Economic Reforms in India A Critical Assessment,* ILO-ARTEP, New Delhi.

Neuwirth, Robert. 2005. *Shadow cities: A billion squatters, a new urban world.* New York: Routledge.

Nigam, R.K. (2008): Application of Remote Sensing and Geographical Information.

ODA, 1995, 'Urban development review paper', Aid Economics and Small Enterprises Department and Engineering Division, London: ODA.

Olds, K., Dicken, P., Kelly, P., Kong, L. and Wai-Chung Yeung, H. (eds) 1999 *Globalisation and the Asian Pacific: Contested Territories,* London: Routledge.

Olsen, W. K. (1996). *Rural Indian Social Relations.* Delhi, Oxford University Press.

Olsen, W.K. (2001). "Social Statistics and the Indian Labour Market." Journal of Critical Realism 4: 11-16.

Olsen, W. K. (2006). "Pluralism, Poverty, and Sharecropping: Cultivating Open-Mindedness in Poverty Studies." *Journal of Development Studies*, forthcoming.

Olsen, W.K. and S. Mehta (2005) The Right to Work and Differentiation in India, conference paper, the Indian Society for Labour Economics, Delhi. Available from the authors.

Palnitkar, S and Kundu, D. (2005): Achieving the Millennium Development Goals, Financing Housing, Water and Sanitation in the Cities of Middle-Income Countries: The Case of Delhi, (mimeo) UNDP

Paolisso, M. and Gammage, S., 1996, 'Women's response to environmental degradation: poverty and demographic constraints. *Case studies from Latin America*', Washington: ICRW.

Papola, T. S., A.N. Sharma, et al. (1999). *Gender and employment in India*. New Delhi, Indian Society of Labour Economics and Institute of Economic Growth Delhi in association with Vikas Pub. House.

Park, R.E., Burgess, E. W. and McKenzie R. D. (eds) 1967 *The City*, Chicago: University of Chicago Press.

Park, Robert Erza. 1915. 'The city: Suggestions for the investigation of human behaviour in the city', *American Journal of Sociology*, 20: 577-612.

Patel, Sujata and Kushal Deb (eds). 2006. *Urban Sociology* (Oxford in India) Readings in Sociology and Social Anthropology series). Oxford University Press, New Delhi.

Patel, Sujata. 2006. 'Bombay and Mumbai: Identities, politics, and populism', in Sujata Patel and Kushal Deb (eds.): *Urban studies* (249-273). New Delhi: Oxford University Press.

People's Union of Civil Liberties-Karnataka. (2003, September). Human rights violations against the transgender community: A study of *kothi* and *hijra* sex workers in Bangalore, India. Bangalore.

Peterson, Jon, 1983. The Impact of Sanitary Reform upon American Urban Planning, 1840-1890. in Donald A. Krueckeberg, editor, *Introduction to Planning History in the United States*. New Brunswick, NJ: Center for Urban Policy Research, Rutgers University.

Planning Commission (1983): *Task Forces on Housing and Urban Developments*, Government of India, New Delhi.

Planning Commission (1997): Ninth Five Year Plan 1997-2002, Government of India, New Delhi.

Planning Commission, 2002. National Human Development Report 2001. Delhi: Government of India, March.

Poitevin, G. and H. Rairkar (1993 (orig. French 1985)). Indian Peasant Women Speak Up. London, Orient Longman.

Porter, J. 1965 *The Vertical Mosaic*, Toronto: University of Toronto Press.

Portes, A. (ed.) 1995 *The Economic Sociology of Immigration*, New York: The Russell Sage Foundation.

Portes, A., Castells, M. and Benton, L. (eds) 1989 *The Informal Economy: Studies in Advanced and Less Developed Countries*, Baltimore: Johns Hopkins University Press.

Pradhan, P., Perera, R. (1998), "Socio-economic Impacts and Natural Resources Management conflicts in the Urban Fringe Areas", Asian Institute of Technology, Bangkok, Thailand.

Racine, Jean Luc (ed.) (1997): *Peasant Moorings: Village Ties and Mobility Rationales in South India*, Sage, New Delhi.

Raghuram, P. (2001). "Caste and gender in the organisation of paid domestic work in India." *Work Employment and Society* 15(3): 607-617.

Ramachandran, V.K. (1990). *Wage Labour and Unfreedom in Agriculture: An Indian Case Study*. Oxford, Clarendon Press.

Ramasubban, R. (1995). Patriarchy and the risks of STD and HIV transmission to women. In M. Das Gupta, L. C. Chen & T. N. Krishnan (Eds.) *Women's health in India: Risk and vulnerability*. Bombay: Oxford University Press.

Ramasubban, R., & Rishyasringa, B. (2002). *Sexuality and reproductive health and rights: Fifty years of the Ford Foundation's population and health programme in India.* New York: Ford Foundation.

Rao, P.S.N. (1999): "Financing Urban Infrastructure—The Emerging Trends", Papers of the International Seminar on Financing and Pricing of Urban Infrastructure, Human Settlement Management Institute, New Delhi.

Ray, C.N. 2008. 'The traditional neighbourhoods in a walled city: *Pols* in Ahmedabad', *Sociological bulletin,* 57 (3): 337-52.

Rege, A. (2002). A decade of lesbian hulla gulla. In B. Fernandez (Ed.) *Humjinsi: A resource book on lesbian, gay and bisexual rights in India.* Mumbai: India Center for Human Rights and Law.

Rodriguez, N.P. and Feagin, J. R. 1986 'Urban Specialisation in the World System', *Urban Affairs Quarterly* 22(2): 187-220.

Rogaly, B. (1997). "Embedded Markets: Hired Labour Arrangements in West Bengal Agriculture." Oxford Development Studies 25(1): 209-223.

Roy, K. (1995). "Where women are worshipped, there the gods rejoice. In U. Butalia & T. Sarkar (Eds.) *Women and the Hindu right.* New Delhi: Kali For Women.

Ruggiero, V. and South, N. 1997 'The late-modern city as bazaar: drug markets, illegal enterprise and the barricades', *The British Journal of Sociology* 48(1): 54-71.

Sachar, A. 1990 'The global economy and world cities', in A. Sachar and S. Oberg (eds) *The World Economy and the Spatial Organisation of Power,* Aldershot: Avebury.

Saith, Ashwani; M. Vijayabaskar and V. Gayathri (eds.). *ICTs and Indian social change: Diffusion, poverty, governance.* New Delhi: Sage Publications.

Santos, M., De Souze, M. A. and Silveira M. L. (eds) 1994. *Territorio Globalizacao e Frag-mentacao,* Sao Paulo: Editorial Hucitec.

Sarkar, T. (1996). Colonial lawmaking and lives/deaths of Indian women. In R. Kapur (Ed.) *Feminist terrains in legal domains: Interdisciplinary essays on women and law in India.* New Delhi: Kali For Women.

Sassen, S. 1990 *The Conscience of the Eye,* New York: Knopf.

Sassen, S. 1991 *The Global City: New York London and Tokyo,* Princeton: Princeton University. (Updated edition 2000.)

Sassen, S. 1994 *Flesh and Stone: The Body and the City in Western Civilisation,* New York: Norton.

Sassen, S. 1996 *Losing control? Sovereignty in an Age of Globalisation,* the 1995 Columbia University Leonard Hastings Schoff Memorial Lectures. New York: Columbia University Press.

Sassen, S. 1998 *Globalisation and Its Discontents,* New York: New Press. *(ed.)* 2000 *Cities and Their Crossborder Networks,* Tokyo: UNU Press.

Satterthwaite, D., 1995a, 'The under-estimation and misrepresentation of urban poverty' in IIED, 1995, 'Urban poverty: Characteristics, causes and consequences' *m Environment and urbanisation,* Vol. 7 No. 1.

Satterthwaite, D., 1995b, 'Viewpoint—the underestimation of urban poverty and of its health consequences', *Third World Planning Review*, Vol. 17 No. 4.

Saunders, Peter. 1985. *Social theory and the urban question* (2nd edition). London: Hutchinson & Co.

Sawers, Larry. 1984. 'New perspectives on the urban political economy', in William K. Tabb and Larry Sawers (eds.): *Marxism and the metropolis: New perspectives in urban political economy* (3-17). New York: Oxford University Press.

Saxena , Aruna (2008): Monitoring of urban fringe using Remote Sensing and GIS techniques, Research Paper, 2008

Sen, A.K. (2000), Role of Urban Local Bodies in Poverty Alleviation Programmes, Shelter, Vol. 3 (2), April.

Seshu, M. (2005). Organising women in prostitution: the case of SANGRAM. In R. Ramasubban & B. Rishyasringa (Eds.) *AIDS and civil society: India's learning curve.* Jaipur and New Delhi: Rawat Publications.

Shaked, M. (2005). 'The Social Trajectory of Illness: Autism in the ultra-orthodox community in Israel', *Social science and medicine,* 61: 2190-2200.

Sharan, P. (2006). "Need for epidemiological Work on Autism in India', *Journal of the Indian association of Child and Adolescent Mental Health* 2(3): 700-701.

Shariff, Abusaleh (1999), India Human Development Report: A Profile of the Indian States in the 1990s, Delhi: National Council for Applied Economic Research.

Sharma, M. (1985). "Caste, Class, and Gender Production and Reproduction in North India." Journal of Peasant Studies 12(4): 57-88.

Short, John Rennie and Kim, Yeong-Hyun I999 *Globalisation and the City,* Essex: Longman.

Short, John Rennie and Yeong-Hyun Kim. 1999. *Globalisation and the city.* Harlow, Essex: Addison Wesley Longman Limited.

Sida, 1996, *Promoting Sustainable Livelihoods: A Report from the Task Force on Poverty Reduction,* Stockholm: Sida.

Singh Kulwant & Maitra, S. (2000), Urban Poverty in India: Approaches and Initiatives, Shelter Vol. 3 (2), April.

Sinha, D. (1988). 'The family scenario of a developing country and its implications for mental health: The case of India', in Dasen, P.R. Et al (eds), *Health and Cross Cultural Psychology: Towards applications.* Newbury Park: Sage Publications.

Sivaramakrishna, and Singh, B. N. and Kundu, A. (2005): Handbook of Urbanisation, Oxford University Press, New Delhi.

Sivaramakrishnan, K.C., Amitabh Kundu and B.N. Singh, 2005 *Handbook of Urbanisation in India: An Analysis of Trends and Processes,* Delhi, pp. 5-7.

Skeldon, R. I997 'Hong Kong: Colonial City to Global City to Provincial City?', *Cities 14(5).*

Skillington, T. 1998 'The City as Text: constructing Dublin's identity through discourse on transportation and urban re-development in the press', *The British Journal of Sociology* 49(3): 456—74.

Sklair, L. 1991 *Sociology of the Global System: Social Changes in Global Perspective,* Baltimore: Johns Hopkins University Press.

Skoufias, E. (1992). "Labour market opportunities and intrafamily time allocation in rural households in South Asia." *Journal of Development Economics* 40: 277-310.

Skoufias, E. (1993). "Seasonal Labour Utilisation in Agriculture: Theory and Evidence from Agrarian Households in India." *American Journal of Agricultural Economics* 75: 20-32.

Skoufias, E. (1995). "Household Resources, Transaction Costs, and Adjustment through Land Tenancy." *Land Economics* 71(1): 42-56.

Smith, D.A. and Timberlake, M. 2000 'Cities in global matrices', in S. Sassen (ed.) *Cities and Their Crossborder Networks,* Tokyo: UNU Press.

Smith, David l995 'The New Urban Sociology Meets the Old: Re-reading Some Classical Human Ecology', *Urban Affairs Review* 30(3): 432-57.

Snow, David and Anderson, Leon (eds) 1993 *Down on Their Luck: the Lives of Homeless Street People,* Berkeley: University of California Press.

Srivastava, Ravi S. (2003): "India's Uneven Development: An Analysis of Some Recent Trends and their Implications" *The Indian Journal of Economics,* July 2003.

Stree, S. (2002). Women coming together. In B. Fernandez (Ed.) *Humjinsi: A resource book on lesbian, gay and bisexual rights in India.* Mumbai: India Center for Human Rights and Law.

Stren, R. 1996 'The Studies of Cities: Popular Perceptions, Academic Disciplines, and Emerging Agendas', in M. Cohen, B. Ruble, J. Tulchin, A. Garland (eds) 1996 *Preparing for the Urban Future. Global Pressures and Local Forces,* Washington D.C.: Woodrow Wilson Center Press (distributed by The Johns Hopkins University Press).

Surjadi, C. and McGranahan, G., 1995, 'Jakarta: environmental problems at the household level', in I. Serageldin, Cohen, A. and Sivaramakrishan, K. (eds), *The Human Face of the Urban Environment,* Proceedings of the Second Annual World Bank Conference on Environmentally Sustainable Development, World Bank, Washington.

Suttles, G. D. 1968 *The Social Order of the Slum,* Chicago: University of Chicago Press. Taylor, Peter J. l995 'World Cities and Territorial States: The Rise and Fall of their Mutuality', in P. J. Taylor and P. L. Knox (eds) *World Cities In a World-System,* Cambridge: Cambridge University Press.

Suttles, G. D. l996 'On the Nation-State, The Global and Social Science', *Environment and Urban Planning* A28: 1917-28.

Takru, Rajiv (1997), *Issues of Slum Development in India,* Paper Presented At National Seminar on Future Cities - Urban Vision 2021, Delhi.

Tendulkar, S.D. (1998), *Indian Economic Policy Reforms and Poverty: An Assessment* in I.J. Ahluwalia and IMD Little (ed.) 'India's Economic

Reforms and Development: Essays for Mohan Singh', Oxford University Press, New Delhi.

Upadhya, Carol and A.R. Vasavi (eds.). 2008. *In an outpost of the global economy: Work and workers in India's information technology industry.* New Delhi: Routledge.

Vanita, R. & Saleem, K. (Eds.) (2000). *Same-sex love in India: Readings from literature and history.* New. Delhi: Macmillan.

Watson, S. and G. Bridges (eds) 1999 *Spaces of Culture,* London: Sage.

Wilson, W. J. 1987 *The Truly Disadvantaged: The Inner City, the Underclass and Public Policy,* Chicago: University of Chicago Press.

Wilson, W. J. 1997 *When Work Disappears,* New York: Alfred A. Knopf.

Wilson, William H. 1983. Moles and Skylarks. in in Donald Krueckeberg, ed., *Introduction to Planning History in the United States.* New Brunswick: CUPR Press.

Wirth, Louis. 1964/1938. 'Urbanism as a way of life', in Paul K. Hatt and Albert J. Reiss Jr. (eds.): *Cities and society: The revised reader in urban sociology* (46-63). New York: The Free Press of Glencoe, 1964.

World Bank (1995b): Better Urban Services: Finding the Right Incentives, World Bank, Washington DC.

World Bank (1998): *Reducing Poverty in India: Options for More Effective Public Services,* World Bank, Washington, D.C.

World Bank (2002), *Poverty in India: Challenge of Uttar Pradesh,* World Bank, Delhi.

Wratten, E., 1995, 'Conceptualising urban poverty', in IIED, 1995, 'Urban poverty: characteristics, causes and consequences', *Environment and Urbanisation,* Vol. 7 No. 1.

Wright, T. 1997 *Out of Place,* Albany: State University of New York Press.

Yuval-Davis, N. 1999 'Ethnicity, Gender Relations and Multiculturalism', in R. Torres, L. Miron and J. X. Inda (eds) *Race, Identity, and Citizenship,* Oxford: Blackwell.

Zukin, S. 1991 *Landscapes of Power,* Berkeley: California University Press.

Zweigenhaft, Richard L. and Domhoff, G.W. 1999 *Diversity in the Power Elite: Have Women and Minorities Reached the Top ?* New Haven: Yale University Press.

INDEX

D

E

F

G

H

I